POVERTY AND WEALTH
Citizenship, deprivation and privilege

LONGMAN SOCIOLOGY SERIES

Series Editor:
ROBERT BURGESS, University of Warwick

Editorial Advisors:
JOE BAILEY, Kingston University
ANGELA GLASNER, Oxford Brookes University
CLAIRE WALLACE, University of Lancaster

Published Titles:
Social Europe
Joe Bailey (ed.)

Women and Career
Julia Evetts (ed.)

Forthcoming Titles:
Frontiers of Identity
Robin Cohen

Gender and Technology
Juliet Webster

LONGMAN SOCIOLOGY SERIES

Poverty and Wealth
Citizenship, deprivation
and privilege

John Scott

LONGMAN
London and New York

Longman Group UK Limited,
Longman House, Burnt Mill,
Harlow, Essex CM20 2JE, England
and Associated Companies throughout the world.

*Published in the United States of America
by Longman Publishing, New York*

© Longman Group UK Limited 1994

First published 1994

ISBN 0 582 080894 PPR

British Library Cataloguing-in-Publication Data

A catalogue record for this book is
available from the British Library

Library of Congress Cataloging-in-Publication Data

Scott, John, 1949–
    Poverty and wealth : citizenship, deprivation and privilege / John
Scott.
      p. cm. — (Longman sociology series)
    Includes bibliographical references and index.
    ISBN 0–582–08089–4
    1. Poverty. 2. Wealth. 3. Equality. 4. Poverty—Great Britain.
    5. Wealth—Great Britain. 6. Equality—Great Britain. I. Title.
    II. Series.
    HC79.P6S338   1994
    330.1'6—dc20
                                        93–43275
                                         CIP

Set by 500 in 10 on 11pt Times Roman
Produced through Longman Malaysia,VVP

CONTENTS

LIST OF FIGURES AND TABLES

SERIES EDITOR'S PREFACE

The Longman Sociology Series is a new series of books which are written specifically for first and second year undergraduate students. Each title covers one key area of sociology and aims to supplement the traditional standard text.

The series is forward looking and attempts to reflect topics that will be included in syllabuses for sociology and social policy in the 1990s. It provides a range of volumes that bring together conceptual and empirical material. In addition, volumes in the series also examine key controversies and debates drawing on commentaries using conceptual and empirical material from a range of authors.

Each volume in the series whether authored or edited, will cover an area that would be commonly found in sociology and social policy syllabuses. The focus of each volume will be upon theoretically informed empirical work with policy relatedness.

The volumes are intended for an international audience and therefore comparative material is introduced where appropriate in a form that will be suitable for first and second year students.

This volume brings together some of the contemporary issues concerned with poverty and wealth. John Scott uses a range of data to focus on British society in the past as well as the present. All together he highlights areas of concern and points the way forward for future research by sociologists.

Robert G Burgess,
University of Warwick

PREFACE

My aim in this book is to develop a specific thesis about the relationship between poverty and wealth. These features of the social distribution of resources have often been studied in inappropriate and un-useful ways. Poverty, for example, is typically seen in terms of an assumed standard of physical subsistence, leading many to elide the idea of poverty with that of starvation. Wealth, on the other hand, has generally been seen in purely statistical terms, with the wealthy being identified as the top percentage group in the distribution of resources. Such a statistical approach is, inevitably, arbitrary, as it is impossible to specify in any objective way whether the wealthy are the top 1 per cent, top 5 per cent, top 10 per cent, or some other intermediate category.

The work of Peter Townsend has suggested a way of avoiding these difficulties. Poverty, he has argued, occurs when a person's resources are so limited that they experience social deprivation. This condition of deprivation, he goes on, can be understood only if it is seen in *relative* terms. To be deprived is to lack the powers and opportunities that form the normal taken-for-granted expectations of all members of a society. As these normal expectations change, so does the point at which deprivation is recognised.

My use of this relative concept of deprivation does not involve a denial of the real and very important differences that have existed in the *absolute* levels of living that are found in different societies and at different times in the same society. It is undoubtedly true that the poor in nineteenth-century Britain, for example, had a standard of living that was lower in real terms than that of their counterparts today. Variations in absolute standards of living and the extent to which particular groups approach or fall below a starvation level are important matters for social investigation. But so are the relativities in living standards that exist within any differentiated society. Poverty, I argue, is a term that should be used to describe such relativities. Poverty is a state of deprivation relative to those standards of living enjoyed by others in the same society.

The thesis that I have tried to develop is in two parts. First, I argue that Townsend's claims about the relativity of poverty and deprivation must be understood in relation to the idea of citizenship and the associated idea of participation in the public sphere of social life. Linking the work of Marshall on citizenship with that of Townsend on deprivation yields a powerful understanding of poverty. The second point of my thesis is less obvious. I argue that privilege is a parallel condition to deprivation. Privilege, understood in relative terms, is a condition in which people are able to enjoy advantaged powers and opportunities, life chances that are superior to those that are normal in their society. Wealth occurs when a person's resources are such that they experience privilege.

Wealth, like poverty, is a term that defines a particular pattern of relativities within a society. To describe a group as wealthy is to refer to their advantages relative to other members of the society. Absolute variations in the level of advantages enjoyed by groups at different times and in different societies have no necessary relationship to the relativities grasped by the concept of wealth. Just as 'poverty' must be distinguished from starvation and absolute want, so 'wealth' must be distinguished from any absolute level of luxury that it might be possible to identify.

I have tried to develop this thesis in relation to the British case. I have used the available evidence on poverty and wealth and I have tried to show how these data can be reinterpreted in the light of my thesis. I have not attempted to give a comprehensive summary of research on poverty, its causes and its distribution. The data that I present derive from the leading social investigations of poverty, which are used to further the argument of the book. The second part of my thesis, concerning the nature of wealth, must remain a little more speculative until far more research has been undertaken. Nevertheless, I feel able to conclude that the approach I have outlined has sufficient validity to form the basis of a powerful research programme.

In Chapter 1, I trace the development of welfare policy and liberal citizenship in the nineteenth century, and I use this as an opportunity to set out the basis of my thesis. Chapter 2 draws on empirical evidence from the leading social investigators to explore the ways in which poverty and wealth were viewed between the 1880s and the 1940s. The major figures in this chapter are Charles Booth and Seebohm Rowntree, who pioneered methods of social investigation into poverty and inequality and whose research results, for all their limitations, must be regarded as landmarks in the history of sociological analysis. No such towering figures exist in the study of wealth, though it is possible to turn to such data as do exist in order to discern the broad outlines of privilege in the first half of the century. Chapter 3 returns to the theme of the relationship between citizenship and social policy, and it traces the transformation of the 'social services' into the 'welfare state' alongside the development of 'liberal' citizenship into 'social democratic' citizenship. The studies undertaken by

Townsend himself have pride of place in Chapter 4 where I attempt to explore the co-existence of poverty and the welfare state in the second half of the century. Once again, studies of wealth have been less useful in their concerns, but it is possible to explore many of the aspects of advantage in Britain today and to suggest the relationship between poverty and wealth.

The British case is central to my concerns, but it cannot stand alone. The historical approach that I have taken requires a complementary comparative perspective. In Chapter 5 I have attempted to sketch the broad outlines of poverty and wealth in other capitalist industrial societies. The purpose of that chapter is not, however, to give a comprehensive picture of these societies – an impossible task within the space available – but to provide a backdrop from which the features of the British case can be highlighted. The final chapter continues this comparative focus at a more general level. I set out my thesis in summary form and develop some of its theoretical implications, and I examine some recent trends in citizenship in modern Britain. A discussion of the debate over the so-called underclass in Britain and the United States shows how changing patterns of citizenship have led to similar issues arising in these two societies.

Much work remains to be done in order to develop the thesis further. In particular, it is necessary to explore in much greater depth the relationship between poverty and wealth on the one hand and the class structure on the other hand. Research on poverty and wealth has largely been undertaken in isolation from mainstream debates about social stratification, and the two need to be more closely integrated. Although the book closes with some suggestions in this area, it remains a major task for the future.

ACKNOWLEDGEMENTS

The initial idea of linking deprivation and privilege arose when Peter Townsend asked me to co-operate in a part of his study of levels of living in London. The thesis was elaborated in papers at the Cambridge Stratification Seminar, the University of Bath, the Annual Conference of the British Sociological Association, and the Economic and Social Research Council (ESRC) Workshop on 'Citizenship, Civil Society and Social Cohesion' held in February 1991. I am grateful to Peter Townsend, Adrian Sinfield, Alan Walker, Ray Pahl, Graham Cox, and Harry Collins for their helpful comments on earlier drafts at these and other meetings. The general framework for the study first appeared in Scott (1992b). I am grateful to Mike Scott for his help in correcting the page proofs during his Christmas vacation.

CHAPTER 1

Poverty, wealth and policy

'Wealth has accumulated itself into masses, and Poverty, also in accumulation enough, lies impassably separated from it; opposed, uncommunicating, like forces in positive and negative poles' (Carlyle 1831, cited in Keating 1976: 1). Thomas Carlyle's remarks, written in 1831, set the scene for much of the debate on poverty and wealth in the nineteenth century. The industrial revolution, it was felt, had unleashed massive changes in the structure of British society, creating huge and expanding towns and cities in which a gulf was emerging between those who benefited from the new society and those who did not. The wealth that was created by capitalist industry was distributed in such a way as to produce riches for the expanding middle classes. Poverty, equally a product of industrial capitalism, had become the fate of ever larger numbers in the working classes. The Conservative prime minister Benjamin Disraeli (1845), for example, had depicted the emergence of two nations within Britain: the nation of the rich and the nation of the poor.

This image of class polarisation has become most familiar to us today from the way that it has been discussed within Marxist theory (see, among others, the contemporary study in Engels 1845). For Marxists, the polarisation that was produced by capitalist development would be ended only by revolutionary action on the part of the working class. The mainstream of public opinion, however, saw things in a different light. Class polarisation came to be seen by nineteenth-century commentators, of all political persuasions, as being a fundamental feature of the new 'industrial' society. Whereas Marxist and socialist writings saw a solution to this growing social problem as lying in an attack on wealth and privilege, mainstream opinion saw no problems in wealth holding. Victorian social policy was, in fact, structured by a concern to overcome social polarisation through eliminating the problem of poverty.

The framework of Victorian policy efforts was provided by the Poor Law Amendment Act of 1834. Coming between Carlyle's statement of 1831 and Disraeli's of 1845, this legislation set the course of welfare policy for almost a hundred years. The Act was the outcome of a Royal Commission whose policy proposals also informed a growing literature of social 'exploration', a body of ethnographic work on urban poverty that included a number of early sociological investigations. Journalists, novelists and sociologists took on the task of exploring the depths of poverty and deprivation that could be found in Britain's towns and cities. In doing so, they uncovered living conditions of which most members of that society were only dimly aware. Novelists such as Charles Dickens and Elizabeth Gaskell are, perhaps, the best-known exponents of this literary genre, but a number of systematic factual investigations were undertaken by writers such as Henry Mayhew (1861), John Hollingshead (1861), and, towards the end of the century, Charles Booth. This literature of exploration is admirably discussed and selected in Keating (1976). The principal concern in these factual investigations was the state of London's East End – which had been described by William Booth, the founder of the Salvation Army, as being 'Darkest England'. The analogy that was drawn with 'Darkest Africa' was explicit, as the 'unknown continent' was currently being 'opened' by British explorers. By interviewing the poor and those responsible for them and, in some cases, by undertaking participant observation, these social explorers into 'unknown England' made clear the extent of poverty and deprivation in the heart of the Empire's capital.

The works of the social explorers suggested that the inhuman and degrading conditions in which the poor lived were a problem for a minority of the population. For the majority of the population the problem was the financial question of how best to ameliorate and, eventually, eliminate these conditions. By the final quarter of the century the economic prosperity that had been generated in Britain – the 'workshop of the world' – was seen as having resolved many of the social problems that had been apparent in the 1830s and 1840s. The newly wealthy financiers and manufacturers were frequently perceived as being merely a part of a very large and affluent 'middle class' of solid citizens to whom the future of Britain and its democracy could be entrusted. Manual workers were acquiring attitudes of thrift and 'respectability', aspiring to the lifestyle of the middle classes, and only a small rump of the 'rough' working class in the urban slums was likely to experience any real poverty. For most people, then, 'wealth' was not a problem, for the majority were prospering, and 'poverty' was a problem only for the very few.

Official statistics suggested that the proportion of paupers in the population had fallen from one in nine at the turn of the century to one in twenty-three by 1870 (Perkin 1969: 412). In this context of apparently declining poverty, the distinction between the 'deserving' and the 'undeserving' poor that had emerged in earlier policy debates was drawn more sharply by public opinion. The deserving poor were seen by the middle classes as being, in many respects, 'one of us'; they were deserving of help because they had the desire and the ability to improve their circumstances and could, in time, return to the autonomy and independence of respectable society. Their poverty was a temporary condition that could and should be ameliorated through effective social policies. The undeserving poor, on the other hand, were felt to be responsible for their own poverty because of their inappropriate attitudes and aspirations. The aim of policy was not to support them in their poverty but to prevent them from contaminating the attitudes of the deserving poor and to control and confine them in whatever ways possible. Some radicals, such as Henry George, rejected this view and railed against the advantages of the propertied and the disadvantages of the poor, but they formed a minority strand in public opinion. Social investigation was, however, to show them to be closer to the truth than was informed middle-class opinion. The late nineteenth century in Britain was a period in which resources were, if anything, even more unequally distributed than had been the case during the 1830s, and the problem of poverty was truly massive.

These changing views on the extent of social inequality shaped a complex cultural outlook on the nature of poverty and its relation to the life of the majority of British citizens. Poverty as a 'social problem', as an object of social policy, was a product of the nineteenth century, and the attitudes and ideas that arose then still set the terms of the debates on poverty and welfare today.

The Poor Law system

Until 1834 welfare provision for the poor had been based on the Elizabethan Poor Law (the so-called Old Poor Law). Under this system, each parish in England and Wales was obliged to support its own aged and disabled poor and to ensure that all of its able-bodied population was engaged in work.[1] The distinction that was made between the 'able-bodied' and those, such as children, the elderly, and the disabled, who were unable to look after themselves was fundamental to the whole system. The 'impotent' poor – those who were not able-bodied – were seen as having a legitimate right to expect a degree of support from the parish in which they were born. They were to be given relief as of right. The able-bodied poor, on the other hand, would receive relief only through the Houses of Correction, where they could be given supervised work at an appropriate rate of pay. This policy depended upon an assumption that work was available for all who needed it. Although it was understood that agricultural conditions might limit employment opportunities in the short term – because, for example, there had been a bad harvest – it was generally held that all those who wished to work would be able to find employment. If an able-bodied person was unable to provide for his family, and was unemployed, this was seen as reflecting an inadequate or inappropriate work motivation.[2] The person's attitudes were in need of 'correction'. The Houses of Correction, by establishing a link between welfare and work, were seen as mechanisms for instilling an appropriate sense of work obligation.

During the eighteenth century the inherent problems of the Old Poor Law system became more apparent, and the strains that they created came to be seen as intolerable. The Houses of Correction had, in many areas, become places of detention for the aged, the insane, and the infirm, while the able-bodied poor were generally receiving 'outdoor' relief. In addition, poverty became more widespread as the century progressed. Britain's rapid industrialisation from the 1780s, together with an associated restructuring of agriculture through enclosure of the open fields, brought the system to breaking point. Growing numbers of people who were in employment were unable to meet the rapidly rising cost of food, and many Poor Law officers began to supplement low wages with poor relief. The best-known case of this practice was at Speenhamland in Berkshire, where magistrates drew up a scale of relief based upon estimates of the minimum sum that was felt to be necessary for the subsistence needs of a labourer and his family. This subsistence concept of officially recognised poverty was common, and it became the basis of a system that operated widely across the agricultural districts of the country. This solution to the rising tide of poverty, however, required substantial increases in taxation in order to meet the increasing costs of poor relief. Increased taxation, in turn, created a misleading impression in the public mind of too much 'generosity' in the treatment of the poor. Contrary to this view, increasing numbers of people were, in fact, experiencing poverty, in both the countryside and the industrial towns, and a growing body of opinion came to the conclusion that a complete overhaul of the system was needed.

A Royal Commission was set up in 1832 with the tasks of exploring these problems and coming up with some solutions. The Commission was headed by the Bishop of London and its members included two leading liberal reformers, Edwin Chadwick and Nassau Senior. These two became its dominant figures and shaped both its aims and its methods. The Commission saw its role as being to set down the principles of a modern system of welfare that could form the nucleus of a wider reformulation of social policy in the spheres of education, health, housing, and working conditions. The ideas of the commissioners embodied a conception of poverty that had begun to emerge towards the end of the eighteenth century. Classical political economy, and most particularly the works of Smith, Malthus, and Ricardo, were the vehicles through which this particular conception of poverty had been constructed, and it has been said, with some justice, that their work involved the 'invention of poverty' in its modern sense (Dean 1991). The outlines of this view had been set out in Sir

Frederick Eden's (1797) influential work, *The State of the Poor.* Eden described

> a new class of men, henceforth described by the legislature under the denomination of the *Poor*; by which term, I conceive, they mean to signify freemen, who, being either incapacitated by sickness, or old age, or prevented by other causes from getting work, were obliged to have recourse to the assistance of the charitable for subsistence.
>
> (1797, 1: 57)

Poverty was a condition in which a person was unable to meet the basic needs of human existence. A new form of poverty had developed alongside the older poverty that resulted from age or infirmity. This new poverty was that which arose when a lack of employment opportunities meant that people who were completely dependent upon income from employment, because they had no income-generating property, were prevented from meeting their own subsistence needs.

The individualistic beliefs of the rising class of manufacturers and professionals saw each person as responsible for their own actions and their own well-being. The Old Poor Law, on the other hand, had embodied a very different assumption of paternalistic responsibility for the poor on the part of the state and the upper classes. Liberal individualism, as expressed in classical political economy, rejected this and stressed the 'natural' and 'normal' character of the contemporary economic arrangements, of which the market system was the central element. The impersonal operation of the market for goods, it was felt, would ensure the efficient and legitimate distribution of resources. A necessary feature of such a market economy was a periodic restructuring of the labour market in response to changing patterns of demand and supply. Unemployment, then, was also a normal and natural feature of a market economy. It was a mechanism of restructuring that resulted from the normal cyclical fluctuations in the level of economic activity and from structural changes in the overall pattern of production. If unemployment was inevitable in a market economy, then so was able-bodied poverty. Poverty was, however, a condition that individuals could escape, given time, by seeking new employment.

The Benthamite version of this liberal doctrine saw a role for the state in ensuring the unfettered operation of the market. The state was to establish the social conditions under which the market could work most smoothly and it was to ameliorate the circumstances of those who were, by virtue of their age or infirmity, unable to cope with these inevitable and natural features of a capitalist market economy. The crucial question concerned the nature and level of the welfare support that was to be given to the able-bodied. The liberal belief in limiting the role of the state was fundamental to the deliberations of the Royal Commission on the Poor Laws. Its members accepted the need to discover a system of relief that would give public authorities a responsibility only for those matters that could not properly be left in private hands. Their principal targets were the inefficiency and abuses that were inherent in the old system and its failure to reconcile the relief of poverty with the encouragement of proper attitudes to work.

The commissioners and their assistants sent out questionnaires and undertook research visits to parishes across the country in order to collect evidence on how the old system could be restructured to meet the needs of a changing society. The Commission reported in 1834, and its principal recommendations were rapidly implemented in the Poor Law Amendment Act of 1834.[3] Equivalent proposals were introduced in Scotland during 1845. The new system rapidly came to be known as the New Poor Law, and while various minor modifications were made to the new system during the latter part of the nineteenth century, its basic shape remained in place. Parishes were grouped into Unions, each headed by a Board of Guardians, and a national board of commissioners was set up to oversee the whole system. From 1847 to 1871 the national co-ordinating body was known as the Poor Law Board, but after 1871 it was incorporated into the new Local Government Board.

Within each Union, the Boards of Guardians determined the level of relief and of the local taxes – the rates – that were needed to finance this level of relief. The Guardians were elected by the ratepayers of the parishes – originally only the wealthier ratepayers – but those who were receiving relief were not entitled to vote in elections. The franchise in local elections was thus restricted to those who were paying the taxes which financed welfare.[4] The Guardians were responsible for the administration of both 'outdoor' relief and the new workhouses, through which all relief to the able-bodied was to be given. Relief was, for the most part, supposed to be available only to residents of the workhouses in the form of 'indoor' relief. Relief was to be given to the able-bodied who became inmates of the workhouses, but not normally to those who remained 'outdoors'.

This system depended upon the utilitarian belief that people were motivated by the material and mental rewards and costs that were attached to their actions. Individuals were seen as rational calculators of these rewards and costs, and social policy could operate most effectively by changing the pattern of rewards and costs that were attached to different actions. If, for example, the costs of receiving relief were high relative to the actual level of relief, then people would seek to avoid these costs and so would endeavour to increase their incomes through other, less costly means. The system of indoor relief involved the 'cost' of a loss of freedom and so was believed to constitute an effective deterrent to those who might otherwise abuse the system through long-term reliance on outdoor relief.

A crucial support for this system was a belief in the cultural inheritance of poverty. It was held that there was a distinct culture of poverty, which shaped people's attitudes to work and relief. Unless they were appropriately motivated, it was felt, paupers would be unable to improve their situation, and their attitudes to work and to welfare would be passed on to their children. Hence, the workhouses were also to be institutions for the practical and moral training of the children of paupers so as to ensure that they started out their life with appropriate work attitudes and did not fall back into the culture of poverty.

The aims of the system were to ensure that only the truly destitute would receive relief – others would wish to avoid the workhouse and so would find ways to support themselves.

If the able-bodied labourer feared the workhouse, he would provide for his old age; he would join savings banks and benefits clubs to provide for his family. In time, new provident habits amongst the working class would save them from dependence on the parish, and private charity could cope with the residue whom thrift had not been able to protect.

(Crowther 1981: 17)

It was assumed, then, that protracted unemployment was a personal rather than a structural problem. The economy was believed to be perfectly capable of absorbing all those who sought work; those who were unemployed for any substantial period of time were in this condition of their own volition. On this basis, the desire to avoid the workhouse would motivate unemployed labourers who were properly socialised to seek work. Those who failed to acquire the appropriate habits of behaviour would be confined to the workhouse and made to undertake work in return for relief.

Central to the New Poor Law was the principle of 'less eligibility' which was seen as ensuring that appropriate motivational patterns were constructed. According to this principle, poor relief was to be made available under conditions that were inferior to – less eligible than – those of the lowest-paid wage labourer. The basic idea was that benefits should be lower than wages: relief should not be so generous as to remove the incentive to work. Those who were in employment and receiving a wage were assumed to be living at an adequate level and standard. If relief were set at or above this level there would be no incentive for the unemployed to seek new employment. The major difficulty in implementing a principle of less eligibility was that the relationship between poverty and unemployment was not this clear-cut. Wages were often well below the level that most people would have regarded as 'adequate', and the ability of a family to live on a particular level of income depended upon the size of the family and its particular circumstances. Poverty, that is to say, may be as much a feature of employment as it is of unemployment.

What this meant, in practice, was that the level of relief had to be kept above the lowest wage level in order to ensure the basic subsistence of those who were without work. In order to maintain the idea behind the principle of less eligibility this relief was made available within a social and cultural framework that would make it appear to be less desirable than low pay. This has led one commentator to remark that less eligibility 'was conceived in psychological rather than material terms' (Digby 1989: 31). The workhouse, as the ultimate sanction, was the basis of a system of stigmatisation. Through a desire to escape the stigma of the 'pauper' label, those who were in receipt of relief would be motivated to achieve the 'independence' of wage labour as soon as possible. Workhouses

were to be turned into places of discipline and terror; families were to be divided, husbands from wives and parents from children; all would be subject to strict and monotonous regimes, dressed in a pauper's uniform, and made to perform tasks such as stone-breaking or unpicking tarred rope.

(Novak 1988: 47; see also Ignatieff 1978, Goffman 1961, 1963)

Paupers were subject to the stigmatising regime of a total institution: they wore uniforms, family members were separated from one another, and they received education and sick relief in the separate Poor Law Infirmary and Poor Law School. They lost their personal freedom through detention in the workhouse and, following the extension of the franchise in 1867 and 1884, they were also politically disenfranchised. Paupers did retain a right to relief under the Poor Law, but they did not have the civil right to go to law to enforce this right to welfare.

In fact, however, local discretion meant that the able-bodied poor were frequently granted the cheaper form of outdoor relief. The workhouses, as a result, were filled with those who were seen as being incapable of helping themselves. Behind this practice was the widely held moral distinction between the 'deserving' and the 'undeserving' poor. The stigma of the workhouse, then, was applied to those who were already stigmatised as undeserving of help.

Those groups whose destitution was seen as the result of individual moral failing – feckless adults such as mothers of illegitimate children or vagrants – were given indoor relief in the workhouse. Other groups – widows, the temporarily disabled, the old – were seen as retaining respectability since their poverty was *not* perceived as avoidable. These groups were *not* usually relieved in the workhouse.

(Digby 1989: 34)

Those who were 'deserving' were those who had the appropriate attitudes to work or whose poverty was unavoidable because of their circumstances. Those who were 'undeserving' – the 'residuum' – were those who required coercion and whose attitudes and motivations were in need of retraining in the workhouse. This belief was particularly important in the work of the Charity Organisation Society, which attempted to ensure that private charities supported only those who were deserving of their help, and that the Poor Law institutions supported the undeserving poor.

The elderly were especially hard hit by this system. It was only their relatively small numbers – because of limited life expectancy – that prevented this from being perceived as a major national problem. As life expectancy improved, so the problem of poverty in old age became more obvious. For most people, the absence of a pension system meant that there was no provision for old age except that which was available through the Poor Law or private charity. Only those in the middle and the propertied classes were, in general, able to make any proper provision for their old age. Those in professions and trade were generally able to provide for themselves through savings. By investing a part of their income on the stock exchange, for example, they could create sufficient personal assets to generate an income for themselves. For those in the civil and military services there was generally some kind of official pension provision, while managerial and clerical employees of the large railway companies, the gas and water companies, and many banks were provided with private pensions by their employers' schemes. Everyone else continued to work for so long as they were able – and perhaps longer in many cases.

The workhouses became primarily institutions for the undeserving poor and for the elderly and infirm sections of the deserving poor who were unable to look after themselves. In 1860, for example, able-bodied labourers accounted for just 5 per cent of workhouse inmates (Crowther 1981: 72). This fact, created by local discretion and stigmatisation, led many to conclude that the workhouses were operating as intended: the very absence of the able-bodied labourers from the workhouse was, it was felt, a sign that the workhouse deterrent was successful.

Poverty and citizenship

What was established in the New Poor Law was a subsistence-level conception of poverty: people are poor when they cannot secure the means for their own survival. Subsistence needs provided the baseline for the measurement of poverty. This idea of poverty has remained the fundamental point of reference in all subsequent official views of welfare policy. The most influential of the early attempts to formalise it can be found in the work of

Seebohm Rowntree in 1899, whose investigations will be fully considered in later chapters. Rowntree employed a subsistence measure of poverty that was based on actual studies of diet and physiological needs. Using evidence from medical studies of nutrition, he calculated the average nutritional requirements of individuals and families and converted these into their monetary equivalents. This gave him a measure of the amount of money that was needed to secure the basic nutrition of an individual and his or her family, and he added to this an estimate of the minimum costs for clothing, fuel, and housing. The intention behind these calculations was to express in monetary terms the subsistence level below which individuals would experience survival-threatening hardships. People with incomes below this level were living in poverty. Those whose incomes were above the level but who engaged in 'wasteful' expenditure and so failed to meet their basic needs were not deserving of support as their deprivation was of their own making. Rowntree extended and elaborated this subsistence view in a study carried out in 1936, and it became a central plank in the Beveridge proposals for the reform of the welfare system following the Second World War.

This measure of poverty, defined on the basis of basic subsistence, has certain obvious attractions. In particular, it appears to offer an absolute and objective measure of poverty that can be applied to all societies and all times. A precise measure of subsistence needs allows policy makers to identify the specific level of income that a welfare system would need to ensure in order to eliminate, once and for all, the problem of poverty. Researchers can assess how far a particular society has moved towards this goal and can compare the degree of poverty in one society with that in another. Such investigations would be rooted in rigorous and indisputable physiological measures and would inform effective and legitimate anti-poverty policies.

There are, however, a number of fundamental difficulties with the subsistence view of poverty. It tends to equate 'poverty' with the very different idea of 'starvation'. Famine, other natural disasters, or the failure of a society's productive system to generate sufficient resources to feed all its members can produce widespread starvation, or near starvation, but those who are interested in poverty have not generally had such life-threatening conditions in mind. If poverty is equated with starvation, an important distinction is lost. Starvation may be avoided, but people may still be judged to be living in poverty. In practice, all attempts to establish a subsistence concept of poverty have, to a greater or lesser extent, gone beyond mere physiological needs. Rowntree, for example, included an estimate of the costs of clothing that rested upon what he and others of his time felt was 'appropriate' clothing for the low paid. The problem is, of course, that the number and type of underclothes, say, a person needs cannot be assessed with the same precision as the amount of carbohydrate that is required in a basic diet. Clothing needs are not only impossible to assess with any precision, but they also involve an irreducibly subjective element of moral judgement. Similar considerations apply to the nature and type of housing and of domestic goods and services: it is simply not possible, for example, to specify the basic 'subsistence' level of washing machine or vacuum cleaner that is required, or the number and size of rooms that are needed in a house.

Townsend (1974) has pointed out, even more fundamentally, that the physiological baseline can itself be questioned. Physiological needs vary according to age, the type of work undertaken, and other aspects of a person's life circumstances. Heavy manual work, for instance, requires a different calorie intake from a sedentary office job. Furthermore, it is not possible to specify the cost of achieving a particular level of nutrition unless subjective judgements are made about the nature and type of food that should be purchased – such food may not, in fact, be available to those who are regarded as 'requiring' it, and so they may have to spend their income in alternative, but equally legitimate ways. Any concept of subsistence depends upon criteria of what constitutes an 'adequate' or 'viable' way of life, and all such criteria involve subjective and culturally variable judgements rather than absolute measures of 'need'. Perceptions of the kind of food that should form part of a 'balanced' diet, for example, change over time and vary from one society to another.

Townsend drew the conclusion that any view of poverty, however 'absolute' it may seem, is historically and culturally relative. 'Needs' are rooted in social customs and conventions, and the means that are available to meet these needs are only ever available in socially variable forms. This led Townsend to conclude that all measures of poverty are, inevitably, *relative* to social circumstances, and that this fact should be recognised explicitly in any attempt to reconceptualise poverty. According to Townsend, poverty consists not of an inability to meet an apparently absolute subsistence minimum, but of an inability to meet the standards of living that are customary for the society in which the person lives. Poverty has to be measured in relation to – relative to – the living standards that are generally accepted as 'normal' for that society. On this basis, it is not possible to compare the 'absolute' levels of poverty found in Victorian England with those found in contemporary Britain; nor can either of these be compared with, say, the level of poverty in contemporary India. Such comparisons make sense only if account is taken of the radical differences that exist among these societies in terms of the kinds of food, clothing, shelter, and general lifestyle that are both available to and expected by the members of each society.

12 Poverty and Wealth: Citizenship, deprivation and privilege

The investigations of poverty that have been undertaken by Peter Townsend have involved a radical reconsideration of all earlier approaches, leading him to argue for a concept of poverty as 'relative deprivation' (1974, 1979, 1987). Deprivation is assessed relative to the prevailing standards of a society. Townsend's position is based on an implicit concept of 'citizenship'. To be deprived, and hence to live in poverty, is to be excluded from the kind of life expected of a full citizen of the society. To be 'deprived' is to be denied the *power* that is normally accorded to the citizen. As Kincaid has argued:

to be poor is not just to be located at the tail end of some distribution of income, but to be placed in a particular sort of powerlessness, an inability to control the circumstances of one's life in the face of more powerful groups in society.

(1973: 171)

Discussions of citizenship have generally taken the work of T.H. Marshall (1949) as their point of reference. Reviewing trends in British social policy, Marshall set out an account of citizenship that saw the extent of social inequality as being limited by the institutionalised expectation that all full members of British society would participate in 'the essential elements in civilisation or culture'. He argued that 'the standard of civilised life' which underpinned modern British citizenship involved a universalisation of standards that had, through most of the nineteenth century, been held to be appropriate only for 'gentlemen'. The claim to a right to participate in this civilised life was, he argued, 'a claim to be admitted to a share in the social heritage, which in turn means a claim to be accepted as full members of the society, that is, as citizens' (1949: 72). Marshall's argument drew on his observation of the development of the post-war welfare state, which was under construction at the time that he was writing. A central feature of the form of citizenship that emerged in modern Britain, according to Marshall, was 'a universal right to real income' which was not directly linked to power in the labour market. Citizenship, then, involved a partial equalisation between capital and labour, though it did not involve their full equality.

From this understanding of the British situation, Marshall developed his general model of citizenship in modern societies. Participation in a 'cultured' or 'civilised' lifestyle is the central idea in this model. Marshall elaborated on this idea in terms of the enlargement of a 'common culture and common experience' within which different groups participate and which defines the boundaries of citizenship (1949: 121).

'Citizenship' as a sociological concept refers to the rights and lifestyles embodied in the cultural understandings and normative obligations that define full membership in a society. Marshall concluded that

Citizenship is a status bestowed on those who are full members of a community. All who possess the status are equal with respect to the rights and duties with which the status is endowed. There is no universal principle that determines what those rights and duties shall be, but societies in which citizenship is a developing institution create an image of an ideal citizenship against which achievement can be measured and towards which aspiration can be directed.

(1949: 87)

The establishment of a right to a basic level of income gave people the opportunity to participate in the 'material civilisation' of a consumer society (1949: 100). Different categories of worker – manual and non-manual – may differ in their incomes, but they can enjoy the same general standard of amenities, and there is a 'safety net' to prevent people from falling below this level. Under a fully established system of citizenship, the vagaries of the market and of individual circumstances, such as disability, ill health, unemployment, old age, and family size, do not prevent people from enjoying the minimum level of material consumption that is believed to be appropriate for a citizen.

It is through Marshall's concept of citizenship – and the various critical discussions to which it has been subjected – that we can best develop the kind of 'relative' concept of poverty that Townsend advocated. Poverty and deprivation must be seen as relative to the prevailing standards of living that are specified in a society's criteria of citizenship. The attempts by nineteenth-century writers to develop a subsistence criterion of poverty reflected the particular liberal conception of citizenship that informed official policy at that time. It is in this sense that official views of the poor from the New Poor Law principle of 'less eligibility' to present-day views of 'welfare dependency' can be understood. The poor occupy a distinct social status, the status of 'second class citizen, deprived of most of the important rights of citizenship' (T.H. Marshall 1965: 26).

Although there is no legal definition of 'poverty' in Britain today, a *de facto* official criterion has emerged through the use by politicians and civil servants of the social assistance qualification level as a basis for the measurement of poverty. In Britain basic social assistance has been termed, at various times, National Assistance, Supplementary Benefit, and Income Support. While entitlement to social assistance has always been subject to a complex system of regulations, it is nevertheless possible to assess the level at which the right to welfare can be activated. It is possible to measure how the income of any individual or household compares with the amount that the welfare system assumes to be necessary for people in their circumstances: how much, for example, is supposed to be the minimum for a single person, a couple, a family with two children, and so on. The *official* poverty line, then, can be seen as being set at that level of resources at which the government recognises an obligation to step in and to supplement individual or family income with safety-net welfare benefits. The point of view has been made quite clear in official publications:

the purpose of the Supplementary Benefit scheme is to bring the resources of each person up to the appropriate level of requirements approved by Parliament.

(DHSS 1969, quoted in Atkinson 1969: 16)

While governments and their advisers have sought to justify the level at which this is set on 'absolute', subsistence standards, the mere fact that the level changes over time (after allowing for inflation) is sufficient to show that official practice is based on a relative standard of poverty. What might be referred to as the British Official Poverty Line (BOPL) can be drawn at the social assistance qualification level that is current at the time to which the data relate. Such data were tabulated by the Department of Health and Social Security from 1972 to 1985, but they can be calculated – with varying degrees of difficulty – for any period.[5] This has, in fact, formed the basis of many studies of poverty.

Comparative studies ought, in principle, to be able to adopt a similar procedure, using whatever official poverty lines are recognised in the countries concerned. In practice, this has rarely been possible. The system of public welfare that has been established varies considerably from one country to another, and governments vary in the extent to which they regard their social assistance level as defining a *de jure* or *de facto* poverty line. There are, furthermore, national variations in the extent to which public opinion sees 'poverty' as a 'problem' in need of research and policy reform.

Despite these problems, an important approach to comparative research was initiated in the European Community programme on poverty. This defined the poor as 'persons, families and groups of persons whose resources (material, cultural and social) are so limited as to exclude them from a minimum acceptable way of life in the Member state in which they live' (EC 1984, quoted in Room 1990: 40). Because of national variations of the kind that I have indicated, this idea was operationalised on the basis of measures of income distribution. Poverty, it was held, characterised all individuals and families whose disposable income was 50 per cent or less of the national average. Those households with an income at or below this level were regarded as living in poverty.[6] This procedure of setting up what might be described as a European Poverty Line (EPL) involves a departure from the various official standards that have been adopted in member nations of the European Community. It does, however, reflect an attempt to establish a coherent and consistent relative measure of poverty at the European level. Recognising that poverty is defined in custom and convention as well as in official practice, the approach sees poverty as relative to whatever pattern of income distribution is maintained by official social and economic policies within a particular society.

The EPL measure also suggests the possibility of a Europe-wide measure of poverty that is rooted in the international distribution of income. If it can be assumed that there are Community-wide expectations about income minima, then it can be said that poverty exists for any individual or family whose income falls at or below 50 per cent of the average income level for the Community as a whole. An important legal support for such a measure would be the as yet incomplete drive towards a Community-wide conception of citizenship, as envisaged in the 'social dimension' of the recent European treaties (Roche 1992: 208ff). Despite these moves – and despite the existence of a European passport – there is no constitutional concept of a European citizen and no centralised mechanism for welfare provision at the Community level. The 50 per cent threshold suggested here and in the EPL measure is, of course, an arbitrary cut-off point. In this respect it is unlike the officially recognised threshold of the BOPL. It would be possible, for example, to define poverty in terms of 40 per cent or 60 per cent of the national average income. Nevertheless, where studies are concerned with countries that are broadly comparable in their economic and political structures, the EPL can give a useful indicator of the extent of poverty.

Official standards are not, of course, the only standards for assessing poverty. One of the implications of Marshall's argument is that the customary and conventional standards of citizenship that prevail in a society may be only imperfectly reflected in official practices. The institutionalised beliefs of those who live in a society about what is appropriate or normal for one of its citizens may be ignored or even denied in official policy, but this does not make them any the less relevant to the definition of poverty. Poverty, then, can be assessed relative to those 'unofficial' standards that are held by the members of the society themselves. Such standards – expressed in assessments of 'public opinion' – stand in a complex relationship to government policy and official practices, and an important task for researchers into poverty is to uncover these views and to use them in the measurement of poverty.

Whether Marshall intended it or not, discussions of his concept of citizenship have tended to assume a unitary model of citizenship that develops, wherever it arises, in precisely the same way. The form of citizenship that emerged in Britain is seen as being characteristic of all other societies. Bryan Turner has sought to avoid this unitary view of citizenship by advancing a powerful and illuminating typology of citizenship that is rooted in a wider and more all-embracing theoretical framework (1986a, 1986b,

1988, 1990, 1991; see also M. Mann 1988). The concept of the 'dominant ideology', which Turner and his colleagues have critically elaborated in a series of publications (Abercrombie *et al.* 1980, 1983, 1990), plays an important part in his analysis and suggests a way of understanding variations between 'official' and 'unofficial' views within a society. Turner's concern is to reject 'consensus' explanations of social stability: socialisation into a dominant ideology is not an important element in social cohesion. The ideology is, however, important in maintaining the internal cohesion of the dominant class itself, and this ideology finds its expression in many aspects of the operation of the state. The acceptance of state policies by members of the other classes is not normally due to this ideology *per se*, but to a pragmatic acceptance of the core institutions and policies that it legitimates. The idea of 'citizenship', according to Turner, is a key element in the dominant ideologies of modern societies. I shall develop these ideas in later chapters of this book.

Matters of definition

My aim in this book is to provide an overview of those patterns of wealth and poverty that are found in Britain and certain other modern societies. In providing this overview I have tried to take a loose and open approach to technical questions of definition and measurement. All too many studies in this area have become so concerned with technicalities that it is difficult to draw any general conclusions from them. I have adopted the opposite approach. I have assumed that those who are interested in definitional matters will prefer to consult the large number of technical sources that are available and that most readers would find a detailed consideration of these issues to be a distraction from the main purpose of the book. It is important, though, to give some indication of how the principal terms have been defined in the various studies to which I have referred.[7]

I am concerned with the distribution of economic resources and, specifically, with the conditions of poverty and wealth that arise from this distribution. My usage of the term 'wealth' in this book accords with the everyday idea that a person is 'wealthy' when he or she is particularly advantaged in the distribution of economic resources. Wealth, like poverty, is a feature of particular patterns of inequality. This usage is something of a departure from the definition of wealth that is generally employed in studies of distribution. In these studies a distinction is generally made between 'income' and 'wealth', where income is the *flow* of economic resources that a person receives in a particular period, and wealth is the total *stock* of such resources that a person has accumulated. 'Income', then, is the total daily, weekly, or annual value of such things as earnings from employment, interest on savings and investments, grants, state benefits, and so on. Income can be measured both 'before' and 'after' the taxes that are applied to its various components. After-tax income, or *net* income, is the 'disposable income' that a person has available for spending.[8] Personal 'wealth', on the other hand, refers to the monetary value of the physical and financial assets that belong to a person and that he or she has been able to accumulate from income and from other sources. I have used such terms as 'personal assets' or 'personal property' for this idea, in order to retain the word 'wealth' to refer to its original meaning of the advantaged possession of personal assets.

In defining income and personal assets I have referred to the 'person' who receives or owns them. In many cases, however, the family or household is the more meaningful unit of analysis, and many studies do, in fact, refer to family income or household assets. Where such differences are relevant, they will be made apparent in my discussion. Matters are further complicated by the fact that official statistics often refer to 'tax units' or other categories that may include individuals, couples, families, or households, and which may be difficult to translate into more meaningful terms. Fortunately, *trends* in such figures generally move in the same direction, whichever unit is used, and so a clear view of overall trends can be obtained. Wherever this is not the case, I have tried to indicate the differences that exist. More problematic is the varying *level* of inequality that is apparent from statistics based upon different units of analysis. All that can be done in many cases is to put the differing estimates alongside one another with an indication of the respects in which they differ.

Other definitional matters relating to income and personal assets need not detain us here; they will be introduced in the main text whenever they are relevant. It is, however, necessary to say something about the definitions of poverty and wealth that I have adopted. 'Poverty' – as I have already shown – is a highly contested term. In its most general sense, poverty refers to a lack of the economic resources that are necessary for the enjoyment of a basic standard of living, however this is seen in the particular society in question. The poor are those who are 'deprived' of the conditions necessary for an adequate life in the society in which they live. One implication of the work of Marshall and Townsend is that it is possible to conceptualise 'wealth' in parallel terms. To be wealthy is to enjoy a standard of living that is greater than that normal for members of a particular society. If deprivation is the condition of life of the poor, 'privilege' is the condition of life of the wealthy.

Deprivation and privilege should be seen as complementary terms and as indicating contrasting departures from the normal lifestyle of the citizen. If it is possible to recognise a 'poverty line', it may also be possible to recognise a 'wealth line': the poverty line defines the level at which deprivation begins, and the wealth line defines the level at which privilege begins. From this point of view, deprivation and privilege are polarised conditions of life that reflect the polarisation of wealth and poverty. A recognition of this fact forces us to recognise that the causes of poverty cannot be separated from the causes of wealth: indeed, the one may be a necessary condition of the other. Townsend's work has developed the powerful idea of poverty as 'relative deprivation', the concept being designed to overcome the inadequacies of attempts to define poverty in simple subsistence terms as an ahistorical absolute. My contention is that an analogous concept of wealth as 'relative privilege' can go a considerable way towards overcoming the difficulties faced in the assessment of wealth.

Notes

1   More detailed historical considerations can be found in D. Marshall (1965), Rose (1971), Fraser (1973), Digby (1989), and Novak (1988).
2   Here, as elsewhere in official policy, the assumption of the male breadwinner was paramount.
3   See Reports from Commissioners (1834). The text is reprinted in Checkland and Checkland (1974), which also contains a useful introduction by the editors.
4   The ratepayers were the householders, and so many women were excluded from voting. Families in short-term rented accommodation, such as weekly tenants, were also unable to vote.
5   Since 1985 the data have been calculated by the privately funded Institute for Fiscal Studies.
6   Statistics for Britain calculated on this basis can be found in CSO (1990).
7   A good introduction to technical issues can be found in Atkinson (1972, 1973, 1975).
8   It can be argued that a measure of before-tax income should also disregard state benefits and other 'transfer incomes' that are financed from taxation, but this flies in the face of common sense.

CHAPTER 2

Poverty and wealth: the past

The extent of poverty in the nineteenth century was, I have shown, a matter of contentious public debate. Towards the end of the century, however, more systematic research became available through the sociological research of Charles Booth, a wealthy Liverpool shipowner. In 1886 he undertook an investigation into the extent of poverty in London, the first systematic sociological study on such a scale. The final results of his work appeared in a massive seventeen-volume series of books, under the collective title *Life and Labour of the People in London* (1902–3). These volumes contain street-by-street accounts of the living and working conditions of the population of London, reviews of social conditions in all the major occupations, and a comprehensive series of maps showing the social characteristics of the various parts of London.

Shortly before Booth's volumes were published in their complete version a companion study was begun in York by Seebohm Rowntree. Using similar methods to those of Booth, Rowntree explored the extent of poverty in a provincial city, and he laid the foundations for much sociological research. The subsistence measure of poverty that Rowntree used became the cornerstone of official and unofficial inquiries for the next fifty years or more. Most important among these later investigations were Rowntree's own follow-up studies of York.

Booth gave only cursory consideration to the question of wealth, and Rowntree hardly considered it at all. This was hardly surprising, given contemporary attitudes, but it means that there was no attempt to understand the interdependence of poverty and wealth as structural elements in British society. Despite the existence of a major official inquiry into land ownership, undertaken in the 1870s, it was not until the turn of the century that researchers began to explore the relationship between wealth and the general structure of inequality.

Booth and poverty in London

The research that was undertaken by Charles Booth began as an investigation simply of East London. Booth and his research assistants had intended to build up a complete census of all residents, collecting information that was not available in the official Census statistics. The research was to concentrate on the extent of poverty and the conditions that were responsible for this. Such a mammoth task – there were three quarters of a million people living in the district – could clearly not be achieved through direct house-to-house survey methods, and so Booth sought a way of approximating to this. Information was collected from the School Board visitors, each of whom was responsible for all the children of school age who were living in their districts. Booth realised that these officials must have known their districts intimately and would be a fruitful source of information on households. Through detailed interviews with these inspectors and also with the clergy, the police, and various other agencies, Booth tried to build up a comprehensive picture of complete streets and, thereby, of the whole of East London. While he did not undertake house-to-house enquiries – he obtained his data 'second-hand, only rarely obtaining any information directly from the families themselves – the published volumes together provide a unique and comprehensive supplement to the official Census volumes.

Booth aimed to work out from the study of East London to an investigation of London as a whole. In this task he had the support of the then Registrar General and he was permitted to make use of unpublished material from the 1881 Census. Through this work he came to have a major influence over the form that was taken by the 1891 Census, and he worked Census data into his own accounts of London life. East London remained the most thoroughly researched part of Booth's work, but he and his colleagues undertook similar studies of the central London districts of Soho, St Giles, and Bloomsbury, and the south London district of Battersea and its neighbourhood.

As Booth wanted to achieve a complete survey of the whole of London, he altered his approach somewhat as the research developed. His aim was to enable himself to arrive at an estimate of the extent of poverty in London as a whole and in its various sub-districts. As information could not realistically be sought for all families in London – they totalled over four million people – he modified his earlier approach and sought to describe the general condition of every *street* in London. Interviews with the School Board visitors were used to gauge the number of adults and of children in each street and to assess their general standard of living.

The core of Booth's findings is contained in Volumes 1 and 2 of his work (see Figure 2.1). Volume 1, *East, Central and South London*, contains his general accounts, together with extracts from his notebooks giving details on particular streets. Volume 2, *Streets and Population Classified*, goes systematically through each of the London School Board districts, summarising their

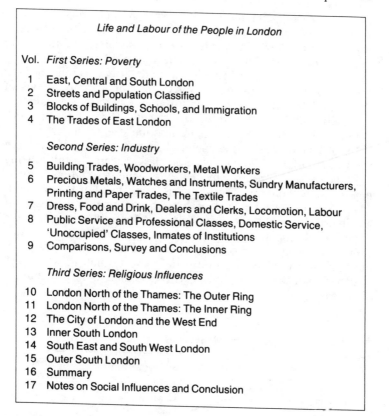

Figure 2.1 **Synopsis of the Booth series**

characteristics and giving examples drawn from particular streets. A *Descriptive Map of London Poverty, 1889* (Booth 1889) was published as a supplement to Volume 2, showing the various districts coloured according to their poverty or wealth.

Booth began his first volume with some detailed house-by-house excerpts from his field notes, though he used pseudonyms to protect the identities of the actual street names. In the second volume, however, he gave further excerpts and provided a list of the real names corresponding to each of the pseudonyms; in an attempt to maintain the anonymity of individuals he used pseudonyms for the people that he mentioned. Streets were classified according to the extent of their poverty, and they were labelled according to the colours that were used on his descriptive maps. Thus the streets of London were described as ranging from the 'black' streets of great poverty, through various shades of 'blue' and 'purple' to the comfortable 'pink' streets and the relatively affluent 'red' and 'yellow' streets. Throughout his work Booth used these colour labels to describe streets and areas.

In order to study the social distribution of poverty and wealth, Booth devised an eight-fold class schema. In this schema households were grouped by the employment situation of their heads and by their 'apparent status as to means'. For Booth, then, 'class' was a concept that described occupational and household income. Related to this class schema was a classification of streets according to the prevailing class character of the households. It was by assigning a colour to each of the street categories that Booth was able to produce the poverty map in which the distribution of colours on the map corresponded to the distribution of classes.

Table 2.1   The class schema of the Booth survey

Street description	Class income*	Class description		Street category
Wealthy: upper class, upper middle class	H	Upper middle class (and above)		Yellow
Well-to-do middle class	G	Lower middle class		Red
Working class comfort, fairly comfortable	E F above 21s	Higher class labour Regular standard earnings	} Pink	} Purple
Ordinary poverty	D } 18s to 21s	Small regular earnings } Poor	Lt. Blue	
Standard poverty	C	Intermittent earnings		
Very poor, chronic want	B below 18s	Casual earnings	} Very poor	Dark blue
Lowest grade, vicious, semi-criminal	A	Lowest class of occasional and semi-criminals		Black

* Income per week. One shilling is the equivalent of 5 pence in decimal currency.

Source: Compiled from Booth (1902–3)

In Table 2.1 the street classification and the class schema are combined, though the correspondence between these two classifications is not perfect. The eight social classes were labelled from A to H, and each was given a description which Booth felt grasped its principal social characteristics. The most important characteristics for Booth were the nature and level of the earnings of household members. Class E, for example, was categorised as 'Higher class labour', and this was qualified as comprising those in highly paid work, those who were regularly employed and fairly paid. Those in class B, on the other hand, were described as following a 'hand-to-mouth existence'.

In many cases Booth's value judgements were made obvious in the descriptions that he gave to the various classes. This is particularly apparent in the street descriptions, where he characterised the streets that were occupied predominantly by members of class A as consisting of the 'lowest grade, vicious, semi-criminals', the 'loafers' who comprise the elements of disorder in the city. More objectively, his street classification added some information concerning the household composition of the various classes. He argued that a defining characteristic of the upper and upper-middle classes was that they had three or more servants (and they paid housing rates of £100 or more). Other members of the middle class, in class G, kept two or more domestic servants. The final column in the figure shows the street colours that were used on his maps, ranging from the golden yellow of the wealthy through to the dense black of the disorderly streets that were inhabited by the lowest classes. The streets of those living in comfort were coloured pink, while poverty-stricken streets were coloured light blue. Booth recognised, however, that many London streets combined both types of families in close proximity, and these streets he coloured purple to indicate their mixed character.

Booth held that the 'poor' (classes D and C, comprising 'those whose means may be sufficient, but are barely sufficient for decent independent life') and the 'very poor' (classes B and A, containing 'those whose means are insufficient' for a decent life) together constitute the problem of poverty. It is worth noting that Booth explicitly adopts a 'relative' view of poverty: poverty is defined by an inability to meet the 'usual standard of life in this country' (Spicker 1990). Booth's estimate of the level at which poverty occurred was based around the assumed needs of a 'moderate family', comprising two adults and up to three children. For the purposes of his research, he set this level at 21s (£1.05) per week . Above this level, he believed, families could avoid poverty, but below this level life became increasingly difficult. The ordinary poor were those whose income was regular but too small (below 21s) to sustain a moderate family in a 'decent independent life'. 'Chronic want' set in whenever income fell below 18s per week. The very poor were those who relied upon casual or illegitimate income that fell so far below the needs of a comfortable life that they were in a permanent state of deprivation.

Booth gave no detailed justification for his choice of a 21s dividing line between 'comfort' and poverty, and, incidentally, he did not use the term 'poverty line'. The level of 'round about a pound per week' (Pember Reeves 1913) was, however, widely regarded as being typical of the mainstream of the working class, and Booth himself took the level of 21s from the actual income that was enjoyed by those wage earners who were just able to meet 'the usual standard of life in this country' (Booth 1902–3, 1: 33). This operational definition, then, assumed some degree of social consensus over the minimum standards of comfort that were necessary in the society of his time.

Table 2.2 shows some of Booth's principal findings. Booth remarked that he was himself surprised by the figures for London as a whole. He had discovered that 35.2 per cent of the population in the East End were living in poverty, and he expected that the figure for London as a whole would be much lower. Instead, he found broadly comparable levels of poverty across the whole of London. Almost one third of London's total population was estimated as living in poverty. The reason for this high average,

Table 2.2 *Poverty distribution in London, 1886–9*

Class		East London	Central London	Battersea	All London (1889)
			Distribution (%)		
H	Upper class and	5.0	5.2	2.0	5.9
G	middle class	3.9	14.4	7.5	11.9
F	Working class	13.6	16.0	18.6	51.5
E		42.3	38.1	38.5	
D	Ordinary poor	14.5	5.2	12.9	22.3
C		8.3	6.5	14.9	
B	Very poor	11.2	13.1	5.1	7.5
A		1.2	1.5	0.5	0.9
Total		35.2	26.3	33.4	30.7

Source: Columns 1 to 3 from Booth (1902–3, 1: 36, 248–9, 284–5), column 4 from Booth (1902–3, 2: 21). The data in column 4 relate to the street survey, in which the distinctions between classes E and F and between C and D could not be made. The division between classes G and H for all London is based on an estimate in Booth (1902–3, 3: 22)

he argued, was the existence of extremely high levels of poverty in parts of south London and in Holborn, which pushed the London average up from the 25 per cent level that he had expected to the 30 per cent level that he actually discovered. Table 2.2 shows some of the more important regional variations within London, with poverty in central London standing at 26.3 per cent and in Battersea, in south London, at 33.4 per cent. Figure 2.2 gives a more graphic picture of poverty in Booth's London, showing the concentration of poverty in the inner London areas closest to the river.

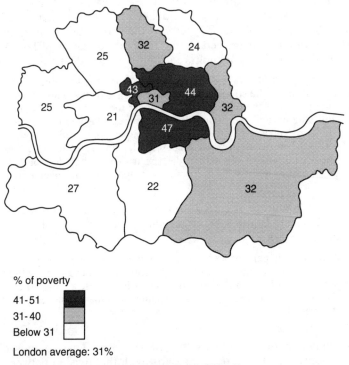

% of poverty

41-51

31- 40

Below 31

London average: 31%

Source: Compiled from various tables in Booth (1902–3)

Figure 2.2 The spatial distribution of poverty (1886–89)

The densest area of deprivation, with 67.9 per cent of the population living in poverty, was found in Southwark, in south London. This was followed by Greenwich with 65.2 per cent and a part of Clerkenwell with 60.9 per cent. The wealthiest areas – or, at least, those with the lowest levels of poverty – were Dulwich (1.3 per cent), Mayfair (2.7 per cent), and Belgravia (5.0 per cent). Although there was a tendency for the western and south-western areas to have lower levels of poverty than the central and eastern districts, there was a complex mixture of wealth and poverty within all districts. The relatively comfortable west-central districts, for example, included both Mayfair, with its 2.7 per cent poverty, and Westminster, with 45.9 per cent poverty.

The majority of the 30.7 per cent of Londoners who were living in poverty were living in what Booth termed 'ordinary poverty', but 8.4 per cent of London's population were found to be living in conditions of 'chronic want'. The very poor he found to consist of occasional labourers, street sellers, and many who were involved in criminal activities, together with those who were reliant on casual work – in the East End the docks were a major source of casual work. Classes A and B together – the very poor – comprised what Marxists have described as the 'lumpenproletariat'. Class A comprised a hereditary subculture of outcasts and deviants:

Their life is the life of savages . . . From these come the battered figures who slouch through the streets, and play the beggar or the bully, or help to foul the record of the unemployed; these are the worst class of corner men who hang around the doors of public houses, the young men who spring forward on any chance to earn a copper, the ready materials for disorder when occasion serves. They render no useful service, they create no wealth: more often they destroy it. They degrade whatever they touch, and as individuals are perhaps incapable of improvement.

(Booth 1902–3, 1: 38)

The casual labourers of class B worked, perhaps, for three days in any week, and Booth saw this as being more a matter of choice than of necessity:

The ideal of such persons is to work when they like and play when they like . . . They cannot stand the regularity and dullness of civilised existence, and find the excitement they need in the life of the streets, or at home as spectators of or participants in some highly coloured domestic scene.

(1902–3, 1: 43)

Booth had more sympathy for the ordinary poor. They comprised both labourers and the poorer artisans, with the division between classes C and D corresponding to that between those dependent on seasonal work and those with regular work. All were, however, in low-paid work. Their ability to avoid poverty depended upon the earnings of their children and on their own habits of providence, thrift, and sobriety. Writing of the labourers in class D, Booth said: 'these men have a hard struggle to make ends meet, but they are, as a body, decent steady men, paying their way and bringing up their children respectably'. He added that 'The comfort of their homes depends, even more than in other classes, on a good wife' (1902–3, 1: 50). It was the thrifty housekeeping of the wife that allowed them to survive on such a small income.

Booth had far less to say about the wealthy. The upper middle class (class H), which included the upper class, was defined as 'the servant keeping class', and they were distinct from the lower-middle class of clerks, shopkeepers, and subordinate professionals (class G). The people in class H were estimated to have made up 5.9 per cent of London's population in 1889. Although he had a definition of poverty as the level of resources that allowed people to live a socially acceptable life, Booth had no corresponding analytical concept of 'wealth' as a level of resources that would allow people to live *above* the normally accepted social level. Instead, the wealthy were described simply as 'class H', the 'upper class and upper middle class' who occupied the 'yellow' streets.

Although he concentrated on describing the lives of the servants and coachmen who served the wealthy, he did give some details of the latter's circumstances. He pointed to the fact that the life of the West End districts surrounding Hyde Park and Kensington Gardens, Mayfair, Kensington, and Belgravia, was dominated by the 'season', the round of exclusive social activities that determined when the lives of the wealthy centred on the country and when on the city. The whole appearance of the area was structured by the seasonal migration of the population:

its gloom in November, the fairy transformation of April, and the marvellous greenery of May and June; the rushing life of the season followed by the emptiness of August, and the weird effect of shut-up houses in the autumn months.

(Booth 1902–3, 12: 93)

Wealthy and poor were interdependent in the London system, and the absence of the wealthy from the city had important consequences for the employment prospects of many ordinary workers throughout the city. Much seasonal work, for example, was geared to the needs of the London 'season'.

Booth gave some further indication of the character of the wealthiest sections of London's population in his survey of trades, where he looked at the 'unoccupied' and at those who were described in the 1891 Census as 'living on own means' (1902–3, 8: pt 3). Just over 60,000 heads of household were living on their own means – relying on private incomes, annuities, and dividends. Taking account of their families, this represented almost 200,000 people in all. To these must be added those who were described as 'capitalists, landowners, etc,' in order to arrive at a full picture of the wealthy. Unfortunately, Booth did not provide this picture in his study.

It is possible to obtain a sense of the depth and subtlety of his analysis of poverty by examining some of his detailed descriptions of streets falling within the black (class A), dark blue (class B), and light blue (classes C and D) categories.

Black areas: Booth analysed a cluster of 'black' streets in the Seven Dials district of Soho in central London, an area that was knocked down and redeveloped very soon after his inquiry began. Almost half of the residents in the larger district were living in poverty – 30 per cent in classes A and B (1902–3, 2: 20, Appendix). The centre of this cluster of 'black' streets was Shelton Street, a narrow street of about forty three-storied houses containing 200 families, most of them living in single-room accommodation. Most of the residents were Irish Catholics working, if at all, as market porters and street sellers. The occupants he described as drunken and dirty; the houses as vermin-ridden. He reported that

Several occupants have said that in hot weather they don't go to bed, but sit in their clothes in the least infested part of the room. What good is it, they said, to go to bed when you can't get a wink of sleep for bugs and fleas? A visitor in these rooms was fortunate indeed if he carried nothing of the kind away with him.

(1902–3, 2: 47)

Sixteen pages were allocated to a systematic description of Shelton Street, with a page or more given to each of the houses listed. At house number 8, for instance, Booth described a woman who lived with her daughter in one room on the second floor, the younger woman earning a living for the two of them through prostitution:

The mother is a notorious drunkard, very violent in her cups, often in trouble with the police, and struck the Protestant missionary in the face in defence of her holy mother of God, backing this up with oaths and foul language.[1]

(1902–3, 2: 52)

Dark blue areas: among these was Old Nicol Street in the Shoreditch district of Bethnal Green, a notorious slum area described later on in a novel (Morrison 1896). It was 'a district where poverty is almost solid' (Booth 1902–3, 3: 94). The houses had formerly been occupied by weavers and contained large rooms that had housed the looms. These had disappeared by the time of Booth's survey, and the large rooms had been subdivided into smaller ones. The houses were old and dilapidated, and families tended, again, to occupy only one room. The residents included street sellers of fruit and baked potatoes, labourers, furniture workers, and box makers. The environment here too was dirty:

In one street is the body of a dead dog and near by two dead cats, which lie as though they had slain each other. All three have been crushed flat by the traffic which has gone over them.

(Booth 1902–3, 3: 96)

The area also contained a number of schools, shops, and missions from which soup kitchens operated. In the surrounding district three quarters of the population lived in poverty, 45 per cent of the population coming from classes A and B. Old Nicol Street itself had 50 per cent of its residents in classes A and B, and a further 25 per cent were members of classes C and D.

Light blue areas: Longhedge Street in Battersea, south London, was dominated by classes C and D, though it also contained some families who lived in extreme poverty. Its residents were mixed in occupational background, and included casual labourers, plasterers, tailors, compositors, and street sellers. This street had 14 per cent of its population in classes A and B, and 70 per cent in classes C and D.

Booth gave rather less attention to the comfortable and the affluent than he did to the poor. Typical of his coverage of the more comfortable are his descriptions of the 'purple' streets – those in which comfort was mixed with poverty. His two-page account of Red Lion Passage in Holborn, for example, comprises a general account with summary details of ten houses. Number 11, for example, was occupied exclusively by one family, comprising a man, his three daughters, and a lodger. The family occupied a four-room house next door to a 'very respectable' public house, and the man ran his own boot shop from the premises. His daughters were 'well-to-do' pupil teachers and the lodger ran a second-hand book shop next door. Number 12, on the other hand, was occupied by four separate households, each in one or two rooms, their members' occupations being carpenter and jobber, box maker, and running a soup shop. The box maker was a woman who supported her mother (aged eighty-five) and daughter: the family 'Just gets along.'

In both sections of the poor – the ordinary poor and the very poor – Booth identified casual or irregular earnings as the single most important cause of poverty (see Table 2.3), though I have

Table 2.3 **Booth's causes of poverty**

	Distribution (%)	
	Very poor	*Ordinary poor*
Loafers	4	0
Casual work, irregular pay	43	43
Low pay	12	25
Drink	14	13
Illness, infirmity	10	5
Large family	8	9
Mixed[*]	9	5

[*] Illness or large family combined with irregular work

Source: Booth (1902–3, 1: 147)

shown that Booth distinguished the two sections in terms of their willingness to take on regular work. The second most important cause among the ordinary, 'decent' poor was low pay. Unemployment in its modern sense was not a separate factor, as the absence of good welfare provision meant that all who were able to do so took on some form of casual or intermittent work. Unemployment, then, was 'hidden' in the general category of casual and irregular work: 'Here are the plentiful materials from which a Sunday mass meeting of the unemployed may be drawn' (Booth 1902–3, 1: 150). Industry needed its reserve army, he said, but the reserve army was currently too large. Booth concluded that it was necessary to examine the structure of industry and employment in London in order to discover the possibilities for expanding the amount of regular employment.

A series of five volumes was published as his survey of industry and employment (see Figure 2.1). These five volumes reviewed various trades in considerable detail, and they also included some notes on pensioners and paupers. The general pattern of information given for each trade was very similar, including statistical and more qualitative evidence on the numbers employed, levels of pay, hours worked, unionisation, and the attitudes of the workers.

Typical of Booth's approach was his survey of the numerous transport workers – cab and omnibus drivers, carmen, railway workers, merchant seamen, and lightermen.[2] He began with a general review of the 154,249 people employed in these trades in 1891, looking at trends in employment over time, at their general conditions of housing, and at the extent of poverty. Poverty was greatest among carmen – 58.3 per cent lived in poverty – and lowest among those in the railway service, of whom 27.8 per cent lived in poverty. From this general survey he moved on to an account of each separate section within the industry.

He began his description of cabmen and omnibus workers, for example, with an analysis of the age distribution in the trade, as compared with that for the general working population, and he compiled a series of tables from unpublished Census Office sources to show where they lived, the numbers of rooms that they occupied, and some of the differences between the various branches of the trades. Booth then drew on his interviews with employers and workers in order to describe the organisation of the work.

London cabmen, he showed, were of two kinds. They were either proprietors who drove their own cabs or drivers who paid a daily rental for cab and horses to an owner. Cab proprietors were generally the better-off members of the trade, though competition was tight and income was generally low. Booth records that average earnings were around 30s per week, though cabbies worked thirteen or fourteen hours a day to earn this.

Proprietors were responsible for all the costs of licensing, stabling, and maintaining their cabs and horses, and they had to meet these costs from their own earnings.

Bus drivers, by contrast, were generally employees of a company or small firm. A busmen's strike had resulted in an agreement for shorter hours, but Booth showed that working hours had risen to around fifteen hours a day. Drivers received 7s 6d per day for this work, while conductors received 5s 6d. The higher-paid inspectors received about 35s per week. As drivers and conductors were paid at daily rates, many of them worked long hours for seven days a week; in this way a driver's earnings could rise to 52s 6d per week.

Booth's descriptions concentrated on male workers, but he covered both men and women in every trade. A number of trades, however, employed women in large numbers. Domestic service, for example, was an extremely important source of employment for women: nearly 400,000 people, 339,101 of them female, were recorded as servants in the London Census of 1891. Booth shows that most domestic servants were employed in private households, but there were many in hotels, inns, clubs, and hospitals. Servants were found in all parts of London, but they were particularly concentrated in the western and central districts. Despite this concentration, 19,773 servants worked in East London.

He concluded from his enquiries that female household servants were of three types: 'those found in the roughest single-handed places', 'a better class of servant also in single-handed situations', and those employed in relatively affluent households. The problems of poverty and exploitation were greatest in the first group, as young and untrained girls were generally recruited to these situations:

The first trial of domestic service by girls whose fathers are casual labourers is made without any training whatever, and often without even a rudimentary knowledge of housework. In too many cases the home they come from is the reverse of clean or tidy, and lacks the simplest necessaries for making it so, whilst that of their mistress may not be much better, she being probably the wife of an artisan or well-paid labourer who does the work of the house herself, with the assistance of a servant.

(Booth 1902–3, 8: 213)

Many of these girls entered service at thirteen or fourteen years of age. Those who came straight from the workhouse schools were generally seen as making better servants as they had received some basic training. These 'lower grade' servants typically earned £5 6s per year at the age of thirteen, rising to £17 14s for those over thirty.

Booth covered the majority of the London trades in his survey, but he failed to come to grips with the structure of the London labour market and its links with poverty.[3] Only in his specialised study of the trades of East London did he come close to assessing this. Booth found that a number of trades were distinctive of the East End, these trades together accounting for a significant proportion of local employment. Dock and canal work, tailoring, boot and shoe making, and cabinet making accounted for about one fifth of all employment in East London. Other distinct trades, though employing smaller numbers, were tobacco work and silk weaving. Combined with general dealing, prominent throughout London, these trades accounted for one third of all employment in the East End. Using Census information, the Reports of the Factory Inspectorate, and interviews with both employers and workers, Booth and his associates documented the conditions in these trades.[4]

The main characteristics of the East London trades, argued Booth, was 'sweating', which included such practices as the subcontracting of employment to foremen and gang masters. In some trades this involved female outworkers undertaking textile work at home. In other cases wholesalers bought directly from individual workers – this was the practice in cabinet making. The common element in the various systems of sweating was long hours of hard work in insecure employment and unsanitary conditions for low pay.

In the docks of Wapping and the Isle of Dogs the labourers who unloaded the ships were of three types: 'permanent', 'preference', and 'casual'. A relatively small number of workers were in permanent – or, at least, regular – daily employment, earning between 20s and 25s per week. Such men were able to keep their families above the poverty line and could follow a 'respectable' life in a rented house in the outlying districts. The bulk of the labourers – estimated by Booth at around 90 per cent of the dock workforce – relied on less regular employment and lived in single rooms in the Tower Hamlets themselves. The 'preference' workers were those who were most likely to get taken on at the daily work call and might expect to earn between 15s and 20s per week. The casual workers had to go for days or weeks without work; although they averaged 12s to 15s per week, this was earned irregularly with well-paid weeks followed by bouts of unemployment.

In the families of men who were employed in the sweated trades of the docks the paid work of their wives was important. But this work too was often carried out under sweated conditions. Women found employment in the textile trades and in such work as matchbox making. In the latter women bought the raw materials from a supplier, enlisted the aid of their children in making the boxes, and then sold the finished boxes to contractors for 2d per gross – resulting in average earnings of 1d per hour (around 8s to 10s per week).

Booth's solution to the problem of poverty was Draconian. He saw the contaminating effects of the loafers and the competition of those seeking casual employment as being responsible for holding down the incomes of the ordinary poor. 'Loafers' were 'those who will not work' and were undeserving of sympathy. He argued for an increase in the work (and, therefore, the income) available to those in classes C and D, by taking work away from those in class B. It was the pressure of the latter that pulled down the former. Members of class B were undeserving of sympathy, unlike those in classes C and D. This solution required state action and could not be left to private charity. The Poor Law, he argued, had to be extended. Members of class B, he believed, should be offered a disciplined life under state supervision in return for regular meals. They should live as families in industrial colonies and should be well housed, well fed, and well clothed. This benefit would be financed, as far as possible, from the work that they undertook. Those who adapted to the system and learned new habits of discipline, hard work, and thrift could return to a normal life above the poverty line. Those who were unable to work hard enough would be transferred to the workhouse. And those who just drifted along would, at least, be financing themselves in their regulated existence. With class B removed from the streets, the authorities could more easily control and eliminate class A. Classes C and D would benefit from the greater work opportunities available to them and would cease to be threatened by poverty.

But even this was merely a partial solution. A complete solution could only come about through 'administrative action and penalties at each point at which life falls below a minimum accepted standard, while offering every opportunity for improvement' (Booth 1902–3, 17: 208). That is, there would have to be state ameliorating action, together with encouragement for hard work.

Rowntree and poverty in York

While many were prepared to accept, with reservations, Booth's findings on the extent of poverty in London, there was a widespread feeling that this reflected the particular features of London itself. Was it likely that such deprivation and squalor would be found outside the capital? This was the question that Rowntree addressed when he began his study of York in 1899. Rowntree's intention was to follow up Booth's study in York, where his family chocolate business was based, so as to compare its level of poverty with that which had been found in London. Subsequent studies were carried out in 1936 and 1950 (Rowntree 1901, 1941; Rowntree and Lavers 1951).

The original 1899 study involved the collection of evidence on 11,560 working-class families, using information that was obtained from members of the clergy and from voluntary workers as well as that from poor families themselves in a direct house-to-house survey. Rowntree compiled a series of research notebooks that contained the information on each household. This information included its size, the ages and occupations of its members, the number of rooms and the quality of housing, along with miscellaneous comments on their cleanliness, religion, criminality, 'respectability', and so on. By excluding those York residents who kept servants – they were seen as comprising the middle and upper classes – Rowntree reckoned to have covered the whole of the city's working class – about two thirds of its total population.

Rowntree adapted Booth's class schema for his own study, thereby adding to Booth's relative standard of poverty an absolute, subsistence standard. In his view, British society consisted of a hierarchy of five social classes, to which he added two additional categories for servants and those living in public institutions. Each class was defined by a particular level of household income, taking account of the earnings of all members of the household. In most cases households comprised a male 'head' together with his wife and children. Where there were older children who were earning more than 7s per week but were still living at home, Rowntree added into the household income the amount that they paid to their parents for their board and lodgings. Rowntree recognised that the subsistence needs of a household varied with its size and so he tried to calculate the income needs for families of varying sizes. To achieve this he estimated the typical income levels for 'moderate' families – those with four to six members – in each social class and he then adjusted this upwards or downwards for larger or smaller families.

Table 2.4 compares the Rowntree social class schema with that used by Booth. While the two schemas were constructed

Table 2.4   **The class schema of the Rowntree study**

Class	Weekly income range	% of population	Booth equivalent
F	'servant keeping class'	28.8	H and G
D	above 30s	32.4	F
C	21s to 30s	20.7	E
B	18s to 21s	5.9	D and C
A	below 18s	2.6	B and A
E	domestic servants	5.7	
G	in public institutions	3.9	

Note: I have rearranged the order of the classes to bring out the implicit class hierarchy more clearly. The equivalences with Booth's classes are approximate only, as the schema are constructed on different bases.

Source: Rowntree (1901)

on different bases, certain broad comparisons can legitimately be made. The working classes comprised Rowntree's classes A, B, C, and D, though domestic servants and many of those in public institutions – the workhouses, hospitals, and prisons – ought also to be included along with them. The largest section within the working class, accounting for almost a third of the total population of York, was made up of those who were in receipt of an income larger than 30s per week. By contrast, 8.5 per cent of the population, in classes A and B, received less than 21s.

Having arrived at his estimates of the distribution of the population according to their household income, Rowntree then set out to calculate the proportion of each class that could be regarded as living in poverty.[5] His main interest was to investigate what he called 'primary poverty', which he defined as the condition of a household whose income was inadequate for it to meet the minimum level of food, clothing, and shelter that was necessary for the physical health and efficiency of its members. In order to identify the line below which households could be said to be living in primary poverty, Rowntree needed to arrive at estimates of the food and other subsistence needs of families and to translate these into their monetary equivalents.

Primary poverty was a subsistence concept that was rooted in the assumed physical needs of nutrition, warmth, and so on. The food needs of individuals were calculated from the calorie equivalents of the proteins, fats, and carbohydrates that Rowntree believed were required in order to maintain their 'physical efficiency'. These calorie values were then converted into a 'standard diet' and the cost of this diet was calculated on the basis of the current prices that were to be found in York shops. The standard diet was, in fact, based closely on the official rations that were set out for the inmates of Poor Law institutions, though Rowntree modified these by making no allowance for the purchase of fresh meat. For this reason, his standard diet was even less generous than that which was allowed to paupers in the York workhouse (Rowntree 1901: 133).

These calculations resulted in estimates of 3s per week as the cost for meeting the dietary subsistence needs of each adult, and 2s 3d per week as the cost for each child. The actual incomes that were required by families of varying sizes in order to meet their needs for food could be calculated by multiplying these figures the appropriate number of times. Two adults and three children, for example, would need 12s 9d per week. To this total must be added an estimate for the actual cost of rent (averaging around 1s 7d for one room and 2s 6d for two rooms) and an allowance for basic clothing, light, and heating. A family comprising two adults and three children, then, was estimated to require a minimum of 4s 11d per week for these purposes.

On this basis, Rowntree arrived at poverty line estimates for families of varying sizes. The family with two adults and three children that has been taken as an example would require 21s 8d per week to meet all their basic subsistence needs. Rowntree was able to calculate the overall proportion of households that fell below his 'poverty line' by calculating the proportion of households in each class whose income fell below the minimum that was required for a family of their size. These were the households that he described as living in 'primary poverty': their income was simply not enough to meet their basic subsistence requirements. In York in 1899, Rowntree claimed, 9.91 per cent of the population (15.46 per cent of the working class) lived below this primary poverty line. This section of the population comprised the whole of class A and significant numbers from class B, together with some from class C.[6]

These were the people whose incomes were inadequate for mere physical efficiency. They could not meet the minimum needs of health and nutrition. It follows that since they could not meet these needs, they were also unable to enjoy such things as a bus ride, a newspaper, or a postage stamp; their clothing could not be more than the very plainest; and they could not afford to drink beer or to use tobacco. When any of these families *did* spend money on such things, concluded Rowntree, it could only be at the expense of their physical well-being by reducing even further the money that was available for food and for rent. This often involved significant gender inequalities. Many poor men, Rowntree observed, were able to smoke and to drink while nevertheless appearing to be strong and healthy workers. Their health was, he argued, gained at the expense of that of their wives and children. A poor woman with an inadequate housekeeping budget would frequently go without food herself and would also deprive her children of food in order to provide a decent meal for a husband who had spent a part of his income in a public house.

In addition to primary poverty, Rowntree analysed what he termed 'secondary poverty'. This existed, he held, where household income was above the primary poverty line but – because of waste or a lack of knowledge – the members of the household failed to meet their main subsistence needs. Their deprivation was not a consequence of low income but of bad budgeting or wasteful expenditure. Rowntree assessed the extent of secondary poverty by measuring the proportion of families above the primary poverty line who at the same time showed signs of 'obvious want and squalor' (Rowntree 1901: 115). Rowntree's assessment of secondary poverty was, however, founded on a rather subjective basis:

Direct information was often obtained from neighbours, or from a member of the household concerned, to the effect that the father or mother was a heavy drinker; in other cases the pinched faces of the ragged children told their own tale of poverty and deprivation.

(1901: 115–16)

Despite his use of such moralistic judgements, Rowntree claimed to have produced an accurate estimate of the extent of secondary poverty in the city. He concluded that 17.93 per cent of York's population (27.94 per cent of the working classes) lived in secondary poverty. Putting the measures of primary and secondary poverty together, Rowntree estimated that a total of 27.8 per cent of the population of York – almost one third – was living in poverty.

Rowntree held that the purpose of the social researcher was to produce findings that had an immediate policy relevance. For this reason, he eschewed 'ultimate' explanations of poverty in terms of the underlying conditions of the whole social and economic system. Explanations that pointed to such factors as the effects on income distribution of land and capital ownership and the redistributive role of the state were seen as too all-encompassing to have any implications for social policy. Rowntree recognised that, in the long run, the overall problem of poverty would not be resolved until the 'social question' had been tackled and the state took action to alter the structure of society, but he decided to focus his attention on the 'immediate' causes of poverty. These immediate causes, he argued, could be tackled in the short term through effective social policies.

He first of all turned to the question of the causes of primary poverty. More than a half of those living in primary poverty, he held, fell below the poverty line because of their low wages. Just under a quarter were poor because they had large families with numerous small children, and one sixth was poor because widowed or 'deserted' women were living with their children. Illness, old age, and unemployment were each responsible for only relatively small amounts of primary poverty. Clearly, then, the most important of the immediate causes of primary poverty was low pay. The bulk of the low-paid families were headed by unskilled labourers working in factories and on the railways. Their wages averaged 18s to 21s per week, and Rowntree concluded that 'the wages paid for unskilled labour in York are insufficient to provide food, shelter and clothing adequate to maintain a family of moderate size in a state of bare physical efficiency' (1901: 133).

For each family living in poverty, the principal cause of their poverty was reinforced by other contributory factors. The effects of low pay, for example, might be exacerbated by the effects of family size or widowhood. Rowntree also pointed to the important effects of the life cycle on poverty, claiming that the chances of a household experiencing poverty depended upon their stage in the family life cycle. He showed that labouring families tended to experience periods of poverty followed by periods of relative comfort as the family went through the various stages of the life cycle. From the age of fifteen until his children were born a labourer would normally earn enough to avoid primary poverty, but an increasing number of children and the withdrawal of his wife from the labour market would force the family into poverty. Such a family begins to escape from poverty again only when the children grow up and begin to earn an income from their employment. Their escape is, however, merely temporary, as the departure of the grown-up children and the arrival of old age once more force household income down below the poverty line.

The causes of secondary poverty, Rowntree argued, were to be found principally in the effects of drink, gambling, or ignorance on the circumstances of a household, though he gave no figures to substantiate this claim. The single most important factor, he held, was drink. National figures suggested that the average working-class family spent 6s 10d each week on beer and other alcoholic drinks. A family of two adults and three children, which needed 21s 8d per week in order to avoid primary poverty, would nevertheless experience secondary poverty if it spent the average amount on drink and had a household income of less than 28s 6d per week. Unlike many of his contemporaries, Rowntree did not over-moralise on the social problems of drink and gambling, and he recognised that those who were employed in arduous and monotonous work for wages that put them only slightly above the primary poverty line could hardly be blamed for seeking solace in the pub or with the bookmaker.

Wealth and inequality

The pioneering studies of poverty that were undertaken by Booth and Rowntree, for all their flaws, provided a clear picture of the grim extent of poverty in Britain at the turn of the twentieth century. Neither writer, however, gave any serious consideration to the holding of wealth or to its relationship to the overall distribution of resources. Wealth is at least as difficult to measure as poverty – indeed, it is perhaps more difficult to measure, despite the availability of some official statistics – and no truly comparable studies of the wealthy were undertaken by any of the early investigators. It is, all the same, possible to turn to some investigations of economic inequality that can offer an overview of the nature and the extent of wealth holding between the end of the nineteenth century and the middle of the twentieth century.[7]

The more recently produced trend data in Table 2.5, presented in a form that is commonly used in studies of wealth, put these contemporary studies in context. The table shows the proportion of the total personal assets of the country that is held by particular 'slices' of the population. Individuals or households are arranged in a hierarchy according to the value of their assets, and such 'slices' as the top 1 per cent, top 5 per cent, and top 10 per cent can be identified. In a relatively egalitarian society, of course, the top 1 per cent of the population would hold close to 1 per cent of the assets, the top 5 per cent would hold close to 5 per cent of the assets, and so on. The greater the discrepancy between the actual figures and this 'egalitarian' baseline, the more unequal is the society.[8]

Table 2.5 shows that the top 1 per cent of the population in 1911 held over two thirds of the total property in private hands.[9] By 1925 their share had fallen below this level, but the top 5 per cent held over four fifths of private property. The obvious but important converse of this fact is that the remaining 95 per cent of the population held a mere one fifth of the total personal property. This 95 per cent included, of course, the one third of the population whom Booth and Rowntree found to be living in poverty, together with the mass of ordinary workers and most of the comfortable middle class. The top 5 per cent were a particularly advantaged group, and the top 1 per cent comprised a highly privileged section of the population. These categories are obviously defined on an arbitrary statistical basis, and they do not directly correspond with actual social groups, but they do give an indication of the massive extent of inequality that existed in British society. Later work has, in fact, shown that the top 1 per cent category forms a useful, if rather crude, indicator of the size of the truly wealthy and privileged section of the British population.

Table 2.5 **Property distribution in England and Wales, 1911–38**

	% of personal property held			
	1911	*1925*	*1930*	*1938*
Top 1%	69	61	58	55
Top 5%	?	82	79	77

Source: Atkinson (1983: 168, Table 7.3)

In the years after 1925 there was a continuous decline in the share of the property that was held by the top 1 per cent of the population, indicating a slow but progressive trend towards greater equality. Despite this trend, the share of personal property in the hands of the top 1 per cent, on the verge of the Second World War, was still in excess of half of the total national assets in private hands, and the top 5 per cent retained more than three quarters of national assets. On the basis of these figures, then, Britain must be regarded as having been a highly inegalitarian society through the whole of the first half of the twentieth century.

The first systematic study of property holding that gave some insight into this inequality was the official government inquiry into land ownership, popularly known as the New Domesday Survey. The late nineteenth century had seen a focusing of radical attention on the issue of land ownership. Concern about the alleged stranglehold that was exercised by landowners – and especially by the largest landowners – on the country's affairs was reinforced in tracts and pamphlets that attacked the concentration of landed wealth. Booth had begun his inquiry into poverty in an attempt to confound the claims of radical politicians, and, with similar intent, the government was persuaded to launch an official investigation of landed property to counter these radical views on its monopolisation. The inquiry was undertaken in 1873 and drew its information from questionnaires that were issued to Poor Law officials in each locality. These officials were asked to compile lists of all the local landowners, with details of the sizes of their holdings, and to return their lists to London for further processing. The returns were grouped into complete county-by-county listings that were then published in immense national volumes (Return 1874a, 1874b, 1876).

The publication of these books caused an immediate national sensation. The government's intention had been to counter radical claims, such as those of John Bright, that a mere 30,000 people owned the whole of the land area of Britain. The report did, in fact, show this claim to be false, and the survey discovered that there were almost one million landowners. It also showed, however, that two thirds of these landowners possessed just one acre or less. The survey's most startling finding was that a mere 7,000 people owned four fifths of the land in Britain.

All those who have used the official report owe a great debt to John Bateman, a minor Essex landowner who produced a digest of the huge official volumes and published them in a far more accessible form (1876). Indeed, most subsequent researchers have used Bateman's digest in preference to the official volumes. Seeing the great attention that had been given to the relatively inaccessible and almost indigestible national volumes, Bateman set himself the task of compiling a biographical 'A to Z' of the largest landowners, a group that he defined as those with 3,000 acres or more and valued at £3,000 or more per year.[10]

The survey had been concerned only with rural land holdings, and so it did not record the urban holdings that were frequently very significant in terms of their values. It remains, all the same, a landmark study of wealth in Britain. Bateman's digest shows that 2,500 landowners held 3,000 acres or more each, and there were a further 1,320 owners of between 2,000 and 3,000 acres. One hundred and fifteen people each held more than 50,000 acres, and forty-four people held more than 100,000 acres. Of most importance in relation to the question of wealth were the values attached to these holdings. A total of 866 people were in receipt of an annual income in excess of £10,000 from their land holdings, while 76 were receiving annual incomes of £50,000 or more. This, it will be recalled, was at a time when the typical wage amounted to just over £50 per year. The largest landowners, then, were receiving annual incomes at least 1,000 times greater than the average wage.

Table 2.6 shows the fifteen wealthiest landowners in Britain for 1873, taking account of both the acreage and the value of their land, and after making allowance for the estimated value of the urban property holdings of such men as the Duke of Westminster. All but two of the top fifteen landowners were peers – the list includes eight dukes, one marquess, and four earls.

The principal researchers to have investigated wealth during the early years of the twentieth century were Leo Chiozza-

Table 2.6 Britain's top landowners, 1873

	Acreage	Value (£)	Main areas
Earl of Breadalbane	438,358	58,292	Perth, Argyll
Duke of Buccleuch	460,108	217,163	Dumfries, Roxburgh, Selkirk, Northants
Marquess of Bute	116,668	151,135	Ayrshire, Bute, Glamorgan
Duke of Devonshire	198,572	180,750	Derbyshire, Cork, Waterford
Earl of Fife	249,220	72,563	Aberdeen, Banff, Elgin
Earl Fitzwilliam	115,743	138,801	Wicklow, Yorkshire
Sir Alex. Mathieson	220,663	26,461	Ross
Sir James Mathieson	424,560	20,346	Ross, Sutherland
Duke of Norfolk	49,866	75,596	Sussex, York
Duke of Northumberland	186,397	176,048	Northumberland
Duke of Portland	183,199	88,350	Northumberland, Caithness, Nottingham
Duke of Richmond	286,411	79,683	Banff, Aberdeen
Earl of Seafield	305,930	78,227	Inverness, Elgin, Banff
Duke of Sutherland	1,358,545	141,667	Sutherland, Ross
Duke of Westminster	19,749	38,994	Cheshire, [London]*

* Acreage and valuation figures do not include London holdings

Source: Scott (1982: 86).

Money, Arthur Bowley, and Josiah Wedgwood, all of whom sought to place the value of landed property alongside other forms of property within the overall structure of wealth holding. Chiozza-Money, a radical Liberal MP, was born Leo Chiozza, but he adopted the additional surname Money when he inherited a fortune under the will of a relative of this name. Appropriately renamed for his purpose, he began an investigation of wealth based upon statistical sources, and he published his results in 1905 (Chiozza-Money 1905). Bowley, an academic who had co-operated with Rowntree in his studies and had also extended this work on poverty, undertook a number of studies of economic inequality during the 1920s. Bowley's studies were sometimes undertaken alone and sometimes jointly with Josiah Stamp, a senior civil servant who became very active in business after his retirement (Bowley 1920; Bowley and Stamp 1924). Last in this group of researchers was Josiah Wedgwood, an economic researcher who later became a managing director of his family's pottery and china company. Wedgwood (1929) undertook his statistical investigations into wealth while working with Tawney at the London School of Economics between 1926 and 1928.

Table 2.7 *Income distribution in Britain, 1903*

	Household income (£p.a.)	Total income		People	
		£m	%	No. (m)	%
1 Rich	More than 700	585	34.2	1.25	2.9
2 Comfortable	160 – 700	245	14.3	3.75	8.7
3 Poor	Less than 160	880	51.5	38.00	88.4
Total		1,710		43.00	

Note: £160 per annum was the exemption level for income tax

Source: Calculated from Chiozza-Money (1905: 28, 42, and other parts of Chs 2 and 3)

Chiozza-Money compiled a detailed and systematic summary of income distribution in 1903, using a model that comprised three social 'classes'. These classes were the 'rich' the 'comfortable', and the 'poor' (see Table 2.8). His 'poor' class, however, was much wider than that identified by either Booth or Rowntree. Chiozza-Money recognised, in fact, that this class in his model included the vast bulk of ordinary working class families as well as the really poor. While his class categories of the 'rich' and the 'comfortable' might be valid for broad sociological analyses – they are compatible with the similar categories that were used by Booth and Rowntree – his category of the 'poor' might better have been termed 'ordinary and poor'.[11] Nevertheless, Chiozza-

Money's three-class model serves a useful purpose in highlighting the broad features of income distribution.

If income had been equally distributed among all members of the population in 1903, individual incomes would have amounted to around £40 per annum; a typical family of five would have received about £200 per year. Chiozza-Money's figures show that this was very far from being the reality. The average worker's wages at this time were around 20s 6d per week, and only one million families had annual incomes of more than £160.

The three classes in Chiozza-Money's scheme were defined by the level of their household income, the 'rich' and the 'comfortable' comprising those whose incomes were sufficiently large to push them above the income tax threshold of £160 per annum – just over £3 per week. The 'rich' and the 'comfortable' were, quite simply, the income tax paying classes. Chiozza-Money gives no direct indication of the share in national income taken by the top 1 per cent of income recipients, so his work is not directly comparable with the data of Table 2.6, but it can be seen from Table 2.7 that just under 3 per cent of the population received over one third of the total personal income of the country. This group of the 'rich' – the top 2.9 per cent of the population – were identified from statistics compiled from the returns for the Inhabited House Duty. Chiozza-Money holds that people having an annual income greater than £700 were likely to be living in houses that were valued at an annual level of £60 or more for the purpose of the tax. For this reason, payment of the tax at this level could be taken as an indicator of high income. Official statistics showed that the quarter of a million houses that were valued at this level contained 1.25 million people, and Chiozza-Money allocates these to his 'rich' category.

D'Aeth (1910) subsequently attempted to transform Chiozza-Money's data into a more adequate conceptual framework. He identified seven social classes, defining these on the basis of their typical income levels. The class structure, he agreed, could be seen as being organised around two 'standards of life'. These standards he termed the 'standard of refined and educated necessities', which required an annual income of around £600 per year, and the 'standard of simple necessities', which required an income of at least 25s per week for an average family. D'Aeth, then, had set his basic standard at an income that was slightly higher than the level that Booth and Rowntree had recognised as the level at which poverty could be avoided. The basic standard defined the level of income that was required for 'ordinary' families to meet the basic comforts of a decent life. Classes A, B, and C of D'Aeth's scheme comprised the principal elements of the 'old working class' and were structured around the basic standard of life. Some of them enjoyed a reasonable degree of comfort, while others slipped constantly into poverty. Those who fell closest to the basic standard, held D'Aeth, were the ordinary labourers of class B, some of whom could enjoy the corresponding comforts and others of whom were in danger of slipping into class A.[12] The standard of refined necessities, on the other hand, was essentially the ground floor for access to the middle- and upper-class lifestyles enjoyed by those in classes E, F, and G. While those in class F enjoyed 'the full degree of cultured life', those in class E were in danger of slipping below this level, and those in class G had 'the satisfaction of luxurious habits' (D'Aeth 1910: 271).

Comparison of Table 2.8 with Table 2.7 shows a certain similarity between the categories used by D'Aeth and by Chiozza-Money. D'Aeth's basic standard of life was very close to the £160 per annum income tax exemption level that Chiozza-Money had used to demarcate the 'comfortable' from the rest of the population; and the refined standard of life was not too far below the £700 level that Chiozza-Money had used to identify the 'rich'. Thus, D'Aeth's class G made up Chiozza-Money's 'rich' class, classes E, D, and C made up the core of his 'comfortable' class, and class A was equivalent to the core of his 'poor' class. Classes F and B were, in different ways, 'intermediate classes' in the schema.

Table 2.8 **Class and income, 1903**

Class	Typical income	Standards of life	Class description
G	more than £2,000 p.a.		'The rich': manufacturers and large business
F	£600 p.a.	Refined necessities	Professional and administrative
E	£300 p.a.		Small business, some lower professionals
D	£3 per week		Clerks, shopkeepers, etc.
C	45s per week		Foremen and skilled labourers
B	25s per week	Simple necessities	Unskilled labourers, shop assistants
A	18s or less		'Irregular labour, or drinks a higher wage'

Source: Compiled from D'Aeth (1910: 270–71)

Evidence from the works of Bowley and Wedgwood allows us to take this picture forward to 1920, as their data on income before tax is sufficiently close to that of Chiozza-Money for some broad comparisons to be made. Annual incomes were divided into a larger number of statistical categories than the three classes of

Chiozza-Money, but there is a closer approximation to the more complex class schema that was used by D'Aeth. In 1910 (see Table 2.9) over 94 per cent of income recipients had annual incomes that were below the income tax threshold of £160. This group would have included all of Rowntree's classes A to D and the majority of those in class F (compare Table 2.4). This income level can be taken as indicative of both the normal and the deprived levels of living that were typical of the majority of citizens in Britain at the time. A very small proportion of the population was in receipt of incomes above this level, though the variation in the size of income at the upper levels was immense. Just over 1 per cent of those with an income received more than £700 per year, but their annual incomes ranged from a bare £700 to more than £45,000. The 1,000 or so incomes that were above £20,000 per year were all at least 125 times greater than the incomes received by over 94 per cent of the population – their incomes were more than 350 times greater than Rowntree's poverty line.

Table 2.9 *Income distribution in Britain, 1910*

Annual income (£)	No. of incomes	%
More than 45,000	327	*
20,000 – 45,000	1,026	*
10,000 – 20,000	2,903	0.01
5,000 – 10,000	8,143	0.04
700 – 5,000	200,000	0.99
160 – 700	880,000	4.40
Less than 160	18,850,000	94.34

* less than 0.005%

Source: Summarised from Wedgwood (1929: 63), who calculated these data from Bowley 1920

While the changed value of money between 1910 and 1920 makes it difficult to compare income levels for the two years, some general conclusions can be drawn. Table 2.10 shows that just under 80 per cent of incomes in 1920 were below £160 per year. A mere 0.1 per cent of income recipients had incomes higher than £5,000, though this was rather more than had been the case in 1910. The overall distribution of income in 1920 was such that just over 2,000 people had incomes that were greater than £25,000, these incomes being at least 150 times greater than those received by the bottom 80 per cent of income recipients. A recent commentator on these data has suggested that an income of £400 in 1920 can be seen as equivalent to one of £160 in 1910

(Waites 1987: 87). Using this baseline and other corrections for inflation, it can be concluded that the Bowley and Wedgwood data indicate that a slight redistribution of income away from those at the top of the hierarchy had occurred. This redistribution was, most probably, a direct result of the changes brought about by the First World War.

Table 2.10   Income distribution in Britain, 1920

Annual income (£)	No. of incomes	%
more than 100,000	165	*
25,000 – 100,000	2,220	0.01
5,000 – 25,000	24,600	0.09
1,000 – 5,000	205,530	1.00
200 – 1,000	2,046,000	9.70
160 – 200	2,031,400	9.67
130 – 160	3,490,000	16.60
Less than 130	13,000,000	62.88

* less than 0.05%

Source: Calculated from Wedgwood (1929: 65, Table II), using data from various dates in the period 1919–20

The method by which Chiozza-Money and Wedgwood had measured the distribution of property involved the use of estate duty statistics. These statistics record the value of the property left by people at the time of their death. Various adjustments were made to these raw figures so that they could be used to estimate the distribution of property among those who were still living. It was assumed that those property holders who die in any particular year can be treated as a statistical 'sample' of the total population of property holders. The 'sample' is adjusted to make it representative of the larger group – for example, by taking account of the differing mortality rates of each group; an accurate estimate of property distribution can be made by multiplying the estate duty figures by an appropriate weighting. This adjustment of the estate duty statistics with what are known as 'mortality multipliers' has become the standard method for measuring the structure of property holding.

Table 2.11 summarises the data from these pioneer investigations of property holding. The figures have a broadly similar structure throughout the period from 1903 to 1924. Chiozza-Money had shown that an equal distribution of property in 1903 would have given each person £300-£1,500 for a typical family of five. In fact, the great bulk of the population held property valued at much less than £100. It must be appreciated that a holding of £100 was not insignificant at this time – its value was equivalent to almost two year's pay for the average worker in 1912. Chiozza-Money also showed that just over 1 per cent of the population, each with assets valued at £10,000 or more, held more than half of the total national property in private hands. In both 1912 and in 1924 well over 90 per cent of the population held less than £1,000 in property, the majority having less than £100. There was, perhaps, some evidence that the years leading up to 1924 saw an increase in the proportion of the population with holdings of between £100 and £1,000, though this was most likely to have been a simple consequence of inflation in the money value of estates.

Table 2.11 **Property distribution in Britain (1903–24)**

Size of holding (£)	Distribution of estates in					
	1903		1912		1924	
	No.	%	No.	%	No.	%
250,000+	2,190	–	1,305	*	2,198	0.01
100,000–250,000	6,780	–	4,580	0.02	7,026	0.03
50,000–100,000	12,570	–	9,890	0.05	15,800	0.07
25,000–50,000	26,850	–	18,106	0.09	34,000	0.16
10,000–25,000	68,640	–	58,160	0.31	109,870	0.51
5,000–10,000 }		–	80,910	0.43	168,220	0.78
1,000–5,000 }	481,740	–	439,000	2.36	942,870	4.39
100–1,000	†	–	1,855,000	9.97	3,658,500	17.04
Less than 100	†	–	16,144,000	86.74	16,523,000	76.98

* less than 0.01%
† not comparable

Source: Wedgwood (1929: 71, Table 4); Chiozza-Money (1905: 68–9)

The top 1 per cent of holdings, in so far as they can be identified from these figures, were in excess of £5,000 each, with the largest estates being far in excess of £250,000. The average worker of 1912 would have had to work for 100 years and spend nothing at all in order to accumulate property worth more than £5,000. Wedgwood estimates that only one in a hundred ordinary workers was able to leave as much as £1,000, and a mere one in a thousand was able to leave £10,000.

The importance of property in generating income is clearly brought out in Wedgwood's analysis of 'unearned' income. This form of income is that which comes from profits on investments and from rent on land, and it is conventionally distinguished from the 'earned' income that derives from employment. Unearned income, like the property from which it derived, was far more unequally distributed than was income from employment. In 1920, unearned income made up just 4 per cent of the total incomes of those who received less than £130 per year, but it accounted for 70 per cent of the income of those who received more than £2,500 (Wedgwood 1929: 66). This finding indicates quite graphically the fact that income-generating property was especially important for those who were in receipt of top incomes.

These statistical surveys produced a clear picture of the structure of income and property distribution and, therefore, of the relationship between wealth and poverty, but they do not give any real indication of the social composition of the wealthy sections of the British population. Booth and Rowntree had examined the labour market position and trades of those who were living in poverty or who were in danger of falling into poverty, but the twentieth-century studies of wealth did not provide an equivalent picture of the rich. Wedgwood's work does, however, supply a brief profile of the social background of the wealthy, which makes it possible to assess the extent to which land still formed the primary source of wealth.

Wedgwood began by drawing a sample of names from the probate registers, which record the raw data from which the estate duty statistics are compiled. His sample aimed to identify the people at the very top of the range of property holdings and it comprised those English residents who had died in the year 1924–5, who had left property valued at more than £200,000 and for whom a predecessor could also be identified in the probate records. Table 2.12 classifies these people according to

Table 2.12 **Social background of top wealth holders, 1924**

	No. of holders	Average holding (£)
Peers, baronets, gentry	15	580,000
Financiers, merchants, manufacturers	34	385,000
Other 'gentlemen'	5	65,000
Professions	6	–
Small manufacturers and shopkeepers	18	8,000
Farmers	2	2,200
Clerks and officials	3	–
Manual workers	4	–
Total	87	

Source: Wedgwood (1929: 166–7)

the social backgrounds of their predecessors, who were, typically, their fathers. One in six of these top wealth holders came from a landed background, while two fifths came from a capitalist background in industry or finance. The wealthiest of the industrial and financial capitalists in Wedgwood's sample was a banker from the Hambro family, who left over £2 million, and his list of the wealthy included such names as Hulton (publishing), Pilkington (glass), Everard (brewing), and Sassoon (banking). His sample also included, interestingly, a Rowntree who left £220,336. Industrial and financial property, however, was generally the basis of smaller estates than was land. If the minor 'gentlemen' are included along with the larger landowners, the total proportion of top wealth holders coming from land, industry, or finance amounted to two thirds of the total. The industrial, financial, and landed categories should not, of course, be regarded as totally distinct from one another. Many landed peers, for example, held directorships on the boards of City companies, and many of the younger sons of landowners had entered full-time City careers. The remaining one third of top property holders had risen from the middle classes or from the artisanal working class, though the two wealthy clergymen that Wedgwood had classified among the 'professionals' would probably have come from established landed families.

Wedgwood's sample covered only those from the wealthy who had identifiable forebears listed in the probate registers, and this highlights a key point in all the studies that have been considered. All the writers assumed that the *inheritance* of property was the fundamental factor responsible for the unequal distribution of economic resources. If low pay and unemployment were the principal causes of poverty, inheritance was the principal cause of wealth.

This assumption was the cornerstone of Chiozza-Money's conclusion that the polarisation between the 30 per cent living in poverty and the 1 per cent or so living in wealth was to be explained by what he called the 'error of distribution'. This was the mechanism through which the benefits of economic growth were denied to a vast section of the population because of the privileges and advantages that were enjoyed by the wealthy:

43,000,000 people in the United Kingdom work to produce certain commodities, and a part of this output is exchanged with commodities produced in other lands. We produce, we export, and we import, and our home production increased by our imports and decreased by our exports constitutes a great income which is divided up amongst us in such a manner that some of us are rich and some of us are poor.

(Chiozza-Money 1905: 6–7)

Because poverty and wealth are interdependent consequences of this underlying 'error of distribution', Chiozza-Money holds that the polarisation can be ended only through a social policy of redistribution. This redistribution would require a structural reorganisation of British society, including such things as the formation of the major services into public monopolies, but it would centre on an effective system of redistributive taxation. Progressive income tax, a heavy tax on unearned incomes, the removal of all excise duties from the ordinary necessities of everyday life, and a reform of the death duties would, he argued, result in a much fairer distribution of income and property. A similar conclusion was drawn by Wedgwood, who recommended the use of the tax mechanism to remove the inequalities of inheritance. Wedgwood showed that, at the aggregate level of the national economy as a whole, around three fifths of all property in 1904 could be regarded as having been inherited from a previous generation rather than as resulting from the accumulation of new property (Wedgwood 1929: 138–9). His conclusion was that pensions and social security would bring the poor up to the level of the ordinary citizen, while death duties would bring the wealthy down to a more acceptable level.

Table 2.13 shows that almost half of the men in Wedgwood's sample of top wealth holders had predecessors (mainly their fathers) who had left property valued at more than £100,000. The millionaire wealth holders – eight of them, including one woman in the full analysis – were particularly likely to have had very wealthy predecessors. In only one case did a millionaire's predecessor leave less than £50,000, and in six cases they left more

Table 2.13 Inheritance of property, 1924–5: men

Size of predecessor's estate (£)	No. of men leaving:			
	£500,000+	£300,000 – 500,000	£200,000 – 300,000	Totals
More than 1,000,000	3	1	2	6
500,000 – 1,000,000	4	3	2	9
250,000 – 500,000	3	2	3	8
100,000 – 250,000	0	4	12	16
50,000 – 100,000	1	2	5	8
10,000 – 50,000	1	2	6	9
5,000 – 1,000	1	2	3	6
1,000 – 5,000	2	1	3	6
Less than 1,000	4	5	6	15
Total	19	22	42	85

Source: Wedgwood (1929: 156)

than £250,000 (Wedgwood 1929: 157). Wedgwood concluded that around two thirds of all the top wealth holders owed their wealth almost exclusively to the inheritance of property. Wealthy predecessors left, on average, just under a half of their wealth to a single inheritor, who subsequently became a member of the category of top wealth holders.

Evidence from a second sample, drawn from the wider ranks of the top 1 per cent of property holders, showed that about two thirds of them could be regarded as inheritors and the remaining one third as 'self-made' (Wedgwood 1929: 169). By 'self-made' Wedgwood meant that their predecessors left property valued at less than £5,000, still a considerable sum by contemporary standards. Those who fell into this category were likely to have made their fortunes in commercial or financial speculation, and Wedgwood cites a number of stockbrokers and other investors as typical of this group (1929: 175). He remarks:

It is obvious, indeed, that mere 'thrift' never made a poor man rich. And for 'industry' to prove a philosopher's stone, it must take great risks and be combined with exceptional luck or exceptional talent. Both industry and thrift are certainly necessary qualities for the accumulation of property, but they are not in themselves the chief source of great fortunes. No poor man who sticks – as the large majority must, who have family responsibilities – to the securer forms of employment for his labour and savings, can hope to leave much property to his descendants, however great his talents and energy, however miserly his thrift.

(1929: 175–7)

The major factor in the making of a fortune during the first part of the twentieth century was thus the inheritance of property. The greater a person's wealth, the more likely he or she was to have inherited a substantial proportion of this from a wealthy predecessor. About a half of all the inheritors combined their inheritance with a skill for further accumulation; the other half simply consolidated and maintained their inheritance. Particularly important for wealth was the indirect inheritance of property through marriage. To illustrate this point Wedgwood cited the case of his own family. At the beginning of the seventeenth century a Wedgwood had married a landed heiress and the bulk of their property (including the family pottery) was passed on to their eldest son. The youngest son, denied a major part in the inheritance, accumulated a considerable fortune of his own through marriage and inheritance, becoming, in fact, head of the wealthiest branch of the family in his generation. The wealth of this branch of the family, however, was dissipated through the failure of the male members to marry and by the marriage of a daughter into the senior branch of the family. The middle son of the second generation neither inherited from his father nor married into wealth, and his descendants had to rely upon income from employment, becoming potters, sailors, and coal miners.[13]

These studies, then, demonstrate the importance of landed, financial, and industrial capital in producing both high incomes and large personal property holdings. The wealthy were those who benefited disproportionately from the operations of the capitalist economy. The poor were those who were disproportionately disadvantaged by that same system. While some in the British population were excluded from citizen participation by virtue of their exclusion from secure and decently paid positions in the labour market, others were able to gain privileges and advantages because their position in the capital market accorded them opportunities that were not open to those who relied upon employment alone.

Poverty before the welfare state

At the London School of Economics Bowley undertook a series of studies during the inter-war years that were intended to supplement Rowntree's findings on York with comparable data for other English towns. In this way, Bowley aimed to move the debate on poverty to the national level. Using sample survey methods, he investigated the social conditions of 1913 and 1924 in Reading, Northampton, Warrington, Bolton, and Stanley. In these studies Bowley used a modified version of Rowntree's concept of primary poverty and found that an average of 6.5 per cent of working-class families in the five towns were living in poverty in 1924 (Bowley and Hogg 1925; see also Bowley and Burnett-Hurst 1915). Table 2.14 shows that the actual figures ranged from 4 per cent in Northampton to 11.3 per cent in Reading. In all of the towns except Stanley the proportion of the population that was living in poverty had declined substantially

Table 2.14 **Poverty distribution in five towns, 1913 and 1924**

	% of working class families in poverty	
	1913	1924
Stanley	5.5	7.5
Northampton	8.0	4.0
Bolton	8.0	5.0
Warrington	12.5	8.0
Reading	23.0	11.3

Note: Bolton data are for 1914, not 1913. The figures involve rounding made in the original tables, which were not always consistent

Source: Bowley and Hogg (1925: 75, 100, 124, 154, 196)

between 1913 and 1924, the decrease ranging from one third to one half. The town that showed the greatest similarity to the early findings on York was Warrington.

Some interesting features of inter-war poverty are highlighted in Bowley's data for Bolton, later to become famous as the 'Worktown' of the Mass Observation studies (Mass Observation 1943). Bolton was a cotton spinning town in south Lancashire. While most employment was to be found in the cotton mills, substantial sections of the population worked in bleaching, metal working, and engineering. In 1914 the 'natural head' – the male breadwinner – was absent, ill, aged, or deceased in over a half of poor families, and a further one fifth of these families had inadequate wages for the size of their family; in 1924 the proportion with a breadwinner who was absent, ill, aged, or dead was similar. This failure of a male breadwinner to provide for a family was, in 1924, more likely to be a consequence of age or illness, though unemployment was responsible for the poverty of about two fifths of families (Bowley and Hogg 1925: 158). The town experienced especially high levels of unemployment during the 1920s, but much of this was short term. Bowley calculated that if the town's population had enjoyed full employment, then the numbers in poverty would have been around half the level that was actually discovered.

Bowley was also involved in research that aimed to repeat the core of Booth's work in London and to combine this with Rowntree's methods. For 1929 Bowley set a poverty line at 39s for a couple with two children. This figure was calculated as being equal to Booth's figure of 21s, allowing for changes in price levels (Llewellyn Smith 1932: 71). On this basis, as shown in Table 2.15, the survey found that 6.6 per cent of all London families were living in poverty in 1929. This represented 10.7 per cent of working-class families with children, about a third of the level that Booth had discovered forty years earlier (see Table 2.2).

Table 2.15 *Poverty distribution in London, 1929*

	% of London families living in poverty		
	Eastern area	*Western area*	*Whole of London*
Working-class families with children	12.5	8.0	10.7
All working-class families	10.7	7.8	9.1
All families	8.3	5.3	6.6

Source: Llewellyn Smith (1934: 87, 89)

Rowntree himself set out to repeat his earlier study in the mid-1930s, aiming to discover what changes had occurred in York since 1899. He looked at all the working-class families that were earning less than £250 per year – a total of 16,362 families – and he obtained information on their wages from their employers. In 1950 he undertook a third and much more limited study, the first of his poverty studies to use sampling methods instead of a complete enumeration. Sampling and survey procedures had developed rapidly in the inter-war years through the work of Bowley and others, and Rowntree's own analyses showed that samples could yield reliable results for the total population. By comparing his 1936 results with data produced from samples drawn from the whole data set, Rowntree concluded that a 10 per cent sample could yield reliable results about the whole of the working class in York.

Rowntree also set out a new approach to poverty that he employed in his empirical study (1937). He first calculated the level of income that was needed for various sizes of family, using similar subsistence measures as he had done in 1899, but he added to this subsistence minimum the costs of such 'personal sundries' as unemployment and health insurance, trades union subscriptions, travelling costs, postage stamps, a newspaper, a wireless, and an allowance for beer, tobacco, holidays, and so on. In making this adjustment to his earlier definitions, Rowntree was outlining a more fully relative measure of poverty. He held that generally rising living standards in the population as a whole meant that items that had formerly been regarded as superfluous – as 'luxuries' which were not necessary for the mere 'physical efficiency' of an ordinary working class family – should now be regarded as necessities. This approach brought Rowntree to a position much closer to that which had been adopted by Booth.

Rowntree's various concepts of poverty are set out in Figure 2.3. Primary poverty, defined in absolute terms, was measured by the calculation of a physiological subsistence minimum. Secondary poverty, as Rowntree had defined it in 1899, was calculated from the difference between the subsistence minimum costs and actual expenditure. What I have called 'ordinary poverty', by analogy with Booth's term, depends on a culturally and historically variable standard of what is necessary for a normal 'comfortable' existence. Ordinary poverty is measured by a relative standard of need. In the 1936 study the concept of ordinary poverty began to supersede the concepts of primary and secondary poverty as Rowntree moved towards a more adequate relative standard of poverty.[14]

Rowntree's 1936 study, then, approached a more relative conception of poverty (Veit-Wilson 1986), but in order to allow comparisons to be made with the 1899 data, he presented a comparison of primary poverty in both years, using the 1899

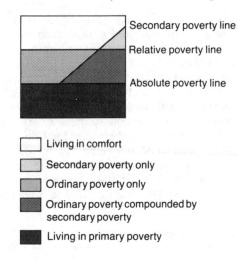

Secondary poverty line

Relative poverty line

Absolute poverty line

☐ Living in comfort

▨ Secondary poverty only

▨ Ordinary poverty only

▨ Ordinary poverty compounded by secondary poverty

■ Living in primary poverty

*Figure 2.3 **Rowntree's three concepts of poverty***

definition of primary poverty. In 1899 the minimum needed for subsistence had been estimated at 21s 8d for a family consisting of two adults and three children. In 1936, taking account of changes in price levels, Rowntree estimated that a similar family would require 30s 7d. By making such calculations for all family sizes and comparing the figures with actual household incomes, he was able to estimate the number of families that were living in primary poverty. In 1899, as stated earlier, 9.91 per cent of the population of York were living in primary poverty; by 1936 the proportion had fallen to 3.90 per cent. Unfortunately, Rowntree made no similar calculation of primary poverty levels for 1951.

The numbers living in primary poverty had declined considerably between 1899 and 1936. The most important factor that was responsible for this, according to Rowntree, was rising wage levels. Wages in York had reached to a high enough level to remove many people from the condition of primary poverty, but changes in welfare provision had increased the number of elderly poor, as more people were now surviving into old age. The most important immediate cause of primary poverty, however, was unemployment. Almost half of the heads of those households that were living in primary poverty in 1936 were unemployed.

On the basis of his new conception of 'ordinary' poverty, Rowntree calculated that the family of two adults and three children needed 43s 6d in 1936 and 77s in 1951 in order to live a life of reasonable comfort rather than one of poverty.[15] These income levels became his yardsticks for measuring ordinary poverty, the actual levels being adjusted upwards or downwards according to the size and composition of the family. It can be seen from Table 2.16 that 17.7 per cent of York's population were living in ordinary poverty in 1936, a total that represented about a third of its working class. By 1951 this figure had fallen to just 1.66 per cent (2.77 per cent of the working class). These conclusions are consistent with Rowntree's findings on primary poverty. The proportion that was unable to meet a very basic subsistence level had fallen considerably between 1899 and 1936, though a third of the working class remained below what most people would have regarded as a barely acceptable level of comfort.[16] By 1951, Rowntree felt, primary poverty had all but disappeared, and ordinary poverty had declined to a very low level.

Table 2.16   **Class distribution, 1936 and 1951**

Class	1936		1951	
	*Typical weekly income**	*% of population*	*Income level**	*% of population*
H	(middle class and above)	35.0		†
E	63s6d and above	20.5	146s and above	34.98
D	53s6d to 63s5d	8.0	123s to 146s	11.90
C	43s6d to 53s5d	10.8	100s to 123s	11.48
B	33s6d to 43s5d	9.6	77s to 100s	1.43
A	below 33s6d	8.1	below 77s	0.23
F	(domestic servants)	4.4		†
G	(in public institutions)	3.6		†

* Calculated as the income level for a man, wife, and three children. Families of other sizes are allocated to an equivalent category. In 1936, for example, a family with three children and income of 43s6d was allocated to class C, while a family with one child is allocated to this class if its income was 38s6d or more
† The 1951 total for the middle class and higher is shown only as a combined figure with that for domestic servants and those in public institutions. This combined figure was 39.98 per cent

Source: Rowntree and Lavers (1951: 30–31); see also Rowntree (1941: 32)

In his original 1899 study Rowntree had set out a life cycle model of poverty, which he developed further in his report on the 1936 study. The demands that were made on household income varied according to the stage of the life course of the family. Households might, for example, fall into poverty when children were young, rise into relative comfort in their middle years, and then fall back into poverty again with old age. For this reason, Rowntree's broad estimate that 31.7 per cent of the York working class were, in 1936, living in poverty underestimated the total number of people who would, at some stage in their life, experience poverty. He calculated, for example, that more than half of all working-class children born in York during the year before his survey were living in households whose income took them below the poverty line. Some of these families would eventually move out of poverty, and a number of the children would, when adults, escape poverty. Similarly, 47.5 per cent of working class people aged over sixty-five were, in 1936, living in poverty. Rowntree's findings clearly show that the experience of poverty in the population at large is much greater than the general figure of 31.7 per cent would suggest.

Rowntree estimated that poverty affected 52.5 per cent of the working class at some stage in their life. He arrived at this figure by estimating that a half of the working class experienced poverty in childhood, a half experienced it in old age, and one quarter experienced it in early middle life (their thirties and early forties). Some people would experience poverty at each of these three stages – they would fail to escape from poverty at any stage in their life. Rowntree gave no estimate of the size of this core of poverty-stricken individuals, and its actual level cannot be guessed. All that can be known is that it could not be more than 20.7 per cent of the working class, as this was the proportion of those aged forty-five to sixty-four who were living in poverty.

As in 1899, Rowntree's 1936 study included an attempt to isolate the principal immediate causes of poverty. Classes A and B were those who, by the new relative standard of poverty, were regarded as living in ordinary poverty. Table 2.17 shows that low pay and irregular earnings together accounted for 42.3 per cent of poor households. If the numbers living in poverty because of unemployment are added to this, more than two thirds of those in classes A and B were poverty stricken because of labour market

Table 2.17 **Causes of poverty in classes A and B, 1936**

	Distribution (%)
Low pay	32.8
Unemployment	28.6
Old age	14.7
Irregular low earnings	9.5
Widows	7.8
Illness	4.1
Miscellaneous	2.5

Source: Rowntree (1941: 39)

conditions. Low pay, unemployment, and casual work were the major sources of poverty. Those in class A – the very poorest – were especially likely to be drawn from the unemployed, whereas those in class B tended to be poor because of low pay. Rowntree concluded that unemployment accounted for about half of the most extreme poverty in the city: 'almost the whole of that poverty would disappear if suitable work could be found'. But this was a long term solution:

Meanwhile we have to fall back upon the unsatisfactory alternative of giving financial relief to those for whom work cannot be found. The relief at present given is not sufficient to raise the recipients above the minimum.

(1941: 47)

Although old age accounted for a smaller amount of poverty than did the labour market, Rowntree found it to be the cause of particularly serious problems. Income deficiency among the elderly was far greater than that for any other group, and Rowntree holds that 'the poverty of old age is more acute than that due to any other single cause' (1941: 66). This was so, despite the existence of old age pensions. The pension, received by only a small number of people in 1936, was itself too low to prevent poverty.

In this chapter I have outlined the research on poverty and wealth that was undertaken by contemporary investigators. The broad picture that was painted by these writers for the period from the end of the nineteenth century to the middle of the twentieth century has withstood the test of time remarkably well. Despite the fact that numerous technical modifications in methods of measurement have been made by later writers, and despite the emergence of alternative conceptualisations of poverty, their depiction of the structure of British society from the 1880s to the 1950s remains largely intact. Putting matters crudely, it may be said that at the beginning of this period 30 per cent of the British population were living in poverty and just over 1 per cent of the population had considerable wealth. By the beginning of the 1950s the proportion that was living in poverty had declined to a much lower level, and the share of the top 1 per cent in national resources had declined slightly. The only qualification to make to this picture, as I will show, is that Rowntree somewhat overestimated the extent of the decline in poverty by 1950.

The benchmark figures on personal property holding that were given in Table 2.5 showed the extent of economic inequality that existed in British society before the Second World War. These figures have been confirmed by the most recent authoritative study of income and property distribution. Using a number of different sources, Rubinstein (1986) has shown that, over a very long period, there have been important changes in the degree of income inequality. From the end of the seventeenth century –

the earliest period for which any reliable evidence is available – income has become progressively less unequal in its distribution. At the turn of the eighteenth century the top 1 per cent of the population received well in excess of 80 per cent of the total national income, a share that they retained until the turn of the nineteenth century. The course of the nineteenth century saw a slight increase in the level of income inequality followed, later in the century, by a degree of redistribution.

This accords with the picture that had been identified by Wedgwood. Reviewing the rather sparse evidence on earlier periods, Wedgwood had concluded that lifetime accumulation of property had been a much more important contributor to national capital in the early- and mid-Victorian periods. The significance of inheritance, he argued, had increased as the Victorian entrepreneurs had consolidated their family property holdings and had passed them on to their sons and daughters. The early and mid nineteenth century comprised an exceptional period that reflected the dynamism of industry as it grew in importance relative to land.

Despite the redistribution that occurred towards the end of the nineteenth century, the top 1 per cent of income recipients at the turn of the twentieth century still received well over 60 per cent of all income. At the end of the nineteenth century the bottom 30 per cent of the population received less than 10 per cent of total national income. From the beginning of the twentieth century the share of the top 1 per cent in national income declined to a figure of 55 per cent in 1938 (Rubinstein 1986, citing Soltow 1968; see also Rubinstein 1981).

Rubinstein has shown that property holding in Britain was also highly unequal at the end of the nineteenth century – far more so than was the case for income. The level of inequality in property had remained extremely high from at least as early as 1740 until just before the First World War. At the turn of the twentieth century about 80 per cent of men who died left no property of any value to speak of, while a small number left estates valued at £100,000 or more. As Table 2.5 showed, the top 1 per cent of property holders owned over two thirds of all wealth in 1911. There was, however, a move towards greater equality during the first half of the twentieth century: by 1950 the share of the top 1 per cent of property holders had dropped to just over a half.

Notes

1 Parts of these descriptions were used in Scott (1990a).
2 This section draws on parts of Scott (1990b).
3 See the study of the impact of the London labour market on poverty in Stedman Jones (1971).

4   Some of these analyses were written by Booth's co-workers. The study of dock workers, for example, was carried out by Beatrice Potter, later to become Beatrice Webb.

5   As will become clear, the income boundaries of the classes were not defined independently of the poverty line, but the general logic of Rowntree's approach is obvious.

6   It is not possible to give an accurate view of the relation between the social classes and the primary poverty line as Rowntree, rather surprisingly, gave no tabulations of these figures.

7   In a later chapter I will look at some evidence about the period which has been provided by recent writers. In this chapter I concentrate on the work of contemporaries.

8   A graph comparing the actual with the ideal typical egalitarian distribution is termed a Lorenz curve.

9   Strictly speaking, the table shows the distribution of national personal 'wealth'. In accordance with the suggestions that I made in Chapter 1 I have generally referred to this simply as personal property.

10 The final edition of Bateman (1876) also included briefer details on those with between 2,000 and 3,000 acres.

11 It might have been better to subdivide the category into the two categories of 'ordinary' and 'poor'.

12 D'Aeth gives rather patronising descriptions of the various classes, referring to such things as the frequency with which they wear collars and whether they can follow a simple logical argument or 'need to be told' what to do. Class A, for example, are 'the loafers', 'the refuse of the race', and so on.

13 Wedgwood includes no information about any daughters in the family.

14 A further change from the earlier study was that class boundaries came to be defined explicitly in terms of the poverty line calculations.

15 He argues that rent, averaging 9s 6d per week in 1936, was a fixed cost for all families and needed to be subtracted before comparisons were made.

16 If ordinary poverty had been measured in 1899, it might have been even higher than its 1936 level, though there is no way of estimating this.

CHAPTER 3

Citizenship, welfare and poverty

I argued in Chapter 1 that T. H. Marshall's concept of citizenship provides an essential basis for understanding the development of social policy. The systems of welfare provision and practice which have been established in Britain are the outcome of changing official views of the rights, obligations, and necessary conditions of citizenship. These official views on what is involved in having 'full membership' of British society are, in turn, shaped by contending political and popular perspectives. Such official views have been embodied in the various policies and practices that have been aimed at the alleviation of poverty and, less often, at the limitation of privilege. Marshall's principal point of reference was the emergence of the 'social democratic' from an earlier 'liberal' view of citizenship, and it is on this basis that he illustrates his general case (1949). It is useful to follow Marshall's discussion in order to obtain an initial understanding of the general idea of citizenship.

There are two fundamental components to citizenship, which may be termed the civil–political component and the social component.[1] *The civil–political* component of citizenship comprises the constitutional and juridical norms that define the legal powers that are possessed by a citizen. A full member of a liberal society must, for example, be able to own property, to enter into contracts, and to take action in the courts of law, whenever necessary, in order to defend and promote his or her property and contractual rights.[2] The rights that are involved in the civil-political component of liberal citizenship include the rights to freedom of speech, thought, and association, which together comprise the freedoms that are enshrined in what Macpherson has called 'possessive individualism' (1962). This component of citizenship also includes rights to participate in the exercise of public power by becoming a legislator, a representative, an elector, or by participating in some other way in political decision-making. To these rights must be added such public obligations as the payment of taxes, the performance of jury service, and, under certain circumstances, the performance of military service under a system of conscription. This cluster of civil–political rights and obligations need not involve a system of full political 'democracy', as this is normally understood, but it does imply a certain degree of democracy among those who are accorded the status of citizenship.

The *social* component of citizenship, on the other hand, involves a person's right to 'share to the full in the social heritage and to live the life of a civilised being' (T.H. Marshall 1949: 74).[3] This means that all citizens must possess the resources that are needed if they are to exercise their rights and undertake their obligations. A citizen, argues Marshall, must be healthy and informed and must have the kind of economic resources that are implied by the obligations of public participation. Education, health, and welfare, therefore, are crucial for the formation of autonomous and responsible citizens. This social component of citizenship includes the right to enjoy an appropriate level and style of living, and to possess the resources that will allow a cultivated lifestyle. Official policies based on the liberal concept of citizenship have, therefore, sought to establish fiscal and economic policies that would maintain a minimum level of living for all citizens. It is this social component of citizenship that will be seen to be central to the understanding of welfare policy.

There has never, of course, been a perfect consensus over the nature and scope of citizenship in Britain. Government positions and official practices have embodied competing and often contradictory conceptions of citizenship, which have also been influenced by diverse popular understandings of the rights and obligations of citizenship. The liberal conception of citizenship that has been used to illustrate the two components of citizenship, for example, has never occupied a unitary and unchallenged position in state policy. British social policy over the last hundred years has, in fact, been shaped by the interplay of two underlying views of citizenship. These are the 'elitist' and the 'universalist' views.

An elitist view of citizenship involves the idea that the status of citizen ought to be restricted to those whose living conditions actually meet those which are expected of a citizen. An elitist interpretation of the liberal conception, for example, would hold that citizenship ought to be restricted to those who actually enjoy a life rooted in the conditions of liberty, equality, and fraternity. The right to be a full member of society can legitimately be withheld from those who lack the material and cultural resources that are necessary for them to act as citizens. Those who, by virtue of inequalities attached to their class, gender, or ethnicity, are unable to participate effectively in their society may be denied the status of citizenship. A universalist view of citizenship, on the other hand, involves the belief that the status of citizen ought to be extended to all adult members of the society. For this reason, a universalist view creates an obligation on the part of the state to establish the material and cultural conditions that are needed for effective citizen participation. A universalist view, then, might require the state in a highly unequal society to follow an economic policy of redistribution and a social policy of welfare provision.

The citizens of a society may, therefore, comprise a small 'elite', as in the classical world, or a large 'mass'.

British political thought has shown a gradual development from predominantly elitist to more universalist views of citizenship. This shift has, though, been both slow and uneven and it has been shaped by the social process that Elias has described as 'functional democratisation' (1970; see also Turner 1990: 194). This process involves the emergence of a degree of equalisation in the balance of power among the principal classes and status groups. The relative equalisation of power chances among groups that were formerly characterised by massive power differentials has meant that the state has become rather more responsive to the demands and interests of subordinate groups. Functional democratisation, a process that is integral to the rise of modernity, has resulted in a marked tendency for the status of citizen to become universalised.

Citizenship in Britain was restricted to *propertied men* until the end of the nineteenth century. It was only gradually extended from those with property to all of those who were regarded as being 'economically active' in the labour market. Economic participation has been structured by 'viriarchy' – 'neo-patriarchal' social relations (Waters 1989; M. Mann 1986) – and most women remained effectively excluded from full citizenship throughout the modern period. Only very slowly, and after considerable struggle and conflict, was their civil and political exclusion lifted, and there remain many respects in which women are denied the full rights of citizenship. Most notable among these gender-based restrictions on citizenship are those that still apply in the areas of taxation and welfare. Most recently, there have been similar struggles over the extension of citizenship to ethnic minorities and to migrants from overseas.

It is important to underline the fact that there is no 'inevitability' to this process of universalisation in citizenship rights and obligations, though Marshall is sometimes held to have seen it as being so (Giddens 1981). The struggles of classes and status groups in Britain have, however, resulted in an effective universalisation of the status of citizen. This universalisation has been the driving force behind the establishment of the welfare state, which Marshall saw as being such a significant feature of recent British history. The universalisation of the status of citizen has required the establishment of policies of income redistribution and of welfare provision that have together removed some of the social inequalities that are integral to the operations of a capitalist economy.

The rivalry of elitist and universalist views has structured political debates in Britain, and has generated the three principal interpretations of modern citizenship. These three interpretations can be termed the liberal, the social democratic, and the radical conceptions of citizenship. Each involves a specific definition of citizen rights and obligations and of the social preconditions for the exercise of these.[4] Although they are rarely found in their 'pure' form, they are useful yardsticks for the analysis of actual systems of citizenship. They are ideal types through which the complexities and contradictions of official practices can be understood.

Marshall based his original account of the British welfare state on the assumptions of one particular conception of citizenship, the social democratic, which he saw as developing from an earlier liberal model.[5] Although this social democratic view was, indeed, influential in the formation of the institutions of the post-war welfare state, these institutions also reflected the continuing impact of the assumptions and practices of a more restricted 'liberal' concept of citizenship. I shall try to illustrate this argument in this chapter.

Social services and liberal citizenship

A concerted move towards a centralised system of social provision, aimed at tackling the problem of poverty in a selective way, was undertaken between 1906 and 1914. The package of policies and practices that was introduced by the Liberal governments of this period marked a sustained attempt to establish a 'social service' system that was rooted in a liberal conception of citizenship. This liberal conception rested on an elitist view of the rights and obligations of citizens and, in consequence, it involved a selective targeting of benefits towards only the most 'deserving' of recipients.

The documentation of poverty that was produced in the research carried out by Booth and by Rowntree had reinforced a shift in official policy towards the poor that had already become apparent by the end of the nineteenth century. The election of thirty Labour MPs to the 1906 parliament provided the final push towards the establishment of a system of social services. Liberal politicians were, however, extremely concerned to differentiate their proposed 'social' legislation from the specifically 'socialist' policies that were advocated by the Webbs and their parliamentary supporters. These socialist policies rested on more universalist principles and implied a comprehensive system of collective welfare. The pre-emptive establishment of a social services system by the Liberals, it was felt, would take much of the steam out of the growth in working-class electoral support for the Labour Party and its policy of collective welfare (Digby 1989).

The policies that were enacted were intended to deal with the worst of the causes of poverty that had been identified by Booth and Rowntree. These were the problems of old age, sickness, and unemployment. The system of pension provision and National Insurance was focused on a resolution of these conditions, which were seen as causes of poverty that were not directly soluble by individuals themselves under the existing social arrangements. There was no intention to alter these social arrangements themselves, which Rowntree had identified as the 'ultimate', underlying causes of poverty. The basic economic and political structure of British society was regarded as an unchallengeable absolute that was not to be tampered with. Indeed, a social policy aimed at alleviating the immediate causes of poverty was seen as a means of strengthening support for the existing social pattern.

Pension provision for the aged, introduced in 1908, was the first plank of the social service system. The reasoning behind old age pensions was that they would provide for the needs of the current aged poor and encourage younger workers to make adequate savings for their old age. State expenditure on pensions was, therefore, seen as a temporary expedient that was required to resolve the massive problem of poverty that had been inherited from the nineteenth century. Those who were currently living in poverty needed direct financial support in order to alleviate their situation, but the total level of spending on old age pensions would decline over time as the members of this generation died. Those younger people who were currently in work were expected to make provision for themselves through private savings schemes. In this way, old age pensions would, in due course, cease to be a central government responsibility needing to be financed out of redistributive taxation. Pension provision would become self-financing, reflecting a long-standing liberal concern to encourage thrift and self-help.

The pension proposals that were enacted in 1908 established a statutory right to receive a pension at the age of seventy, and the full pension of 5s per week was set at around one fifth of the average wage. This was however a means-tested right, as it was available only to those whose income fell below a specified level. Those who earned more than £31 10s per year received no pension. This level – just over a half of the average wage – was, in effect, regarded as the level at which an elderly person should be able to support herself or himself. The only conditions attached to this right were that the person should have no record of drunkenness or indigence.

The National Insurance system that was established in 1911 was aimed at offsetting some of the worst consequences of sickness and unemployment. The system did not, however, involve direct payments by the Exchequer from taxation. Unlike the old age pension, National Insurance was a contributory scheme in which benefits were treated in the same way as the benefits arising from any scheme of private insurance: individuals contributed their 'premiums' to the insurance scheme, which paid out benefits if, and only if, they were unfortunate enough to experience either of the insured perils of sickness or unemployment.[6]

The health insurance scheme, which was available only to those in employment, provided for medical treatment in times of ill health or disability, and was administered through friendly societies, trades unions, and insurance companies. The unemployment insurance scheme provided for benefits during involuntary unemployment, the payments being limited to a specified number of weeks. Neither scheme was seen as a means of collective state provision. The element of state provision remained that which was available through the machinery of the Poor Law, which was now seen as a fall-back safety net for the uninsured. The National Insurance system, therefore, involved a voluntary principle: neither the health nor the unemployment scheme was compulsory. The system was also operated along strictly commercial lines, with the benefits that were paid out being financed from a fund that was built up from the individual contributions that had been made to the scheme.

The practices and institutions of the social service system that was established in 1908 and 1911 embodied the principles of liberal citizenship. National Insurance was intended to provide a public framework for self-supported, semi-private insurance schemes that would involve no *net* drain on public expenditure. The old age pension was seen as a temporary expedient that would last only until such time as the new generation of workers were able to make their own, private pension arrangements. The schemes also involved the exclusion of women from certain of the benefits that were enjoyed by men. Women who contributed to the National Insurance scheme received lower sickness benefits than their male counterparts, and married women who were not members of the scheme received no health insurance benefits through their husbands' memberships.

The assumption that pension provision would, in due course, become less of a burden on the state proved ill founded. The majority of those at risk of poverty in old age were, while in employment, unable to afford to make adequate savings for their retirement. As a result, the cost of pension provision increased rather than diminished. In 1925, therefore, the pension system was brought within the National Insurance scheme in an attempt to prevent the cost of pension provision from soaring. Under the new arrangements the National Insurance scheme was extended from health and unemployment to retirement, and, at the same time, the age of retirement was lowered to sixty-five. Contributions to the scheme were made compulsory for all workers who were earning less than £250 per year. The principal advantage of the new scheme was that the old age pension ceased to be means-tested. Now that it had become a National Insurance benefit it was seen as being owed to the insured person as of right.

The National Insurance scheme was aimed at manual workers, who formed the lowest-paid sector of the workforce. Most non-manual workers and all of the self-employed were excluded from the scheme as they were assumed to be able to meet their own needs through private insurance arrangements or through membership of a company pension scheme. As state provision for retirement had been so severely restricted during the nineteenth century, there had been some pension provision by companies for their own employees, but this had been, for the most part, a perquisite only for the better off.[7] On the whole, occupational pension schemes had been limited to the employees of the railway, gas, and water companies. From the turn of the century, however, many more companies began to set up their own pension schemes. These were generally managed from within the companies them-selves as 'self-administered' company schemes. From the 1920s other forms of private pension provision supplemented these self-administered schemes. The so-called group schemes were offered by insurance companies, and involved the administration of pension provision on behalf of large numbers of companies by the insurers. Both forms of company pension provision were *funded* systems. That is to say, the 'members' and their employers paid contributions into the scheme in order to create a fund that could be invested on the stock exchange so as to generate an income. This income was then used to meet the costs of the scheme and to pay the pensions of retired members. The size of the fund that a self-administered scheme can build up is, of course, limited by the size of the company, and so an adequate spread of risks was possible only for the largest of companies. That is why the smaller firms, and many companies that lacked any internal investment expertise, found the group schemes more attractive. In these schemes the investment funds could be swelled by contributions from the numerous participating companies.

The self-administered schemes of the nineteenth century had been formed as integral elements of the business operations of the companies, and so the pensions of members were closely tied to the financial well-being of their company. Twentieth-century schemes, on the other hand, have found the formation of a pension 'trust' a useful way of overcoming this dependence. A trust is legally and financially independent of the company, even though it is normally managed by company executives. For this reason, the trust's moneys cannot be used by the company for its normal business activities, and if the company goes bankrupt, the assets of the pension fund are unaffected.[8]

The number of occupational pension schemes grew during the period from 1900 to 1925, paralleling a growth in large-scale corporate enterprise that also involved a wider restructuring of the employment relationship (Hannah 1976). These schemes emerged as elements in the bureaucratisation of employment and they reflected, at least in part, a managerial policy that was aimed at limiting the antagonism between capital and labour. They reflected, therefore, a strategy of 'incorporation' through the establishment of internal labour markets for 'core' workers: the size of the pension was geared to a person's length of service, and so pensionable workers were tied to their employers through a fear of losing their pension entitlements if they changed jobs (Hannah 1986: 22–4).

The economic dislocations of the inter-war period brought about wholesale industrial collapse and consequent long-term structural unemployment. The growth in unemployment put considerable pressure on the National Insurance system, which had been designed to deal with relatively short-term 'frictional' and cyclical unemployment (Digby 1989: 49ff). Under the original National Insurance scheme, the length of time for which unemployment benefit could be drawn was related to the length of time over which contributions had been made. When their benefits ceased, workers had to resort to Poor Law provision. Longer periods of unemployment for larger numbers of workers made this system impossible to sustain and, in 1927, a system of 'transitional payment' was introduced.[9] This allowed long-term unemployed workers to continue to draw benefit and so separated their status as contributing and, therefore, fully entitled citizens from that of their uninsured counterparts, who were dependent solely on the Poor Law safety net. Transitional payments were not a straightforward entitlement as of right, as their receipt depended upon a test of means and character that was, in effect, no less stigmatising than those applied by the Poor Law authorities.

Economic problems resulted in the collapse of this system of transitional payments in 1931, and it was replaced by a system of Public Assistance. The committees that managed Public Assistance were, in fact, the successor bodies to the Poor Law Guardians, and the new system marked the effective merger of the National Insurance and Poor Law systems for handling long-term unemployment. Those who were out of work for more than twenty-six weeks no longer had any right to receive unemployment benefit, and in order to receive any help at all they had to apply for Public Assistance, when they were subjected to a household means test. Because of regional disparities in both practices and payments – whose costs had to be met by the Treasury – an Unemployment Assistance Board was established in 1934 to handle claims made by the insured long-term unemployed. When, in 1937, the Unemployment Assistance Board took over responsibility for all long-term unemployment benefits, for both the insured and the non-insured, the Poor Law institutions were left with only a restricted and residual responsibility, which was finally swept away after the Second World War. The National Insurance and Unemployment Assistance system had, though, established a modified two-tier system of contributory benefits combined with a means-tested safety net.

Welfare and social democratic citizenship

In 1941, following trades union pressure, the wartime coalition government announced the establishment of a committee of inquiry into the national schemes of social assistance. The members of the committee, with the exception of the chairman, were representatives of the various ministries that had a direct interest in these matters, but the leading role in all aspects of the committee's inquiry was taken by its chairman, Sir William Beveridge. The ministry representatives sat on the committee as advisers and assessors, with Beveridge having been given a free hand in the policy recommendations that he drew up. Beveridge had been one of the civil servants responsible for the introduction of the 1911 unemployment benefit scheme and had subsequently followed an academic career at the London School of Economics and Oxford. Re-entering the senior levels of the Civil Service during the Second World War, he was an obvious choice to head the committee. Although he appears to have been chosen as a 'safe' appointee who would meet the government's aims of minimising change, Beveridge came to see the committee as an opportunity to devise the kind of social assistance scheme that he had long advocated. As the scale of the changes that he wanted to introduce became apparent, the minister insisted that Beveridge alone should sign the Report and should not identify the ministerial representatives with his views.

Beveridge (1942) pointed out that the various reforms that had been introduced since the end of the nineteenth century had been simply piecemeal changes and that no account had been taken of how each new policy measure related to the wider system. The experience of wartime conditions had created a mood of opinion in official circles that there should be fundamental changes in the structure of social policy as soon as post-war reconstruction was possible. It was, Beveridge argued, 'a time for revolutions, not for patching' (1942: 6). In Beveridge's 'revolution' the system of social assistance was to be reshaped so as to eliminate 'want', and other reforms in the spheres of health, education, and employment would be needed to attack the social problems of disease, ignorance, squalor, and illness. The revolution was, however, a liberal revolution in which a principle of social insurance would ensure the appropriate co-operation between the state and the individual:

The state in organising security should not stifle incentive, opportunity, responsibility; in establishing a national minimum, it should leave room and encouragement for voluntary action by each individual to provide more than the minimum for himself and his family.

(1942: 6–7)

Beveridge began his report with a review of the available evidence on the extent of want in Britain, drawing on the work that Rowntree and other researchers had carried out during the inter-war years. These studies, he concluded, showed that the levels of social assistance given to those who were without work were far below the subsistence levels that had been recognised in the poverty studies and that the system failed to adjust the payments according to the needs of families of different sizes. Beveridge therefore advocated an increase in the level of assistance and the introduction of a new system of child allowances. The poverty of old age and childhood would have to be eliminated through retirement pensions and child allowances that were paid at flat rates, while the alleviation of poverty for all other sections of the population would need to be dealt with through a social insurance principle.

In the social insurance system advocated by Beveridge all those who were employed, self-employed, or non-employed would pay a contribution akin to an insurance premium, though the level of contribution for each of these three groups would differ.[10] Men in each group would pay a higher contribution than women, so as to provide a benefit for married women who paid no contribution. The assumption behind this differential was that the man was the normal breadwinner in a family and that single women – who would eventually marry – needed to pay only a small contribution. The growth of female employment was seen as a temporary war-time phenomenon, and Beveridge held that married women would, after the war, once again become financially dependent on their husbands. As a result, he recommended that married women receive lower pensions and lower benefits for unemployment and sickness than men. Once they were married, they would benefit from the higher contributions that were paid by their husbands. All those of working age would thus be entitled to appropriate levels of unemployment and disability benefit, adequate medical care, and a retirement pension.[11] The wives and children of working men would also be supported by maternity benefits and child allowances.

It was Beveridge's intention that contributions would produce a social insurance fund from which the various benefits would be met, without a means test. The scheme would – like any insurance scheme – be self-financing, and this would remove any element of stigma from the scheme: 'Management of one's income is an essential element of a citizen's freedom. Payment of a substantial part of the cost of benefit as a contribution irrespective of the means of the contributor is the firm basis of a claim to benefit irrespective of means' (Beveridge 1942: 12). Direct government expenditure, Beveridge argued, should be limited to such things as maintaining the overall level of employment and the provision of education and public health; it should not be used to undermine the insurance principle through the payment of non-contributory benefits.

The Beveridge system of social insurance was to ensure that families avoided the ordinary poverty that had been identified in Rowntree's work. Beveridge recognised that post-war price levels could not be anticipated, but he estimated that the post-war assistance level would need to be set at around 40s per week for a man and wife, with a further 8s per week for each child. A couple with two children, then, would get 56s in times of unemployment, compared with just 36s under the pre-war system.[12]

Beveridge's proposals aroused much opposition within the government, but a skilful mobilisation of public opinion forced the government to introduce draft legislation along the main lines of the report. It was not until the return of a Labour government after the war, however, that the legislation was actually introduced to parliament for enactment. Because of the climate of public opinion that resulted from the wartime conditions, the Beveridge Report became the official charter for social democratic citizenship in the field of welfare. This conception of citizenship was strengthened by the public reception of the report, which expressed the ideals of 'one nation' and national unity that underpinned the wartime consensus. It became the foundation for the Labour government's enactment of a series of reforms that set up the modern welfare state between 1946 and 1948. The emergent welfare state involved two principal areas, so far as the issues of wealth and poverty were concerned. These were National Insurance and National Assistance, which were set up along with the Family Allowance and various income tax reliefs. Family Allowance was a payment given for the second and subsequent children, and it was a universal but non-contributory benefit. As it was taxable, the degree of benefit varied with family income, giving relatively more, after tax, to low-paid families. This allowance was supplemented by a system of tax reliefs which covered exemptions for dependants, private pensions, and so on. Such reliefs were, of course, benefits only for those who earned enough to pay income tax.

National Insurance, the cornerstone of the welfare state, comprised the system of retirement pensions, unemployment benefit, sickness and injury benefit, and other benefits for widowhood, maternity, and death. This system of National Insurance was an amalgamation of the various pre-war contributory schemes. The benefits were *universal* and were based on a uniform flat rate, not on earnings-related contributions. In principle, the scheme was a *social* insurance scheme, as the employers' and employees' contributions were subsidised by a contribution from general taxation. The amount of redistribution that this involved depended upon the level of the subsidy. In fact, the governmental tax subsidy was generally kept at a small proportion of the total insurance fund, resulting in only a very limited degree of income redistribution.[13]

National Assistance – renamed Supplementary Benefit in 1966 and Income Support in 1988 – was a non-contributory, means-tested supplement to income. The levels of assistance were based around the establishment of a threshold level of income below which an entitlement to a supplementary income would bring recipients back above the threshold. The assumption was that the contributory National Insurance scheme would meet all the main needs of families and that National Assistance would be used to supplement the incomes of those who were outside the schemes. It was argued that as the National Insurance benefits were increased and its schemes were extended to the whole population, there would be a declining need for National Assistance. The universal, contributory benefits would provide for everybody, and the means-tested benefits would disappear. These expectations were never met. Beveridge's intention had also been that benefits would show a gradual increase in real terms, but this aim was never achieved, nor even seriously pursued. The initial National Insurance rates were set at such a low level that many people had to be supported from National Assistance.

The official poverty line – the level at which National Assistance became payable – was calculated as a part of the National Assistance scheme, and its calculation involved similar methods to those that had been followed by Rowntree in his 1936 study. Indeed, Rowntree and Bowley were members of a small sub-committee that Beveridge appointed to advise on this matter. This involved the identification of a threshold level of income that would trigger payments. The actual level that was set in 1948 was £1 14s for a single person, reflecting not simply a calculation of 'need', but also Treasury constraints and political expediency to keep payments low. The benefit rates were about one third less than Beveridge had intended. The threshold has been periodically revised in order to take account of inflation and changing patterns of expenditure, but these revisions have continued to reflect fiscal constraints and political expediency. National Assistance, under one name or another, has continued to be paid, as many have remained below this income threshold – not least because retirement benefits, unemployment benefits, and other benefits have generally been set at levels below the official poverty line. Much of the money paid out as National Assistance has, in fact, been paid to retirement pensioners. Other be characterised not simply by the end of poverty, but also by the end of class and of class-based politics.

Rowntree's research had been intended to test such views. To do this he had constructed various hypothetical distributions of poverty, each assuming different social conditions. His aim had been to measure what the level of poverty in 1950 might have been if the level of welfare and the level of unemployment had remained at the same level as they had been in 1936.

le 3.1   The effects of welfare and full employment

	Actual figures (%)		Hypothetical figures (1950)		
	1936	1950	Without welfare	With high unemployment	
	20.5	34.98	27.58	28.04	
	8.0	11.90	10.22	8.70	
	10.8	11.48	8.97	10.32	'poverty line'
	9.6	1.43	10.49	3.35	
	8.1	0.23	2.84	1.37	

tals in the columns do not add up to 100 per cent because middle class,
ants and those in public institutions are not included

ated from the various estimates in Rowntree and Lavers (1951: 39, 48);
.4

-war welfare reforms had not been made, argued
 proportion of the population of York that was
ty – classes A and B in Rowntree's scheme – would
3 per cent in 1950 instead of the 1.66 per cent
found (see Table 3.1). Rowntree concluded that
n had made a major and continuing difference
 poverty, and that this was especially true for
He made a similar calculation to estimate the
oyment, which in York in 1936 had been at a
nt. Rowntree calculated that if unemployment
his level in 1950, but welfare benefits were
ctual 1950 levels, then only 4.72 per cent of
d have been found to be living in poverty. He
roportion of the population living in poverty
if the level of unemployment were to rise
ut the improved system of welfare benefits
rising to anywhere near its 1936 level.
re further underlined in Rowntree's analysis
 in 1950, in which he sought to highlight
ered still to be matters of serious concern

problems have included the fact that social assistance cannot be paid to those in employment, no matter how low their pay, and no one may receive benefit that would give them an income higher than that which they would get from employment. Thus, people deemed eligible for employment in low-paid jobs have been denied benefit.

Beveridge's pension scheme was aimed at bringing everybody into a social insurance scheme. It was to be based around universalism rather than selectivity. But universalism had the paradoxical effect of allowing the wealthy to benefit from the welfare system. The 1946 Act extended state provision to the middle classes, who had previously been excluded. Thus, the position of the middle classes – who generally had private pension arrangements – was significantly improved. The position of the working class – who were dependent solely on the state pension – was affected only at the margin. The benefits that were given to the middle classes were only partly offset by the remaining element of means testing through Supplementary Benefit and Income Support for poor working-class families.

The post-war system of pension provision was altered somewhat in 1961, when a graduated pension system was introduced alongside the flat rate scheme. Contributions to the new scheme were graduated according to earnings, meaning that the higher-paid employees contributed more. The benefits were, in turn, graduated. Those who made higher contributions would receive higher pensions when they retired. There was a provision for those who were in private occupational schemes to 'contract out' from the state graduated scheme. The advantages of the graduated scheme were not, in fact, great enough to compete with the private schemes, and there was a massive growth in private pension provision. Such schemes covered around half of the workforce by the middle of the 1960s.

The 1960s and 1970s saw a number of unfulfilled plans for pension reform. In 1969 the Labour government announced an expansion of the earnings-related scheme, combined with a redistribution of benefits from the better off to the worse off. This plan fell with the 1970 general election, and a rival Conservative plan – formulated by Sir Keith Joseph and announced in 1973 – also fell with the election of 1974. In 1978 Labour's Barbara Castle reverted to the 1969 plan, though trying to accommodate it to the powerful private schemes. Her State Earnings Related Pensions Scheme (SERPS), however, simply resulted in a much higher level of contracting out, as the costs of staying in the state scheme were extremely high in relation to the benefits.

The private schemes that people were contracting into had grown alongside the state scheme, as they were seen as a way of limiting the extent of public provision. As the insurance company and similar group schemes became more important, so many industrial and commercial enterprises began to delegate the management of all or part of their internal schemes to the financial institutions. As a result, the financial institutions of the City of London became central to the whole system of pension provision, both through the operation of group schemes and through the management of 'self-administered' schemes. The contributions of workers and their employers swelled pensions funds, which came increasingly under the financial management of City institutions. The growth of such pension funds was far greater in Britain than it was in the United States and most other capitalist societies (Hannah 1986: 51).

From the very earliest days of private pension provision it had been possible for the schemes to become 'captive funds'. Instead of being invested in a wide range of securities the resources of a company pension fund could be heavily invested in the shares of the company itself. This would have the effect of boosting the capital that was available to the company without resulting in a dispersal of its shares: instead of sharing control with outside investors the directors of a company could buttress their own controlling position through the investment power of their own company pension fund. Thus a company pension scheme could become one of the largest shareholders in its own company and so become an integral part of the structure of ownership and control. This was the case with many of the early railway and utility companies. Most schemes, though, invested their funds in fixed-interest government securities until the middle of the century. Only from the 1950s did investment in company shares become a major element in pension fund investment, and it was in this period that the number of captive funds increased; with the changes that had occurred in the financial system, a new kind of captive fund emerged. Because of the growing role played by the City institutions, which had begun to invest in company shares in the 1930s, pension funds became the captive funds of the institutions: the power and influence of the City institutions were boosted by pension contributions, but the contributors had little say in the uses to which their funds were put (Minns 1980, 1982).

Furthermore, many of those who worked for the companies in which the institutions invested their funds were not themselves covered by company pension schemes, yet the profits that they produced were meeting the costs of the pensions of those who were members of schemes. Their work generated the profits that paid the dividends that, in turn, paid other people's pensions. A simplified model of this circuit of pensions is presented in Figure 3.1, which shows the structural relations between City institutions, companies, and the workforce. The circuit of contributions and pension payments is simply one part of a larger flow in which the productivity of non-pensioned workers contributes

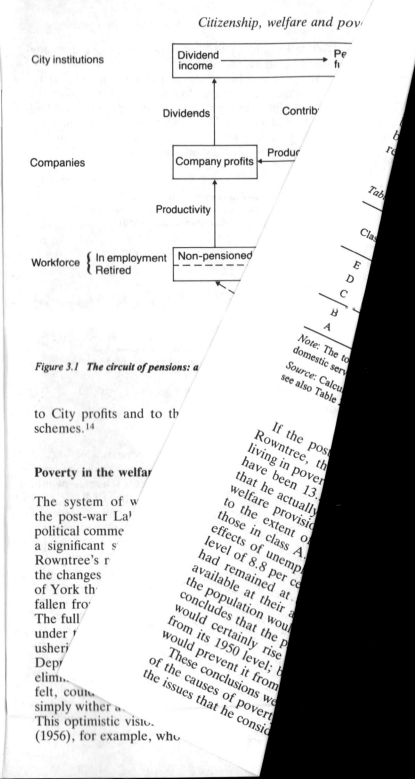

Figure 3.1 The circuit of pensions: a

to City profits and to th
schemes.[14]

Poverty in the welfa

The system of w
the post-war La¹
political comme
a significant s
Rowntree's r
the changes
of York th
fallen fro
The full
under ¹
usheri
Dep
elim
felt, coun
simply wither a
This optimistic visio.
(1956), for example, who

Table 3.2 *Causes of poverty, 1950*

	Distribution of households %
Old age	68.1
Sickness	21.3
Death of wage earner	6.3
Large family	3.2
Low wages	1.1

Source: Rowntree and Lavers (1951: 34)

in the struggle against poverty. He found that the principal conditions that were associated with poverty were old age and sickness (see Table 3.2). In a period of relative affluence and full employment, such as the 1950s, low wages and unemployment no longer generated significant amounts of poverty. Both wages and employment levels had risen in real terms between 1936 and 1950. Unemployment benefits had also increased, but they remained below Rowntree's poverty line. For this reason, an increase in unemployment would still result in a substantial increase in poverty. Nevertheless, so long as full employment and affluence could be maintained, poverty would constitute a problem mainly for the aged, the infirm, and the disabled. Rowntree was very optimistic about the elimination of this 'residual' problem of poverty. Looking forward to the effects of the 1951 budget, he argued that the changes in the level of pensions that were announced might be expected to reduce poverty by more than a half – though he pointed out that inflation would partly offset any improvement.

Rowntree's findings, then, were widely seen as documenting, in the words of the *Manchester Guardian*, 'The Ending of Poverty'. This judgement was, perhaps, premature. The number of adults who were receiving National Assistance in 1949 – the end of the first full year of the scheme – was 1.8 million. This number, like all such estimates, is a minimum figure, as the claimants are only a fraction of those actually living in poverty as it was officially defined. The reason for this is that many of those who would be eligible for welfare benefits do not apply – and people in low paid jobs are, in any case, not eligible, no matter how low their income may be. Atkinson's (1969) study attempted to correct this and estimated that the actual number of people living in poverty in 1967 was between two and five million, somewhere between 4 and 9 per cent of the population. Unfortunately, there are no more reliable estimates for any year in the post-war period, but the actual figure is certainly substantially higher than Rowntree's estimate suggested.

A sceptical view about the elimination of poverty was put forward in the early 1950s by Peter Townsend, who can be regarded as a critical and radical follower of Booth and Rowntree. While he rejected many of their leading theoretical ideas, as well as their political assumptions, he has undertaken empirical research on poverty that lies directly within their tradition of work. His first major study (1952) held that existing measures of poverty were rooted in a very narrow and restricted view of the 'necessities' for an ordinary life. Researchers such as Booth and Rowntree had failed to move far enough towards an adequate, *relative* concept of poverty and so they remained too closely tied to absolute, subsistence-level measures. Research that Townsend undertook with Brian Abel-Smith (Abel-Smith and Townsend 1965), along with the related work of Titmuss (1962) was very influential in elaborating this argument, and in the middle of the 1960s Townsend began a major national investigation of poverty. This resulted in a number of important monographs (Marsden 1969; Land 1969) and culminated in the appearance of a massive national volume (Townsend 1979). Since that study Townsend has undertaken a major study of London, cast directly in the mould of Booth's investigations of one hundred years earlier. Townsend's work on poverty and deprivation stands alongside the landmark works of Booth and Rowntree, and must be reviewed at length. In the remainder of this chapter I will outline the theoretical basis of his work, and in the following chapter I will discuss his empirical findings.

Citizenship and relative poverty

Townsend set out a definition of poverty that was intended to break, conclusively, with the assumptions of 'absolute', subsistence-level measures. This concept of poverty was given a provisional outline in the early 1970s (Townsend 1974) and was subsequently elaborated in his empirical work. His view was that poverty must be seen as relative to historically and culturally variable conceptions of an acceptable standard of life. As such, it is always defined in relation to prevailing social standards. He argues that

Poverty . . . is the lack of the resources necessary to permit participation in the activities, customs and diets commonly approved by society.

(1979: 81)

Townsend's starting point is that poverty must be defined in terms of *deprivation*, as this is judged by the customary levels of living that prevail in a society:

Individuals, families and groups in the population can be said to be in poverty when they lack the resources to obtain the types of diet, participate in the activities and have the living conditions and amenities that are customary, or are at least widely encouraged or approved, in the societies to which they belong. Their resources are so seriously below those commanded by the average individual or family that they are, in effect, excluded from ordinary living patterns, customs and activities.

(1979: 31)

Galbraith's influential work, *The Affluent Society*, put forward a similar view of poverty, cast in his characteristically pithy prose:

People are poverty-stricken when their income, even if adequate for survival, falls markedly behind that of the community. Then they cannot have what the larger community regards as the minimum necessary for decency; and they cannot wholly escape, therefore, the judgement of the larger community that they are indecent. They are degraded for, in a literal sense, they live outside the grades or categories which the community regards as acceptable.

(1958: 261)

To live in poverty, then, is to be deprived of those opportunities that are open to most other people in that society. Poverty is an inability to meet the costs that are associated with the social expectations that define a normal life within one's society (Townsend 1987). For this reason, poverty must always be defined in relation to a socially recognised standard of living. There is, therefore, no single and unambiguous 'absolute' definition of poverty that can be applied to all societies and to all times. No 'subsistence minimum', for example, can be applied to all societies and all periods in a culturally neutral way. Any measure must take account of changing social expectations.

But the social expectations that are institutionalised in a particular society rarely specify a single lifestyle as that which is obligatory or expected for all the members of that society. They specify, rather, the general standard and style of living that a full member of society is expected to pursue, but they do not enjoin rigid conformity to a uniform code of behaviour. Social expectations define a range of alternative and equally acceptable modes of living. Despite the greater uniformity that has been engendered by the mass media, there are still many important and socially significant variations in 'legitimate' lifestyles. Such lifestyles are often differentiated according to age, sex, and locality, but many ways of living are mere matters of preference. It may be believed that all elderly people ought to have a daily hot meal, though public opinion is also likely to believe that they should be able to choose whether this meal is a cod mornay, an Irish stew, or a vegetarian hotpot. Put more generally, social expectations may define strict minima – and maxima – for levels of living, but they will tend to allow considerable discretion in the actual content of those levels of living. Social expectations are concerned with the kinds of things that people *can* do, rather than with specific acts that they *must* perform.

People engage in the same kind of activities rather than the same specific activities . . . The style of living of a society consists more of elements which are heterogeneous, but ordered and interrelated rather than rigidly homogeneous.

(Townsend 1979: 54, 249)

There are thus a number of equally acceptable ways of meeting the socially expected standard of life that prevails in a society. 'Deprivation', according to Townsend, consists in an inability to meet *any* of these expectations. It involves not simply limited resources, but a complete lack of choice about one's way of life. Deprivation occurs whenever the resources that are available to a household are insufficient for it to meet the socially sanctioned and legitimated needs and expectations that are placed upon its members.

The crucial element in Townsend's relative conception of poverty, then, is the idea of the existence of socially institutionalised standards of living. The 'customary', 'conventional', or 'accepted' styles of living in a society create 'needs' and 'expectations' on the part of the members of the society. Those who are unable to meet these needs and expectations are deprived, and the cause of their deprivation is their lack of resources. Societies vary in the standards that they require of their members, and so the extent of poverty and deprivation will also vary from one society to another. Two societies may show the same degree of inequality in the distribution of their resources, but they will have differing levels of poverty if the social expectations that are placed upon their members differ. This same point applies with respect to changes over time within any particular society. The extent of inequality may decrease, but if social expectations remain the same or are rising, then the amount of poverty that is recognised in that society will increase.

This argument can best be understood by relating it to the idea of citizenship that I have already discussed. While the word 'citizenship' is not used by Townsend, the concept permeates the whole of his work. This is very clear in his statement that those who live in poverty are 'deprived of the conditions of life that ordinarily define membership of society' (1979: 915). To be deprived is to be excluded from even minimal participation in what Marshall called the 'material civilisation' of a society. This means that people lack the income that would permit 'adequate' housing, nutrition, education, or leisure, say where 'adequate' is defined in terms of socially variable conceptions of citizenship. Conceptions of deprivation and, therefore, estimates of the numbers of those who are deprived must always be made relative to particular conceptions of citizenship.

Conventions of citizenship become institutionalised through legislation and through other socially structured processes. Most obviously, welfare legislation creates a pattern of entitlements to income and resources. Similarly, health and housing legislation creates a framework of environmental requirements and expectations, education and the mass media generate expectations about work and leisure, legislation on schooling requires certain levels of parental expenditure, business operations generate a particular pattern of demand for products, and so on (Townsend 1979: 50–51). Townsend sees law and other institutionalised requirements and obligations as being central elements in the whole complex of conventions that surround socially accepted styles of living. It is the prevailing view of citizenship that defines and sustains these standards. The core conventions of citizenship are those that are embodied in the policies and practices of the state. Where the framework of citizenship accords a legitimacy to the expression of public opinion, this will also carry a prescriptive force.

Three elements enter into the conventions of citizenship. These can be termed 'empowerments', 'legitimate wants', and 'induced obligations'. *Empowerments* are those prescriptive expectations, both positive and negative, that are embodied in official views and public opinion. The positive elements are the rights on which Marshall's work concentrated. To be a citizen means to be empowered to do certain things: to go to law in defence of one's interests, to vote, to act as a magistrate. The 'negative' elements in empowerment are prescriptions to the effect that citizens should not be prevented *de facto* from exercising their rights. They must not, for example, be prevented by lack of income from exercising their rights.

Legitimate wants are those things that it is felt all citizens ought to be able to enjoy, if they so choose. The citizen, in the modern capitalist world, is regarded as a 'consumer' and, through such processes as advertising, is encouraged to want certain things. Those wants and desires that become routinised as elements in the consumption patterns typical of the majority of citizens come to be seen as legitimate wants for all citizens: they become features of the normal, expected, and taken-for-granted lifestyle of the citizen.

Induced obligations are not specified in particular social prescriptions, but they acquire their force by virtue of those legitimate wants and empowerments that are established in the society. The prescription that all children should attend school, for example, engenders expectations of parental support and encouragement and creates the obligation for parents to provide the kinds of facilities that will allow their children to benefit from their schooling. Such facilities might include the provision of books, a place to study, and foreign exchange visits.

The 'official' view of poverty in a society is that which is defined in the officially institutionalised criteria of citizenship and their associated empowerments, legitimate wants, and induced obligations. The official 'poverty line', – even when it is not defined in those precise words – is drawn at the level of resources at which the institutionalised system of welfare regards people as falling below socially expected standards.

But citizenship must not be seen only in 'official' terms. I have already shown that legally institutionalised ideas are buttressed by a whole package of other institutionalised requirements and expectations. An implication of Townsend's position is that popular as well as official perceptions of deprivation and poverty are formed on the basis of particular conceptions of citizenship. Customary expectations rarely reflect a monolithic normative consensus. A lack of consensus over these matters will result in varying views of the rights and duties of full membership; 'unofficial' views may, then, depart from the officially institutionalised conventions of citizenship. These unofficial, popular views may coalesce into competing conceptions of citizenship, which political parties and movements may then attempt to build into the official machinery of the state. More generally, they constitute those looser conceptions of what is 'normal' and expected. They find their expression in everyday actions and attitudes and they can be uncovered in attitude and opinion surveys.

Measuring poverty

Townsend recognised that measures of the extent of poverty and deprivation in a society will vary according to which standards – *whose* standards – are taken as the point of reference. Poverty is a contested concept, and researchers must make clear the standards that are being used in their research. Townsend initially used a variant of the 'social democratic' concept, according to which majority public opinion – imperfectly reflected in official standards – is the arbiter of acceptability and deprivation. He argued that it is necessary, ideally, to survey the whole range of lifestyles that are current in a society in order to discover 'the elements common to, or approved by, the majority of the population' (1979: 249). That is to say, it is necessary to look at the extent to which particular items and activities are 'representative', 'frequent', 'important', and so on, to the majority of the people. The absence of these items in a particular household could then be regarded as a sign of its deprivation relative to prevailing social standards. Unfortunately, Townsend did not follow through the full logic of this view. Lacking the time and resources to undertake such a survey, he concentrated on a list of some sixty items relating to diet, housing, environment, welfare, and education. These items were arrived at through informed professional judgement and were, Townsend felt, adequate surrogates for properly measured indicators of deprivation. A count of the number of items that were lacking for a particular household produced a 'deprivation score' for that household: 'the higher the score the lower the participation' in normal social life (1979: 251).[15]

Townsend showed that the deprivation scores for those in his national sample varied with their income: the lower the income, the higher the deprivation score. But such a measure of deprivation does not, in itself, yield an objective way of defining the overall level of deprivation in a society. There is no obvious way of deciding the score at which 'deprivation' begins. It would be necessary to search for a criterion according to which it is possible to say that people with a score of greater than X on the index are deprived, while those with a score of less than X are not. This level would need to be defined independently of any measures of income or other resources if it is to show the proportion of the population falling into each category. Townsend does not, unfortunately, achieve this important task in his own research. It is paradoxical that while Townsend argues that poverty must be defined in terms of relative deprivation, he does not, in fact, attempt to identify the level of his own deprivation index at which objective deprivation can be said to occur.

What he does, however, is to identify a 'poverty line' in the distribution of resources. He argues that poverty can always be defined by some 'line' in the distribution of resources, though he does not follow the approaches used by Booth and Rowntree to identify this line. Instead, he attempts to identify an objective poverty line from a theoretical model of the relationship between institutionalised standards and resource distribution.[16]

We would expect, he argues, participation in social life to vary with resources. It should be possible, therefore, to draw a graph showing these two 'variables'. On such a graph (see Figure 3.2), it would be possible to identify varying levels of normal participation

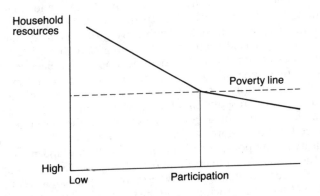

Source: Simplified and modified from Townsend (1979: 261, Figure 6.4).

Figure 3.2 *The poverty threshold*

and a lower range of deprived participation. There would also be a correspondence between the point at which deprivation begins and the point at which household resources fall below a level capable of sustaining normal participation. This point in the resource distribution is the poverty line. The poverty line, then, marks the level of resources at which normal participation gives way to deprived participation.

Townsend has argued that there is a qualitative difference between normal and deprived participation. If he is correct in this assertion, the poverty line might be expected to mark a point of 'catastrophic' change in the level of resources. He claims that

At relatively low levels of resources people find they are unable to enjoy a wide representation of consumer goods, customs and activities and are able to enjoy only cheaper versions of some goods, customs and activities. The range is reduced proportionately to falling levels of resources. The reduction is more gradual than the diminishing resources would suggest, because of the need to maintain social cohesion or integration. . . . But at still lower levels of individual and family resources, economical forms of social participation become impossible to provide. People's participation in the national style of living diminishes disproportionately.

(1979: 59)

As resources fall, so people try to cover up and 'make do'. At the lowest levels of resource this becomes impossible:

It may be hypothesised that, as resources for any individual or family are diminished, there is a point at which there occurs a sudden withdrawal from participation in the customs and activities sanctioned by the culture. The point at which withdrawal 'escalates' disproportionately to falling resources could be defined as the poverty line.

(1979: 57)

It is important to note that the existence of a sharp threshold at the poverty line is a hypothesis. Poverty can, and does, exist without there being such a sharp threshold, but the absence of a point of escalation makes the drawing of a poverty line more difficult. Townsend seems to be arguing that the existence of a point of escalation makes the identification of an objective, though still relative, measure of deprivation much easier: the researcher can simply identify the point of escalation on the graph and then read off the corresponding point at which deprivation begins.

In the absence of a point of escalation, the researcher must proceed in the more logical, but more difficult way of first identifying the point at which deprivation begins and then reading off the level of the poverty line from the graph. Such an approach would need to define deprivation by a particular score on a deprivation index, such as that constructed by Townsend. Poverty could then be said to exist where resources are such that people have a deprivation score at or above this level.[17] Consider, for

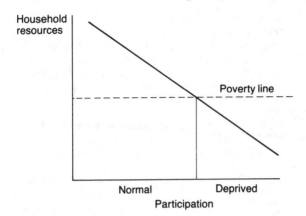

Figure 3.3 Poverty and resources

example, the graph in Figure 3.3, in which there is no point of
sharp escalation, no 'elbow' in the line showing the relationship
between resources and participation. The poverty line on such a
curve can be identified only after the dividing line between normal
and deprived participation has been identified. This procedure can
be followed when the researcher has no information about the
overall distribution of resources, so long as the resources of those
just above and just below the point at which deprivation begins
are known.

Despite the sophistication of Townsend's approach, much of his
actual research concentrated on officially recognised poverty. That
is, he focused on poverty and deprivation as measured relative
to official standards and the underlying view of citizenship.
His research findings and those of subsequent researchers are
reviewed in the following chapter.

Notes

1 Marshall separates the civil from the political in his own account and
   so recognises three components. For my purposes here, a two-fold
   distinction is more useful.
2 I use the term 'right' to refer to any *legitimate* expectation. It is
   not restricted to formal, legal rights. It is in this sense that people
   may come to have a right to welfare or to a reasonable standard
   of living.
3 Turner (1988) has, in a related way, pointed to the relationship
   between the 'political' aspects of status and its 'cultural' aspects of
   lifestyle.
4 Turner (1991: 44) has contrasted 'liberal' and 'communitarian'
   approaches to citizenship. Unfortunately, he conflates the liberal
   and the social democratic conceptions that I wish to distinguish.

5   A further limitation to Marshall's viewpoint is that he generalises his whole model of citizenship from the British social democratic case.

6   The National Insurance scheme was not a funded insurance scheme of the kind described later in this chapter, as payments were met from current contributions and taxation rather than being financed from accumulated investment income. It was, nevertheless, a legally constituted system of insurance.

7   The following discussion draws on Hannah (1986).

8   The legal limitation is not water-tight, as evidenced by the misuse of the Mirror Group pension funds by Robert Maxwell.

9   This was based on a similar scheme introduced, on a smaller scale, in 1921.

10   Employees were also to have their contributions supplemented by their employer.

11   A comprehensive national health scheme, separate from the system of cash benefits, was proposed by Beveridge. He left open the question of whether this National Health Service would be financed, in part, from insurance contributions.

12   Pre-war benefits stopped after thirteen weeks; Beveridge wanted to abandon this and to continue benefit for as long as unemployment lasted.

13   Indeed, the practice of financing payments from current funds, rather than from the investment of contributions, has resulted in the use of general tax revenue to maintain basic payments.

14   In this diagram I have ignored other forms of personal savings and investments in order to highlight the circuit of pensions itself. I have also ignored wages, which flow from companies to employees. Each of these is involved in its own circuit. See, for example, Marx's attempt to describe the circuit of capital in relation to wages (1864). It is important to note that dividends are also a source of profits for other forms of personal savings which benefit, disproportionately, the middle and the capitalist classes.

15   The later *Breadline Britain* survey followed Townsend's ideal strategy of surveying public opinion. See Mack and Lansley (1985).

16   Townsend often resorts to a consensus assumption. Although there are a number of ways of measuring deprivation, he feels that there will be one which corresponds closely to the central assumptions and structures of the society and that this will correlate with the resource distribution.

17   This procedure was adapted in the *Breadline Britain* survey, which used an opinion survey to construct an index of deprivation and a cut-off threshold. Desai (1986) has shown that there was a close agreement between the threshold level identified by Townsend and that identified by the *Breadline Britain* researchers. Townsend seems to have used an adequate index of deprivation and to have correctly hypothesised a point of escalation.

CHAPTER 4

Poverty and wealth: today

The work of Peter Townsend has dominated the debate on poverty since the 1950s. His relative concept of poverty – rooted in the framework of citizenship and social participation – must rank as one of the most influential ideas of the twentieth century. Like his predecessors Booth and Rowntree, Townsend has allied his theoretical and political commitments to empirical investigations, and he has produced a number of important studies. Townsend has, however, been able to take advantage of advances in research methodology that have occurred since the pioneer studies.

The early studies that were undertaken by Booth and by Rowntree were detailed investigations of particular cities, and only Rowntree's final survey had made any use of sampling methods. Townsend's work, on the other hand, used modern survey methodology, which allowed him to make a national sample study. In addition to this national investigation, four surveys of poverty in 'poor' areas – Salford, Neath, Glasgow, and Belfast – were carried out.[1] A subsequent study of London was undertaken independently of the national study, and provides a useful comparison with Booth's earlier work on London.

Of all the work that has been done in the wake of Townsend's own investigations, the *Breadline Britain* study is, perhaps, the most important. While it extended and updated the national level data that Townsend had produced, its principal significance lies in its use of public opinion to measure relative poverty in relation to contemporary standards of citizenship. Taken together, these studies have resulted in a considerable sophistication of our understanding of poverty.

Research on wealth, by contrast, has hardly advanced since the pioneer studies that were reviewed in Chapter 2. While the research of such investigators as Atkinson and Rubinstein is technically more proficient than that of Chiozza-Money and Wedgwood, the greater reliability of their results has not been matched by an equivalent advance in the conceptualisation of wealth. Studies of wealth holding have remained firmly wedded to the statistical approach that was used in the pioneer studies: the wealthy are defined simply as the top X per cent of the population, with little consideration being given to the sociological rationale for using any particular cut-off level. As a result, some impressive ethnographic data notwithstanding, accounts of the wealthy remain rather unsatisfactory. In Chapter 6 I will suggest a way forward for research into wealth.

Townsend on levels of living

Townsend planned his national study as a sample investigation from the very beginning, and he used a detailed schedule of questions as the basis for formal interviews with respondents. The pilot study for the national survey was undertaken in 1965–8, the schedule was tested in 1967, and the main survey was completed in 1968–9. The national sample was a multi-stage stratified sample. Parliamentary constituencies were chosen in each of the twelve standard regions of the United Kingdom, giving a selection of fifty-two constituencies balanced for their degree of urbanism. Using Census information, wards within these constituencies were grouped by their demographic characteristics, and a sample of wards in each constituency was drawn. As Townsend's aim was to achieve a comprehensive sample of households, rather than a sample of individuals, the sampling frame that he used was the local rating records, together with some unpublished information that had been collected to update the electoral register.

From this selection procedure, a sample of 2,495 households was produced, and their members were approached for interview. A total of 2,052 households (containing 6,098 individuals) co-operated in the research, an 82 per cent completion rate. Those interviewed were 'the housewife and all wage-earners (and other income recipients) in the household' (Townsend 1979: 102; for more details see his Appendix 1: 927–54). An interview schedule running to 175 complex questions was used, the questions covering such areas as housing and living conditions, employment, income and savings, health and disability, and related matters. The interviews lasted, on average, between one and a quarter hours and two and three quarter hours.

The London study began in 1985. Over the following two years a large number of interviews were carried out and statistical information was collected for analysis (Townsend *et al.* 1987). The core of the work consisted of a random sample of 2,700 adults living in Greater London. More detailed investigations of two London boroughs at opposite poles of the distribution of resources were also undertaken. A general sample was drawn from 30 wards selected from a list of all 755 London wards, which had been ranked by an index of 'multiple deprivation' in order to ensure that the sample gave a good representation of all levels of living in the city. The index of multiple deprivation itself combined a number of indicators – such as the level of unemployment, overcrowding, and the number of pensioners in one-person households – into a single 'z-score', which was used as an indication of the general level of deprivation characteristic of each ward. This measure had been devised by the Intelligence Unit of the Greater London Council and, in the light of the results of the earlier national study and related investigations, Townsend regarded it as a useful provisional measure of overall deprivation for the purposes of his initial data selection. Positive values on the measure indicated deprivation, while negative numbers indicated an absence of deprivation, the z-scores varying from +8.42 in Spitalfields to − 11.01 in Cranham West (Havering).[2] The 30 wards that were chosen for the general sample were drawn at regular intervals from between these two extremes. By combining ward scores into overall borough scores it was possible to identify extremes of poverty and affluence for the more detailed case studies.

To represent a 'poor' area − or, at least, one with significant pockets of deep poverty and an overall low level of income − Townsend chose Hackney in the East End, and to represent a relatively affluent area he chose Bromley in the south-east. Interviews were carried out with 400 residents in each of these boroughs, and a series of further interviews was undertaken with local employers.

Townsend's starting point in both of these studies was to explore the official poverty line, the level of resource at which the government sees supplementary income as being necessary to bring people up to an appropriate standard of living. This is the British Official Poverty Line (BOPL) measure of poverty that was defined in Chapter 1, which it will be recalled, takes the National Assistance, Supplementary Benefit, or Income Support levels of entitlement as the basis for the measurement of poverty. Townsend shows that 7 per cent of British households were living below this official poverty line in 1968.

Townsend's national investigation used the procedures that had first been set out in *The Poor and the Poorest* (Abel-Smith and Townsend 1965), which involved adjusting the social assistance thresholds so as to take account of the additional discretionary payments that were available over and above the basic rate. Using the BOPL, he regarded receipt of an income that was less than 140 per cent of the Supplementary Benefit level as an indicator that people were living 'on the margins' of officially recognised poverty (see Table 4.1). He estimated that almost one third of households in Britain in 1968 were living below or on the margins of the official poverty line, which amounted to 15.2 million individuals (Townsend 1979: 272). This figure of 31 per cent compares with the estimates of 30.7 per cent for London in 1886 and 27.8 per cent for York in 1901 that were found by Booth and Rowntree using their differing measures of poverty.

The relationship of poverty to inequality can be glimpsed in

Table 4.1 *Poverty distribution in Britain, 1968*

	% of households	% of population
In poverty*	7.3	6.4
On the margins†	23.3	21.5
Total	30.6	27.9

* Income at or below Supplementary Benefit level
† Income less than 40% above Supplementary Benefit level
Source: Townsend (1979: 275, Table 7.2)

Table 4.2 *Income distribution in Britain, 1968*

Net income as % of mean	% of households	% of persons
200 or more	4.0	4.3
140–99	9.5	9.8
110–39	15.6	16.0
100–109	7.9	8.2
90–99	10.1	10.6
80–89	12.7	12.3
70–79	11.3	11.1
50–69	18.2	18.5
Less than 50	10.6	9.2

Source: Townsend (1979: 280, Table 7.6)

Table 4.2, where the distribution of households into various income categories is shown. From these data it is possible to calculate the European Poverty Line, defined as 50 per cent of average income. The 10.6 per cent of households receiving an income that was less than half of the national average income included most – if not all – of the 7.3 per cent that were living below the BOPL (see Table 4.1). At the top of the hierarchy were 13.5 per cent of households with incomes more than 140 per cent above the national average, many of whom had incomes of 200 per cent or more above the Supplementary Benefit level.

Table 4.3 gives some further, though limited insight into those at the top of the distribution. The top 1 per cent of income recipients come closest to being those who could be regarded as living above an officially recognised 'wealth line', as this is the upper level that has been identified in official reports on income distribution. It is, however, an arbitrary statistical categorisation, lacking the foundation in citizenship that characterises the official poverty

Table 4.3 **Households distribution, 1968**

Quantile group (slices)	% of income received	% of assets held
Top 1%	6.2	26.0
2–5%	10.0	25.0
6–10%	9.4	13.0
11–20%	15.0	15.0
21–100%	59.4	21.0

Source: Townsend (1979: 342, Table 9.1)

line. Nevertheless, it can be employed as a useful indicator of wealth. Townsend's research showed that if income and assets were combined into a single distribution, all of those in the top 1 per cent of the distribution had incomes at least ten times the Supplementary Benefit level. If 7.3 per cent of the population lived a deprived existence at an income level below the Supplementary Benefit rate, and 23.3 per cent lived on the margins of deprivation at 140 per cent of the Supplementary Benefit level, 1 per cent of the population lived a relatively privileged existence on incomes of 1,000 per cent or more of the Supplementary Benefit level.

Townsend attempted to substantiate his hypothesis that there was a 'point of escalation' in the distribution of resources, his aim being to compare the numbers living below this level with the numbers living in officially recognised poverty. The distribution of resources among the households studied did indeed show the pattern that was hypothesised in Figure 3.2, and he identified 25 per cent of households as falling below the 'elbow' point in the distribution of resources. If he is correct in his hypothesis, we would expect to find that many of those who were living on the margins of official poverty were also to be found among those households that fell below the point of escalation. Those who actually live in officially recognised poverty would constitute the most deprived group below the threshold.

The conditions that arise at this threshold level have been described by Lockwood (1986, 1987) as those of 'civic deficit'. Although citizenship rights may be formally enjoyable by all, there are certain groups with very limited resources who are unable to exercise these rights, and so are unable to enjoy full citizenship. In the terms that I introduced in the previous chapter, they are not fully empowered as citizens. Lockwood argues that these groups tend to become stigmatised by the pattern of citizenship itself. The very fact that the legal institutions of citizenship specify a range of state welfare benefits that are available to all those whose resources fall below an officially recognised standard of adequacy creates a division within the status of citizenship. This division is one between the ordinary citizen and the citizen who is dependent on welfare benefits. Those who are in receipt of supplementary benefits, state pensions, and unemployment benefit, for example, will tend to experience public derogation as 'second-class citizens', as 'claimants', because the official machinery of welfare provision relies on means testing and on a scrutiny of their personal affairs. Such stigmatisation may actually undermine the moral claims that these people make to greater resources.[3]

Townsend's national survey data relate to 1968, and he drew on other sources in order to outline any changes that had taken place in the ten years between the completion of his survey and its final publication. Using official data, he showed that the share of the top 1 per cent of wealthy households fell over this period, though this fall had not resulted in any redistribution of resources to the bottom 80 per cent of households. At the same time the proportion of those 'at risk' of poverty – the elderly and the unemployed – had increased at a greater rate than had the population as a whole over the period. Official estimates from the *Family Expenditure Survey* showed that, as a result, officially measured poverty declined slightly in the early 1970s and then increased again from 1975 to 1979. In 1976, Townsend claims, there were 2.3 million individuals living in poverty and 8.5 million living on the margins.

These figures can be put in a wider context by using official data analysed by the Child Poverty Action Group, which updated the estimates to 1987. This research showed that the proportion of the population living in poverty and on the margins of poverty, as measured on the BOPL, stood at 22 per cent in 1979 and 28 per cent in 1987. This would seem to show a marked reduction in inequality between 1968 and 1979, followed by a sharp rise over the following decade. The figures for those actually living in poverty increased from 6.4 per cent in 1968 to 12 per cent in 1979 and to 19 per cent in 1987 (See Table 4.4). The extent of poverty, then, showed a continuous increase over the period following

Table 4.4   **The population in poverty, 1979 and 1987**

% of population	1979	1987
Below Supplementary Benefit level	4.0	5.0
At Supplementary Benefit level	8.0	14.0
On the margins[*]	10.0	9.0
Total	22.0	28.0

[*]See Table 4.1

Source: Oppenheim (1990: 22, Figure 1)

Townsend's survey. Some idea of the degree of deprivation involved can be seen from the actual level of Supplementary Benefit entitlement. In 1987 this stood at £70.15 per week for a couple with two children aged under eleven, after allowing for the costs of housing. Turning to the European Poverty Line measure, the Child Poverty Action Group survey found that the proportion of the population living at or below 50 per cent of average income stood at a similar level in 1979 as it did in 1968. The 1979 figure of 9 per cent of the population had, however, risen to 19 per cent by 1987, confirming the impression of a marked increase in poverty during the 1980s (Oppenheim 1990: 28, Figure 3).

The highest incidence of poverty in the Townsend survey was to be found in one-person households. Ten per cent of these families lived in poverty and 39 per cent were on the margins – almost a half, therefore, were 'poor' in the broadest sense. The next highest incidence of poverty was found in large households containing five or more people. Poverty was also strongly associated with age and with gender: women were more likely to live in poverty than were men, and the highest incidence for each sex was among those aged over sixty-five. It was found that over half of men and women above the age of sixty-five were living in poverty or on its margins. Indeed, Townsend supports Rowntree's life cycle argument, claiming that about a half of all households would experience poverty at some stage in their life cycle (1979: 285, 898). Poverty was, of course, related to employment conditions. Fifteen per cent of manual workers lived in poverty, with 32 per cent on the margins. This figure compared with just 1 per cent of managerial workers, mainly the retired (1979: 292). A more recent survey by the Child Poverty Action Group confirmed many of these demographic findings. Families living in poverty in 1987 included 21 per cent of children, but children in one-parent families were especially at risk: 70 per cent of such children were living in poverty (Oppenheim 1990: 24).

Townsend described the conditions of some of the families in his study. A couple with three children in a four-roomed council flat in Oldham were said to be living in damp and insanitary conditions, and the family had no money to heat the flat adequately. The husband was medically unfit for work and the wife – herself unwell – had had to give up her own job in order to look after him. The family were living, in 1968, on a total of £12.20 per week. When Townsend's team intervened with the authorities, the allowance was increased by 35p per week. Little had changed four years later, though the eldest son was then out at work and earning £7.94 per week. Townsend concluded: 'The evidence of deprivation is as strong and in some respects stronger, than in 1968. They go to bed early to save fuel. Mrs Nelson buys second-hand clothing at jumble sales. For breakfast, she cooks porridge for the children but she and her husband have nothing.

They are used to days without any cooked meal' (1979: 308–9). The husband died four years later, aged forty-three. Other poor households included a retired woman living on her own, who was said to have 'one cooked meal each day – mince or a piece of meat not more than three times a week – and she is fond of tripe. She has half a pint of milk each day' (1979: 311). A young woman whose husband was in prison was supporting two children on £5.96 per week. Because of support from her extended family, she was able to survive on this, and could afford to smoke ten cigarettes a day.

'On the margins' of poverty were a couple with two children, living in a terraced house. They received up to £13.98 per week from employment, which was supplemented by a 40p family allowance and subsidised rent. They managed some small savings and could eat regularly, but they had no holidays and few outings. Their housing was 'tied' to the work, and they would become homeless if the husband lost his job.

At the other end of the scale, Townsend's sample located few of the small number of wealthy families. One of the wealthiest that he interviewed was an elderly couple with a resident maid. They owned houses valued, in 1968, at £30,000, they had about twice this amount invested in stocks and shares, and they received income from investments and from an army pension. Their total assets were around £100,000. The man came from a shipping family and his wife from the landed gentry. The husband remarked:

'No healthy person need be poor . . . I think the Welfare State has done an awful lot of harm by leading the population to expect the government to do everything for them. It has undermined the feeling of responsibility that a man owes to his family.' (Townsend 1979: 357)

Poverty in London

Townsend's national study discovered that poverty was particularly concentrated in the northern and western parts of the country. The highest level of official poverty was recorded in Northern Ireland and the lowest levels were to be found in Greater London. The proportion living in poverty in Northern Ireland was twice that for London. This result may appear surprising in view of Booth's early work on London, but it should be remembered that Townsend's data refer to Greater London as a whole, and not just to the inner London areas on which Booth had concentrated. The Greater London area includes a number of prosperous suburban areas, and one aim of Townsend's separate study of London was to provide more detail on the distribution of poverty within London. Using data from official sources, Townsend calculated that 1.8 million people in London were living in or on the margins of poverty (see Table 4.5). This level represents over a quarter of London's

Table 4.5 *Official poverty in London*

	No. (000s)	% of London households
Below Supplementary Benefit level	300	4.42
At Supplementary Benefit level	600	8.85
On the margins*	900	13.28
Total	1,800	26.55

*See Table 4.1

Source: Calculated from Townsend *et al.* (1987: 47, Table 5.2; based on official sources)

population, a proportion that is very slightly lower than that found for the country as a whole. About a half of these people – those with incomes at or below the Supplementary Benefit level – were actually living in poverty. Townsend estimated that the levels had doubled since the early 1960s.

Townsend saw the causes of poverty as being firmly rooted in the structure of the labour market. As in Booth's original study, Townsend sought to relate living conditions in London to the particular structure of its labour market. As I have shown, this explanation of poverty became less fashionable in political circles after the Second World War, when economic affluence and full employment were widely seen as having eliminated all but the 'natural' deprivation of old age and sickness. Researchers ignored the labour market and concentrated on the ability, or inability, of the welfare system to deal with these residual problems. Townsend's survey, undertaken when the 'affluence' and full employment of the 1950s and 1960s seemed as distant as the Depression and mass unemployment of the 1930s had seemed to Rowntree during the 1950s, aimed to reorient poverty research into the investigation of the links between poverty and the labour market.

This reorientation was directly in line with the conclusions of his national study, where it had been shown that poverty among unskilled manual workers and their families could be explained as the combined result of low income and an above average number of dependants. Those on low incomes were those with low pay from employment, together with those who were in receipt of a low income because of unemployment or retirement. Roughly one third was poor because of low pay from employment, another third because they had retired from employment and were dependent on a pension, and a further one third because disability or illness prevented them from working. To their economic deprivation, then, was added 'the denial of access to other than intermittent or insecure forms of employment, with few rights or no rights to sick pay, paid holidays and other benefits, lack of assets, greater chances of becoming sick or disabled, and poorer coverage under the provisions of the national insurance and industrial injuries schemes' (Townsend 1979: 409–10). The poor, that is to say, experienced multiple inequalities and exclusions:

Many people, and overwhelmingly married women and children, are not in poverty by virtue of any personal characteristics so much as indirectly by virtue of the labour market, wage or social security characteristics of the principal income recipient of the family unit.[4]

(Townsend 1979: 899)

The London survey pursued this line of investigation. It pointed in particular to the fact that high levels of unemployment were linked to specific features of the labour market:

There are structural divisions – between non-manual and manual, skilled and non-skilled, permanent and temporary, public and private sector, manufacturing and service industries – which explain where the axe of redundancy is likely to fall, and fall most quickly.

(Townsend *et al.* 1987: 13, grammar corrected)

Certain sectors of the labour market predisposed their occupants to the risk of unemployment and, hence, poverty. Those sectors that were prone to unemployment were also those that tended to be characterised by casual or insecure unemployment and by low pay. The labour market was, of course, organised geographically, and so the risk of poverty was concentrated in certain localities within the city. In January 1986, for example, the unemployment rates in Hackney and in Tower Hamlets were over 22 per cent, while the rates in Sutton and in Kingston were around 6 per cent. The London average was 11.9 per cent (Townsend *et al.* 1987: 15–16).

There was, Townsend argued, an increasing polarisation between boroughs such as Hackney, Tower Hamlets, Islington, Lambeth, and Newham, where income and employment were low, and the more affluent boroughs such as Harrow, Sutton, Bexley, Bromley, and Havering. With this polarisation of resources went a polarisation in living standards. The research showed that life expectancy in men ranged from sixty-eight years in Tower Hamlets to seventy-three years in Harrow. Mortality rates for people aged forty-five to sixty-four varied from 18.92 per 1,000 in St Mary's (Tower Hamlets) to 4.74 per 1,000 in West Wickham (Bromley).

The labour market was also structured by gender and by ethnicity, concentrating women and members of ethnic minorities in the 'peripheral' and most insecure areas of employment. Thus the 1985 unemployment rates among young West Indians in London averaged more than 30 per cent, and the rate for young Asians was only slightly lower. Although women appear to have had lower rates of unemployment than men, much female unemployment was 'hidden': many women who were seeking employment but who did not qualify for unemployment benefit simply did not register as unemployed. This led Townsend and his colleagues to conclude that there had been an increasing 'feminisation of poverty'. The hidden unemployment of women and their concentration in low-paid jobs, the increasing number of female lone parents (often with large families), and the large numbers of elderly women living alone are factors that combine to make women disproportionately likely to experience poverty.

Townsend's policy proposals for the elimination of poverty are more radical than those of Rowntree. Where Rowntree had eschewed any search for the structural causes of poverty, these are the very focus of Townsend's attention. He advocates the abolition of excessive wealth and income, combined with a redistribution of resources in such a way as to break down the distinction between 'earners' and 'dependants'. This would need to be associated, he argues, with a right to work and a right to a minimum income that would, in turn, require alterations in the structure of ownership, control, and authority at work (1979: 926).

Breadline Britain

The *Breadline Britain* study, undertaken in conjunction with a television series, was explicitly intended to update the work of Townsend.[5] It aimed to explore the impact of economic recession and a sustained period of Conservative government on both the extent of poverty and the nature of popular attitudes towards it. The first phase of the survey took place in 1983, using a national quota sample of 1,174 people. This sample had been designed specifically to include a large number of poor households for detailed analysis, but the general results were adjusted in order to give a nationally representative sample of attitudes and opinion. The second phase of the research took place in 1990 and allowed the researchers to document trends over the seven year period that separated the two phases of the research.

Mack and Lansley, the authors of this study, followed Townsend in using a relative concept of poverty, according to which poverty comprises a condition of deprivation relative to socially accepted standards of living. Those living in poverty – or, more strictly, those who are 'deprived' – are 'excluded from the way of living that is expected and customary in society today'. The poor 'are excluded from the way of life that most people take for granted' (Mack and Lansley 1985: 9, 15). Mack and Lansley go beyond Townsend in their use of social survey methods to measure these standards directly. They aimed to explore, in contemporary Britain, the 'accepted' or 'conventional' level of living that was regarded in public opinion as the minimum that was appropriate for a citizen. Their approach follows closely that of Sen (1982: 16–17), who has argued that a study of the actual standards and conventions that prevail in a society is not, in itself, a prescriptive or purely subjective task: the minimum standards appropriate to the status of membership or citizenship can be identified objectively through normal social scientific methods.

I noted in the previous chapter that there may be a number of competing conceptions of citizenship in a society, and Mack and Lansley's research goes some way towards recognising this by shifting the focus of research away from 'official' conceptions and towards 'popular' conceptions. They remain firmly wedded, however, to a viewpoint that assumes that an unambiguous level of poverty can be identified wherever there is a perfect consensus in society over the minimum acceptable standard of living for a full member. This is, of course, true: but perfect consensus is extremely rare. In fact, Mack and Lansley fall back on a measure of majority opinion: the state of opinion in society as a whole can be based on a measure of the opinions of the majority. This sleight of hand is unwarranted from the standpoint of their own concept of poverty. An adequate research programme would need to explore systematically the divergence between the majority and various minority viewpoints, relating each to the conceptions of citizenship that I have identified. Despite these reservations, the Mack and Lansley study can be seen as a particularly powerful exploration of public opinion on the minimum standard of living appropriate for a citizen in Britain today.

Mack and Lansley made the extremely important point that estimates of poverty that are based on these standards may not correspond with popular beliefs about the extent of poverty in society. There may be a consensus that certain items are necessities, but if people are unaware of how many of their fellow citizens are denied these items they may underestimate the extent of deprivation. This is particularly likely if people's conception of 'poverty' runs counter to their conception of 'necessities'. It is quite possible, for example, for the majority in a society to adopt a very strict subsistence conception of 'poverty' and to believe that few people fall below this level, while, nevertheless, recognising as 'necessities' numerous items which many people are actually denied. People may be mistaken about the nature and extent of deprivation in their own society, even when this deprivation is measured by their own standards of need. To use prevailing standards of need as the basis for the identification of deprivation does not, then, involve an acceptance of the accuracy of people's knowledge about the extent of the deprivation that is around them. As Mack and Lansley argue,

it seems perfectly possible that there will be people who see 'poverty' as simply about starvation but who take a broader view about what constitutes necessities.

(1985: 39)

The *Breadline Britain* study found a high degree of consensus over these necessities, and it also discovered that accepted standards pointed beyond mere subsistence to a broader quality of life. In operational terms they regarded 'necessities' as those things that were so regarded by a majority of the sample – ranging from the near unanimity over heating and an indoor toilet, through the widely recognised need for self-contained accommodation, leisure, and a holiday, to the bare majority regarding a television and a garden as necessities (Mack and Lansley 1985: 54).

Table 4.6 Socially recognised necessities, 1983

Item	% rating as necessary
1 Heating	97
2 Indoor toilet	96
3 Damp-free housing	96
4 Bath	94
5 Beds for everyone	94
6 Public Transport	88
7 Warm, waterproof coat	87
8 Three meals a day for children	82
9 Self-contained accommodation	79
10 Two pairs of shoes	78
11 Separate bedrooms for children over ten	77
12 Refrigerator	77
13 Toys for children	71
14 Carpets in living-rooms and bedrooms	70
15 Celebrations on special occasions	69
16 Roast meal once a week	67
17 Washing machine	67
18 New, not second-hand clothes	64
19 Hobby or leisure activity	64
20 Two hot meals a day for adults	64
21 Meat or fish every other day	63
22 Presents for friends or family once a year	63
23 One-week holiday away from home	63
24 Leisure equipment for children	57
25 Garden	55
26 Television	51

Note: Items that were not recognised as necessities by a majority included a telephone, a car, a night out once a fortnight, and cigarettes

Source: Frayman (1991: 54, simplified)

The full list of necessities in 1983 is given in Table 4.6. It can be seen that some items related specifically to families with children, where special requirements were widely recognised, but twenty-two of the twenty-six necessities applied to all types of households. Very few changes were observed between 1983 and 1990; the biggest was the substantial increase in the number of people who saw two meals a day, a meat meal (or its equivalent) every other day, a refrigerator, and children's toys as necessities. By 1990 a telephone, a best outfit, and entertainment and outings for children had come to be recognised as necessities.[6] These items, Mack and Lansley argued, could be used as indicators of the social minimum that prevailed in Britain. They were not, of course, saying that any household that lacked one of these items was deprived. It was an accumulation of such deficiencies that constituted 'deprivation'. In operational terms, they regarded a person as being deprived if they lacked three or more of the socially recognised necessities. The justification for this operational definition will be discussed shortly.

The changes that were observed between 1983 and 1990 point to changing standards and social expectations, and Mack and Lansley correctly see these changes as mere moments in a continuous shift in social standards. Items that were previously felt to be luxuries or matters of legitimate aspiration come to be seen as legitimate wants, as necessities for all. To spend money on travel in the 1880s was an unnecessary extravagance, but in the 1980s it was regarded as a necessity. They also noted that necessities were not judged simply on the basis of subsistence. Majority opinion held that many items were necessary because they contributed to the comfort or enjoyment of life rather than to sheer survival. People were seen as deprived if they were unable to enjoy such 'normal' comforts: 'To go without the necessities of life is not just to suffer hunger or to risk ill-health or even death but also to be demeaned and degraded' (Mack and Lansley 1985: 58). Equally, the growth of a complex industrial society and its system of mass production and mass consumption leads to the emergence of new consumer goods which rapidly come to be seen as necessities. Mack and Lansley point out that some items become necessities not so much in their own right but because they are essential conditions for other necessities. Refrigerators, for example, have come to be regarded as a necessity today because they are essential elements in a normal lifestyle: many people are constrained by work commitments to do their shopping weekly rather than daily, modern homes lack ventilated larders, and many items of food are now sold in pre-frozen form.

What, then, was the extent of deprivation as measured by the *Breadline Britain* survey? The survey asked respondents which of the necessities they actually possessed and whether this was a matter of choice for them. The question of choice was investigated as it is central to the whole question of deprivation. An individual may be without a television, say, but this may be a deliberate act of choice by an otherwise affluent person. It would make little sense to describe such a person as being 'deprived' of a television. The proportion of households that was unable to afford a particular necessity (as opposed to having chosen not to purchase it) varied between 1 per cent and 21 per cent in 1983, and between 1 per cent and 30 per cent in 1990. Table 4.7 shows the items that were most frequently lacking from the lifestyles of households. In both years the inability to take an annual holiday was widespread, with around one fifth of respondents not having had a break away from home. One third of households in 1990 was unable to make regular savings (the question had not been asked in 1983), and savings are, of course, a way of paying for holidays. Linked to inability to save was the fact that 10 per cent of households in 1990 were unable to afford basic insurance. In both 1983 and 1990 large numbers of people were unable to meet the costs of

Table 4.7 Lack of necessities: 'the top ten'

	1983			1990	
	Necessity	*% of households unable to afford*		*Necessity*	*% of households unable to afford*
1	Holiday	21	1	Regular savings	30
2	Two pairs of shoes	9	2	Holiday	20
3	Meat or fish every other day	8	3	Decent decoration	15
4	Hobby	7	4	Outing for children	14
=	Damp-free house	7	5	Insurance	10
=	Warm coat	7	6	Out-of-school activities	10
=	Weekly roast	7	7	Separate bedrooms	7
8	Leisure equipment for children	6	=	Hobby	7
=	New clothes	6	=	Telephone	7
=	Washing machine	6	10	Best outfit	8
			=	Entertaining of children's friends	8

Source: Frayman (1991: 6)

leisure and hobby activities for themselves and for their children. In 1990 many could not afford to support out-of-school activities, children's outings, or basic entertaining for their children. There were, however, some indications of change over the period of the study. In 1983 8 per cent were unable to have a meat or fish meal every other day (4 per cent in 1990), 7 per cent were unable to have a weakly roast meal (6 per cent in 1990), 7 per cent had no warm coat (4 per cent in 1990), and 6 per cent could not afford new clothes (4 per cent in 1990). There was thus a small but noticeable rise in basic living standards, but this was associated with continuing low levels of living in many areas and a general rise in expectations.

Poverty, it is generally recognised, involves multiple deprivation. While it may be significant that large numbers in the population were 'deprived' of one of the items on the *Breadline Britain* list, this cannot be regarded as a true indicator of deprivation unless those who lack one item also lack others. Table 4.8 shows some relevant data for 1983. Around one third (34 per cent) of the adult population lacked one or more of the basic necessities, but one in ten lacked four or more. This was clearly associated with household income: one third of the bottom 10 per cent of households lacked four or more necessities, while only 3 per cent of the top 30 per cent of households were in this situation.[7] Around one in five of low-income households lacked six or seven necessities. Vulnerability to deprivation, the survey found, was characteristic of the whole of the bottom half of the income range, though it was concentrated in the bottom decile. Those whose incomes came from Supplementary Benefit were especially likely to experience deprivation: two fifths of families with young children on Supplementary Benefit and one third of pensioners on Supplementary Benefit lacked five or more necessities.

Table 4.8 *Multiple deprivation, 1983: % lacking necessities*

No. of necessities lacked	All adults	Bottom 10% of income recipients	Top 30% of income recipients
0	66	29	82
1 or more	34	71	18
2 or more	19	52	7
3 or more	12	39	4
4 or more	10	34	3
5 or more	8	29	2
6 or more	5	21	1
7 or more	4	19	0

Source: Mack and Lansley (1985: 107, Table 4.7)

Deprivation of many items is qualitatively distinct from a mere deficiency in one or two. The *Breadline Britain* survey found that where households lacked only one or two necessities, these were likely to be such things as a holiday, a washing machine, and regular meat or fish meals. Households experiencing seven or more deprivations were most likely to go without a holiday, regular meat or fish meals, two pairs of decent shoes, a warm coat, and new clothes.[8] Most multiple-deprived families were also likely to fall into debt as they tried to juggle their household budgets. More than half of all such households were in debt in one way or another: almost two fifths of those that were deprived of seven or more necessities had fallen into serious rent arrears, two fifths had electricity debts, over a half had gas debts, and one fifth had hire purchase debts (Mack and Lansley 1985: 160).

How, then, is it possible to move from a measure of relative deprivation to a measure of poverty? Poverty, argued Mack and Lansley, is an 'enforced' lack of necessities, and so it is important to allow for those who lack one or more necessities through 'choice' – as a matter of taste, preference, or priority. But the crucial problem is that of deciding the cut-off level of deprivation at which poverty can be said to exist: *how many* items must people lack, in an enforced way, if they are to be regarded as 'poor'. They argue that

we assume that poverty is a situation where . . . deprivation has a multiple impact on a household's *way of life*, affecting several aspects of living. Thus, a family which just about manages but to do so does without an annual holiday is deprived by today's standards; in our judgement, however, it is not poverty. Deprivation has to have a more pervasive impact to become poverty.

(1985: 175)

The need is to operationalise this idea of the 'pervasive impact' of deprivation on a household's way of life.

The measure of deprivation shown in Table 4.8 involved an attempt to allow for the effect of taste and preference. Only those households were counted where income was in the bottom half of the national distribution and their lack of a necessity was matched by a cutting back of expenditure in other areas. Choice, Mack and Lansley discovered, was a significant factor among those who lacked one or two necessities, but for those who lacked three or more the deprivation was overwhelmingly enforced. In order to take account of the possible argument that such households were deprived only because of inadequate budgeting and wasteful expenditure of the kind investigated by Rowntree and Booth – families might, for example, spend much of their limited income on gambling, drinking, cigarettes, or other expenditure – Mack and Lansley made a deduction for expenditure on smoking and a general deduction for high spending patterns.

On this basis, they conclude that lacking three or more socially recognised necessities was a sign of poverty, after allowing for the effects of taste. By this definition a total of 7.5 million people, 13.8 per cent of the population, lived in poverty in 1983. A fairly broad band of error must be added to this figure. If adjustments for high spending and smoking are made, the proportion would be as low as 11.7 per cent, but if account is taken of the fact that those who are deprived will lower their expectations and so feel that they are exercising a degree of 'choice' the figure would rise to 17.1 per cent. Taking all the adjustments together, Mack and Lansley concluded that the 7.5 million people living in poverty formed the core of a larger group of 12.1 million (22.2 per cent of the population) who were living in or on the margins of poverty (see Table 4.9).

Table 4.9   *Poverty distribution in Britain, 1983*

% of population	1983
In poverty	13.8
On the margins*	8.4
Total	22.2

* See Table 4.1

Source: Calculated from Frayman (1991: 184, Table 6.4)

Those who lived in poverty comprised the unemployed, single parents, the sick and disabled, pensioners, and the low paid, these categories overlapping with one another. Low pay was an important factor for those on the margins and in the 'mainstream' of poverty, while unemployment became the most significant factor among those who suffered intense levels of deprivation (lacking seven or more necessities). The elderly, argued Mack and Lansley, were a smaller proportion of those in poverty than was found in Townsend's national survey for 1968. The main reason for this, they claimed, was that the economic recession had increased the numbers of the unemployed, the state pension had fared relatively well by comparison with other benefits, and many more of the elderly had occupational pensions.

The final area of measurement to which Mack and Lansley turned was the question of whether there was a particular level of income at which the risk of falling into multiple deprivation escalated. While a 'poverty line' could be drawn at the level of income at which poverty, as defined above, began, their main concern was whether this formed a threshold of the kind that was hypothesised by Townsend, who suggested the existence of a threshold at around 150 per cent of the Supplementary Benefit level. The 1983 *Breadline Britain* survey found a clear threshold at around £70 per week (for a couple), which they show to be roughly 150 per cent of the Supplementary Benefit level after taking account of housing costs. The *Breadline Britain* survey confirmed Townsend's hypothesis: there was a threshold level of 150 per cent of the Supplementary Benefit rates at which the risk of multiple deprivation escalated and at which 'people are forced to withdraw from a whole range of activities and are unable to afford a whole range of goods' (Mack and Lansley 1985: 194).

The *Breadline Britain* studies, then, have advanced the study of poverty by undertaking direct investigations of the customary social expectations that define the normal and acceptable standard of life for those who enjoy the status of full citizenship. This approach has been taken yet a further step forward by Jonathan Bradshaw (1992), whose important study attempted to establish a link between popular perceptions of necessity and the official poverty line. In doing so, Bradshaw modernised Rowntree's 'budget standard' approach.

Rowntree and Beveridge, it will be recalled, sought to establish levels of welfare provision that would meet the basic subsistence needs of households, but they failed to break completely with absolute methods of measuring subsistence. Bradshaw's study sought to move to a fully relative view and to measure basic subsistence on the basis of customary expectations. Those items that the 1990 *Breadline Britain* study found to be recognised as 'necessities' by two thirds of the population were regarded as defining the basic subsistence or 'low cost' budget. The income that was necessary to meet this budget was calculated as £141 per week for a couple with two children living in local authority housing. A more realistic estimate of a 'modest-but-adequate' budget was made on the basis of the prices of popular branded goods for items that are actually possessed by over a half of the population. On this basis, the minimum family income rose to £317 per week. This is the 'prevailing family standard' in Britain today. The Income Support level for such a family was just £105, and Bradshaw concludes that the official level of social assistance was substantially below both the prevailing standard and the subsistence minimum. The Income Support level, for example, was just three quarters of the low-cost budget.

The wealthy

I showed in Chapter 2 that the period from 1900 to 1950 saw a gradual decline in the degree of inequality in the distribution of income and wealth. This decline was especially rapid during the immediate post-war period, when the Labour government introduced the welfare reforms that improved the position of the poorest and increased levels of taxation that put pressure on top incomes. The significance of taxation in this move towards greater equality is apparent from the fact that while the share of the top 1 per cent of income recipients in income before tax fell from 16.6 per cent in 1938 to 11.2 per cent in 1949, their share in income after tax fell from 12.1 per cent to 6.4 per cent in the same period (Rubinstein 1986: 78–9). Declining inequality was not, however, a simple consequence of Labour government, as the trend continued – albeit more slowly – throughout the 1950s, 1960s, and 1970s.

Table 4.10   Share of top 1% in income before and after tax, 1949–74

	% of income held			
	1949	1954	1964	1974
Before tax	11.2	9.3	8.2	6.2
After tax	6.4	5.3	5.3	4.0

Source: Rubinstein (1986: 80, Table 5, drawing on the Royal Commission)

Table 4.10 shows that the share of the top 1 per cent of income recipients continued to fall both before tax and after tax. In the period of Conservative government during the 1950s and early 1960s far less emphasis was placed on the tax mechanism, and after-tax income distribution hardly altered at all over the period. This situation changed with the Labour government of the later 1960s, and the share of the 1 per cent in after-tax income continued to fall through the 1970s. In Table 4.11 it is evident that this trend towards redistribution was largely confined to an internal redistribution within the top 10 per cent and that it hardly affected those at the bottom of the income hierarchy.

Controversy has arisen over the question of whether the Conservative government of the 1980s favoured higher-income groups, at the expense of the low paid, in its social and economic

Table 4.11   Income distribution after tax, 1949–74

	% of income held			
	1949	1954	1964	1974
Top 10%	27.1	25.3	25.9	23.2
Next 40%	46.4	48.4	48.9	49.8
Bottom 50%	26.5	26.3	25.2	27.0

Source: Rubinstein (1986: 80, Table 5, drawing on the Royal Commission)

policies. It is certainly clear that, during the 1980s, the trend towards greater equality in income distribution went into reverse. The proportion of after-tax income that was received by the bottom 10 per cent of the population stood at 3.9 per cent in 1979, but it had fallen to 3.0 per cent by 1987 (Oppenheim 1990: 36). Tables 4.12 and 4.13 compare the positions of the top and bottom sections of the income hierarchy during this period, using varying measures of income. The share of before-tax income that was received by the bottom 20 per cent of the population fell substantially between 1979 and 1987, a period of Conservative government, while that of the top 20 per cent showed a parallel, but more marked increase. Using a slightly broader definition of income, the data in Table 4.13 show that the share of income received by the top 10 per cent increased between 1977 and 1983, while the share of the bottom 10 per cent declined slightly. In the first four years of Conservative government the top 1 per cent of income recipients saw their share of income rise by almost a quarter. While the top 20 per cent enhanced their position over the 1980s, all in the remaining 80 per cent saw their position worsen. The same trend was apparent after taking account of the redistributive effects of taxes and welfare benefits. The tax and benefit systems did achieve a redistribution of income in favour of lower-paid groups, but this redistribution failed to keep in step

Table 4.12 Income distribution, 1977–87

| | % of income held | | | | | |
| | 1977 | | 1979 | | 1987 | |
	Before Tax	After Tax	Before Tax	After Tax	Before Tax	After Tax
Top 20%	44.0	39.0	45.0	40.0	51.0	45.0
Bottom 50%	0.6	6.4	0.5	6.1	0.3	5.1

Note: Before- and after-tax figures include both tax and benefits

Source: Oppenheim (1990: 128, Table 27, drawing on the *Economic Trends*)

Table 4.13 Income distribution, 1977 and 1983

| | % of income held | |
	1977	1983
Top 10%	21.2	23.7
Bottom 10%	3.2	3.1

Source: Rentoul (1987: 26, summarising N. Morris and I. Preston, 'Taxes, benefits and the distribution of income 1968–83', *Fiscal Studies*, Nov. 1986)

with the increasing polarisation of original income that took place during the 1980s. The most recent information available shows that the share of the top 20 per cent of the population in after-tax income increased consistently between 1979 and 1988. Incomes for those in the top 10 per cent of the hierarchy in 1990 were at least 1.8 times the average, while incomes of those in the bottom 10 per cent were around half the average or less (Social Trends 1992).

I have shown that the share in total income that was taken by the top 1 per cent of the population increased during the 1980s. One of the principal reasons for this was a substantial increase in top salaries, which occurred without a commensurate increase in taxation – indeed, the 1980s saw a reduced tax burden. A study of the salaries of chairmen and chief executives of large companies in 1986 found that a quarter of them were receiving salaries that were 23 per cent higher than they had been the previous year – and one in ten of them had received rises of 42 per cent or more (Rentoul 1987: 30). Such top salaries are boosted by a whole range of fringe benefits, including cars, travel, and medical insurance, and by direct cash advances in the form of share options. Under a share option a company grants its top executives and directors the option to purchase new shares at discounted prices. Particularly likely to be found among the highest-paid directors and executives were those who worked for financial companies: almost one third of the highest paid directors in 1986 were directors or executives of merchant banks. The growing internationalisation of the money markets of the City of London has been a major factor in rising incomes, just as the globalisation of economic activity more generally has led to increases in business salaries.

Townsend's London study throws some light on the significance of high salaries, which, he argued, resulted from the occupancy of very specific niches in specialised labour markets. Those at the top of the administrative and professional hierarchies of the government agencies located in London and, more particularly, those who occupy leading positions in the major commercial and financial enterprises of London were operating in an increasingly internationalised labour market and they were able to command extremely high salaries and other fringe benefits (Townsend *et al.* 1987: 64ff).

While the distribution of personal assets remained considerably more unequal over the whole of the post-war period, it too showed a trend towards more equality. It can be seen from Table 4.14 that the share of the top 5 per cent of the population fell from just under three quarters in 1950 to just over a half in 1973, and the decline in the share of the top 1 per cent was even sharper. Research suggests, however, that much of this redistribution failed to touch the poorest sections of society: the share of the bottom

Table 4.14 *Wealth distribution in England and Wales, 1950–73*

	% of total personal assets held					
	1950	*1956*	*1960*	*1966*	*1970*	*1973*
Top 1%	47	45	34	31	30	27
Top 5%	74	71	59	56	54	52

Source: Atkinson (1983), Rubinstein (1986: 95)

Table 4.15 *Trends in wealth inequality, 1966–87*

	% of wealth held				
	1966	*1976*	*1979*	*1986*	*1987*
Top 1%	33	24	24	18	18
Next 9%	36	37	35	32	32
Next 40%	28	34	36	44	43
Bottom 50%	3	5	5	6	7

Source: Oppenhiem (1990: 133, Table 28, drawing on *Inland Revenue* statistics

80 per cent stood at 16.4 per cent in the 1950s and had risen to just 18.5 per cent by 1970.[9] Table 4.15 puts these findings into a larger context.

Personal assets were being redistributed from the top 10 per cent to the bottom 90 per cent of the population, but most of the benefits of this redistribution were going to the middle 40 per cent 'slice' of the hierarchy. There was a reduction in the share of the top 1 per cent between 1966 and 1976 and between 1979 and 1986. Much of this redistribution reflects the growth in home ownership in the period, which significantly increased the assets of many in the lower-middle classes and skilled manual classes. Clearly, while Conservative governments have encouraged top income earners, resulting in an increase in income inequality, they have not favoured the propertied unambiguously: the decline in the share held by the top 1 per cent between 1979 and 1986 was matched by a decline in the share of the next 9 per cent in the hierarchy.

It has often been pointed out that the degree of inequality in personal assets alters significantly if the value of state and occupational pension rights is included in the calculation. The share of the top 1 per cent of asset holders in 1972, for example, stood at 29.9 per cent when only convertible, marketable assets were taken into account. When the assumed value of pension rights is included, their share falls to 17.4 per cent. Corresponding figures for 1981 were 23 per cent and 12 per cent. Conversely, the share of the bottom 50 per cent in marketable assets stood at 6 per cent in 1981, while it was between 8 per cent and 12 per cent when pension rights were included (Rubinstein 1986: 97).[10] In such a measure of assets the value of pension rights is estimated by calculating the amount of money that would have to be invested in order to ensure the receipt of an equivalent income on retirement. It is assumed, therefore, that the right to a pension is equivalent to the possession of a lump sum for investment. This assumption is highly contentious. While pension rights do indeed represent a major addition to a person's life chances, it does not seem sensible to regard them as being the equivalent of money in the bank. State pension rights cannot actually be converted into a lump sum, and there are considerable restrictions on the convertibility of occupational pensions. Convertibility is, surely, at the heart of the idea of wealth.[11]

To fall within the top 1 per cent of personal asset holders in 1986 a person needed to hold assets valued at £190,000 or more, while those in the bottom 50 per cent would have held only an average of £2,500 each.[12] Twenty thousand people – the top 0.05 per cent – were estimated to have been millionaires in 1986 (Rentoul 1987: 43). These very wealthy people had a distinctive pattern of asset holding. Where the assets of the less well off were embodied mainly in their home, those of the very wealthy were likely also to include substantial financial assets, such as company shares. Despite the spread of shareholdings that has taken place with the privatisation of companies that were previously publicly owned, the vast majority of privately owned shares are highly concentrated. In 1981, for instance, the top 1 per cent of the adult population held three quarters of all privately owned company shares.

The principal cause of the extreme degree of economic inequality that existed in Britain for the first half of the twentieth century, according to Josiah Wedgwood and other pioneer researchers, was the inheritance of land and financial assets by the wealthy. Through inheritance, Wedgwood argued, the wealthy were able to maintain and even to enhance their position at the top of the economic hierarchy. A study by Harbury and Hitchens published in 1979 used an extension of Wedgwood's own methods in order to test the validity of his claims and to try to assess whether the argument was still valid for the second part of the century.

Harbury and Hitchens went directly to the probate records in order to investigate the assets of the wealthy and to compare them with those of their parents and their children. Their intention was to investigate the 'top wealth leavers', who, they believed, comprised the top 0.1 per cent of property holders. In order to take account of the changing value of money with inflation, they used a variable cut-off threshold to identify this group. In 1957, they argued, the threshold level would be property valued at £100,000, while for 1973 the threshold level had to be raised to £200,000. Evidence from Chiozza-Money and other early studies suggests that the corresponding figure for the beginning of the century would have been around £5,000. Samples were drawn for the years 1902, 1925, 1957, 1965, and 1973, the samples for the earlier years being drawn so as to include the top wealth leavers and certain others who fell just below this threshold.[13] Using biographical reference books, General Register Office records, and, in many cases, direct approaches to the families concerned, they traced the deaths of the parents of the top wealth leavers and, for earlier years, of the children of those in their samples. The total database, then, allowed Harbury and Hitchens to investigate the profile of the top wealth leavers at each period and also to investigate the sources and the destinations of their wealth.

Harbury and Hitchens defined the 'inheritors' as those whose wealth was equal to or greater than that of their parents, *and* whose parents had themselves been wealthy. Their re-analysis of Wedgwood's data for the 1920s suggested that there had been little change in the significance of inheritance between the 1920s and the 1950s. After 1957, however, they detected some signs of a declining trend in the significance of inheritance among top wealth leavers. Their initial analysis was limited to the inheritance of men from their fathers. Taking as the yardstick of 'wealth' the level of £100,000 (at 1957 prices) that was used to identify top

Table 4.16 Inheritance by top wealth leavers, 1957–73

Amount left by father (£)	1957	Top wealth leavers (%) 1965	1973 Men	1973 Women
More than 1m	9	4	7	4
500,000–1m	10	8	6	12
250,000–499,999	14	12	8	14
100,000–249,999	18	21	15	25
50,000–99,999	12	10	11	10
25,000–49,999	5	13	11	7
10,000–24,999	5	9	13	8
5,000–9,999	3	3	3	1
1,000–4,999	7	3	5	7
Less than 1,000	15	17	21	12

Note: Figures are calculated at constant prices (1957 levels)

Source: Calculated from Harbury and Hitchens (1979: 44, Table 3.3, and 89, Table 5.1)

wealth leavers, it can be seen from Table 4.16 that the proportion of 'inheritors' was 51 per cent in 1957, 45 per cent in 1965, and 36 per cent in 1973. There was, therefore, a constant decline in the significance of inheritance from 1957 to 1973. Within this overall trend, however, the decline over the period of almost twenty years was far less marked among the extremely wealthy than it was for other categories. They found, for example, that 7 per cent of top wealth leavers in 1973 had millionaire fathers, compared with 9 per cent in 1957.

Harbury and Hitchens considered a number of factors that suggested this declining significance of inheritance in the post-war period might be more apparent than real. Their first point was that increases in taxation might be expected to have led to higher levels of tax avoidance among the wealthy. To the extent that the wealthy passed on their wealth to their sons and daughters during their own lifetimes, figures that were based on estate duty statistics would underestimate the true extent of inheritance. The general level of the figures would also be influenced by any tendency for parents to distribute their wealth among all their children rather than simply to an eldest son. The death of a man with, say, £200,000 would result in a single top wealth holder if his wealth passed intact to his eldest son; while an equal distribution of his wealth among three children would produce no top wealth holders. Figures based on *individuals*, then, may underestimate the significance of inheritance within *families*. While this might be expected to have a constant influence at each of the periods investigated, any long-term trend away from primogeniture and towards more equal distribution within families would produce an apparent trend away from inheritance.[14]

While the bulk of their research concerned male wealth, Harbury and Hitchens did undertake some analyses of women's wealth. It can be seen from Table 4.16 that 55 per cent of female top wealth leavers in 1973 were the daughters of men who were themselves top wealth leavers. This figure is far higher than that for men. Indeed, the proportion of female top wealth leavers whose fathers left a substantial amount of money was generally higher than that for men. Inheritance seems to play a greater role in the wealth of women than it does in that of men.

The true significance of inheritance must take account of wealth inherited from all sources, and not simply from a person's father. Harbury and Hitchens went on to examine the wealth that was inherited from mothers and from fathers-in-law as well as that which came from fathers. Looking at those male top wealth leavers who were not the sons of top wealth leavers, they discovered that many of these men had, in fact, still inherited substantial sums from their fathers (see Table 4.16). Fifty-eight per cent of male top wealth leavers dying in 1973 had fathers who left £25,000 or more (at 1957 prices). Of those who did not inherit this much from their fathers, one in seven had fathers-in-law who had left more than this. Taking account of the 'independent' wealth of mothers, rather than simply that which they had inherited from their husbands before passing it on to their sons, had a similar effect on the total level of inheritance.

Although it was not examined in detail, Harbury and Hitchens attempted to look at inheritance from a wider band of kin by constructing a 'wealth tree' for a particular family. This was a simple family tree on to which they entered the size of estates of all the family members that could be traced in the probate records. For this study they used the Wills family, the founders of a major tobacco company in Bristol, which included ten people who each left in excess of £2 million. They started the tree with Henry Wills, who died in 1826 and left property valued at just over £70,000 (at 1957 prices). One of his sons left over £200,000, another left just under this amount, and a third left over £40,000. The two eldest sons, both of whom were active in the running of the firm, produced seven sons who left more than £100,000 each, together with other sons and daughters who left varying substantial sums. Of the seven top wealth leaver sons, one left over £21 million and three others left over £10 million each. In subsequent generations, as the numbers of children and grandchildren multiplied, wealth became more widely dispersed within the family. In the fifth generation there were still to be found twelve top wealth leavers, including six millionaires of whom one left in excess of £9 million.[15]

It is, of course, difficult to assess how typical the Wills family were among industrialists. Harbury and Hitchens found that inheritance had a greater significance in the agricultural sector than it did in any other occupational sector. There were, however, a number of industries in which inheritance played a particularly important role: principally food, drink, and tobacco, metal manufacture, textiles, and distribution. Inheritance was also important for many men who went into the professions. This is not to say that these sectors were dominated by inherited capital. The point is simply that wealthy families based in these sectors were especially likely to have acquired the core of their wealth through inheritance. Those industries in which wealthy people were more likely to be 'self-made' were chemicals, clothing, paper, construction, transport, and finance (Harbury and Hitchens 1979: 105). Harbury and Hitchens concluded that the division between inheritance and 'self-made' corresponded to the distribution of small-sized firms: those sectors with large numbers of small firms allowed relatively easy access for those with limited capital and so provided a basis for the accumulation of entrepreneurial capital by those who were successful in business.

A regular, annual survey of the rich undertaken for the *Sunday Times* newspaper provides some useful insights into the nature of the very wealthy in Britain today. The survey was first published in 1989, and the 1990 survey appeared in book form (Beresford 1990). The book lists the 'top 400' wealthy individuals and families, and claims to be virtually complete for this very top level of wealth. The definition of wealth that was used was constrained by the criteria of visibility and measurability. Thus, land, shares, and houses were included, but cash in bank accounts was not. It is possible – indeed it is very likely – that the very wealthy may have money in high-earning bank accounts in tax havens, and that some may have gold bullion accounts for which the researchers had no information. The same holds true for unit trusts, property bonds, life insurance, and so on. This is, of course, a major limitation to the study, but it affects mainly the absolute values of the wealth that are given, and not the pattern of distribution. The researchers claim that such assets show a similar pattern of distribution to those assets that it was possible to measure directly.[16]

The researchers also point out that much of the wealth is not liquid – it cannot easily be realised for purposes of consumption. A controlling block of shares in a family firm, for example, could only be sold if the owner were willing to lose control of the enterprise.[17] Similarly, the owner of a large stately home could not sell it, assuming that a willing buyer existed, unless he or she was prepared to give up the family's traditional home. This should not, though, be seen as a 'limitation' to the data. It is an ineradicable feature of wealth itself. Indeed, the wealthy are a great deal better off than the mass of ordinary people who could not realise the wealth that is tied up in their family home or car without rendering themselves homeless or without adequate transport.[18]

With these reservations in mind, what conclusions can be drawn from the study? There were 20,000 British millionaires in 1990. The *Sunday Times* list covered the 400 wealthiest of these people, their wealth ranging from £20 million up to £6,700 million. The overall size distribution of these fortunes is shown in Table 4.17. Collectively, the 400 super-rich individuals and families held £543 thousand million in assets, with more than 40 per cent of this being held by the top ten alone. Almost half of the super rich had fortunes valued at over £100 million. Around 40 per cent of the total wealth of the top 400 was held as financial assets, mainly company shares. These financial assets were frequently held through trusts and, for the wealthiest, they were managed through a family office. The most extreme case was that of the Vestey family, which used a complex series of overseas trusts to legally avoid paying any income tax for sixty years (Knightly 1981).

Table 4.18 shows the sources of wealth among the top 400. Just under a quarter of the fortunes, accounting for a third of the total wealth that was held by the super rich, could be

Table 4.17 **The top 400 super rich, 1990**

Wealth (£m)	No.
Over 1,000	12
500–1,000	5
300–499	14
200–299	12
100–199	47
90–99	6
80–89	10
70–79	27
60–69	23
50–59	52
40–49	45
30–39	66
20–29	81
Total	400

Source: Calculated from Beresford (1990: 333–4)

Table 4.18 **Sources of wealth, 1990**

Source of wealth	People and families		% of wealth
	No.	%	
Land	85	21.25	33.0
Property	43	10.75	5.7
Building	20	5.00	2.0
Hotels	11	2.75	2.2
Retailing	32	8.00	14.2
Food production	16	4.00	2.5
Brewing	6	1.25	0.7
Shoes	2	0.50	0.5
Other industry	104	26.00	19.7
Publishing	24	6.00	4.7
Entertainment	20	5.0	2.0
Trading	2	0.50	0.1
Shipping	1	0.25	1.6
Finance	27	6.75	6.0
Other	7	1.75	3.1

Source: Calculated from Beresford (1990: 293)

regarded as landed fortunes, these increasingly involving urban property as well as agricultural holdings. The greater significance of urban property for personal wealth is also apparent from the fact that 18.5 per cent of the super rich derived their wealth from the ownership of companies that were engaged in property development, construction, or hotels.[19] Just under one third of the super-rich fortunes derived from manufacturing industry, which accounted for a quarter of the total wealth. The biggest individual categories of industrial wealth were those that originated in the production of food and drink. The commercial sectors of retailing, publishing, and entertainment made up 19 per cent of the very large fortunes, while financial services (including trading and shipping) accounted for 7.5 per cent of these fortunes. Putting these findings into simplified categories, it can be concluded that roughly one third of the super rich were 'industrialists', one quarter were from the financial and commercial sectors, one third were traditional landowners, and one fifth were involved in corporate landed property.

The landowners, predominantly drawn from the old peerage, were among the wealthiest of the super rich. About a quarter of the top 400 were peers, mainly dukes, earls, and viscounts, but not all of the peers were landowners. To these can be added the Queen and the Prince of Wales, the two wealthiest people in the country. The position of the royal family is, of course, unique: the sheer size of their wealth reflects their identification with the structure of the state and, not unimportant, their exemption for many years from the payment of income tax and estate duty. They do, however, follow a similar approach to that of other major landowners towards the management of their land. Typical of the traditional landowners was the Duke of Westminster (Gerald Grosvenor), the inheritor of land and other property worth £4,200 million. The core of the family estate was acquired 300 years ago, and includes much of Mayfair and Belgravia, together with parts of Oxford Street and Bond Street. An acre of land in Mayfair had an estimated value of £23.5 million: the Duke had 300 acres in Mayfair. During the last 100 years the Grosvenor family acquired additional rural property in England, especially in Cheshire, as well as land in Scotland and Ireland.

Other established landowning peers in the top 400 included Earl Cadogan (owner of land in Chelsea and Perthshire), Viscount Portman (Herefordshire, and in Oxford Street and its vicinity), Lord Howard De Walden (London and Berkshire), the Duke of Buccleuch (Scotland and Northamptonshire), the Marquess of Bath (Wiltshire), the Duke of Northumberland, and the Duke of Devonshire. Few, if any, of these landowners could afford to live on their wealth without acting in a rational way to protect and to enlarge it. Their estates were actively managed for farming and also for shooting, fishing, and forestry. Their houses were often 'open' to the public and, in cases such as the Marquesses of Bath and Tavistock, were managed as leisure park businesses. Management of wealth on such a scale not infrequently brought 'problems' for the landowners: the Duke of Bedford became a tax exile in the 1970s, leaving his son to manage the family estates. Many of these landowning peers had leisure interests in related areas, including horse racing and the management of racing studs. In addition to land and financial assets, their wealth was invested in the works of art that stocked their large houses. The landed peers had direct political participation through their membership of the House of Lords, as well as having indirect political involvement through other family members. Some had been members of the House of Commons before inheriting their titles, and many continued to play a role in county politics. The 'poorest' of the super rich landowners included Lord Home, an ex-prime minister with land in Scotland worth £21 million, and the Earl of Carnarvon and Marquess of Bristol with £20 million each. Much land is tied up in family trusts, which ensure it passes intact from generation to generation, but it is still a source of personal, disposable wealth.

Retailing and property development were particularly important and interlinked areas of wealth generation, forming part of a narrow range of service industries that produced a large number of 'first-generation' super rich.[20] Among the older-established members of this group, however, were Garfield Weston (a third-generation member of the family that owned Associated British Foods), fourth-generation members of the Sainsbury family, third- and fourth-generation members of the Vestey shipping and food family, Gerald Ronson (second-generation property management), Sighismund Berger (second-generation urban property), and Lord Forte and Rocco Forte (first- and second-generation hotel chain).

In banking and trading were found the Swire family (originally Liverpool shippers who went into insurance and property in Hong Kong and who now own Cathay Pacific airlines), the Cayzer family (third-generation shippers and financiers), and numerous members of such long established City banking families as Rothschild, Kleinwort, Hambro, and Keswick. In other areas of business were Lord Rothermere (third-generation publishing), Anthony Pilkington (fifth-generation glass manufacturing), and Samuel Whitbread (seventh-generation brewing).

In assessing inheritance it is, as Harbury and Hitchens pointed out, difficult to date the first generation of true wealth, and it is therefore difficult to separate the 'inheritors' from the 'self-made'. The compilers of the *Sunday Times* survey claimed that only 162 of the top 400 were 'inheritors', these being defined as those who were in an obvious and direct line of inheritance of family wealth. Yet there are other less obvious cases and examples of smaller-scale inheritance, often of an indirect nature. Clearly the number of true inheritors was underestimated, as suggested by the Harbury and Hitchens study. Viscount Hambleden, of the family that owns the firm of W. H. Smith, shows the problems that are involved in dating wealth accumulation. The family firm as an important source of wealth is now in its fourth generation, having expanded after acquiring the licence to supply newspapers on railway stations in the Victorian heyday of the railway. But the family had been involved in the newspaper business in a smaller way for a generation before this time. Indeed, most of the established business fortunes had started in a fairly small way and accumulated substantial wealth within one generation. A related model is that of Sir James Goldsmith, who built up a massive retailing and financial services group, but who inherited considerable capital from both his father and his father-in-law. It was this accumulation of wealth on the basis of 'seed corn' assets that has, in general, been maintained and increased over subsequent generations.

Those among the super rich who showed a fairly clear self-made pattern at an early stage included Sir John Moores (Littlewoods supermarkets and football pools), Robert Maxwell (publishing),[21] Harry Hyams (urban property), Tiny Rowland (trading and publishing), and Alan Sugar (Amstrad electronics). Paul McCartney was, perhaps, the best example of a 'self-made' businessman in the super-rich league. Beginning in the music business in a small rock group, he became, as a member of the Beatles, a multimillionaire through the astute plough-back of his massive earnings at the time of the group's success. In 1987 he was reported to be receiving £3,750 per hour simply from composer royalties. Music, in fact, was one of the most striking routes of entry to the super rich for the genuinely self-made: the top 400 included Elton John, Mick Jagger, George Harrison, Phil Collins, and Rod Stewart. Also included was Richard Branson, who made his fortune through the Virgin music and airline businesses.

In only 23 of the top 400 cases was a woman named as the principal wealth holder. While this may, in part, reflect a lack of knowledge or sexist assumptions on the part of the researchers, it undoubtedly represents the very real exclusion of most women from active participation in the control of their family wealth. Most prominent of the female wealth holders was the Queen, though she was not, of course, typical. One of the very few women shown as a wealth holder in her own right was Anita Roddick of the Body Shop, who was worth £152 million.

There are, analytically, two sections within the wealthy: those with substantial *property* and those who are high *income* earners. There will, of course, be a considerable degree of overlap between these two sections. While land ownership and small businesses remain of considerable importance, the main source of income and assets for the propertied and the high earners is increasingly to be found within the corporate sector of big business. Company shares and other financial assets are the fundamental forms of property, and it is from salaried appointments at the highest level of the corporate system that the high earners receive their incomes. The propertied will, in general, be the more established, as they have accumulated or inherited income-generating assets that can be passed on to the next generation of their families. The high earners will tend to be rather more peripheral and less secure, as they cannot easily ensure the privileges of their family inter-generationally. This can be achieved only if they are able to use their income to accumulate substantial wealth – which is very difficult – or can convert their income into social and cultural assets such as private schooling for their children. This strategy would enhance the opportunities of their children to enter high-earning occupations, but it is a precarious basis for inter-generational social reproduction and passes on to the next generation the problem of the perpetuating of advantages.

There are two primary sources of propertied wealth within the corporate sector of big business: *entrepreneurial capital* and impersonal *institutional capital* (see Scott 1986). Entrepreneurial capital is based in the direct family ownership or control of a business undertaking by an individual or a family. The operations of the enterprises that they own and control determine their personal advantages. The largest of the entrepreneurial firms include those owned by the Vestey, Rothschild, Moores, Cayzer, Sainsbury, and Pearson families, though the bulk of entrepreneurial capital is to be found in medium- and small-sized enterprises that may still generate high levels of personal wealth. It is for this reason that the wealthy include the capitalist class of property owners and income recipients together with substantial numbers of the entrepreneurial middle class (Scase and Goffee 1982).

Many of the wealthiest entrepreneurial families are the descendants of the nineteenth century capitalist entrepreneurs, which suggests the relevance of an inter-generational model of wealth for business families. A small enterprise may grow in size through the ploughing back of profits or through the successful mobilisation of small 'seed corn' inheritances from the wider family. The enterprise or the wealth derived from it will normally be passed on to the next generation of the family. Such an enterprise may eventually reach the stage where it generates sufficient liquid wealth to sustain a large family group of inheritors. This is particularly likely to occur if the enterprise can be formed into a joint stock company and all or part of the family holding can be sold on the stock exchange. In these circumstances, the family wealth can be diversified through investment in a range of assets rather than being tied up in one enterprise. The individuals at an early stage in this generational process will appear to be 'self-made' accumulators of their assets, while those in later generations will appear to be 'inheritors'. At any particular point of time, then, a study of wealth will find some 'self-made' wealth holders, but these people will, in all likelihood, pass on their wealth to the next generation of their family. Today's 'self-made' person is tomorrow's 'inheritor'.

The sector of impersonal, institutional capital comprises those companies that are owned and controlled by financial institutions – banks, insurance companies, pensions funds – and that are themselves controlled in exactly the same way. There is a depersonalised system of ownership and control (Scott 1985) that operates in the interests of the beneficiaries of the institutions. It is often held that the main beneficiaries of the institutional system of investment are the pensioners and ordinary insured persons, but this is not the case.[22] The top income and asset holders are the major beneficiaries of the institutional system of ownership: they are well placed in terms of occupational earnings as directors and executives, they have large private bank trust accounts, substantial unit trust and life assurance savings schemes, and, naturally, generous pension schemes. These people also have direct shareholdings in the companies with which they are involved, and this further boosts their incomes. Many of the propertied rich hold blocks of shares in a large number of the companies in the sector of institutional capital, giving them a *rentier* orientation towards their wealth. Through a strategy of diversifying their wealth, they come to own significant non-controlling stakes in a large number of companies. Where such holdings are substantial, but below the level required for control, they may still be able to influence company affairs or to gain a seat on the company board of directors and so can enter directly into ensuring that the system continues to operate to their advantage.

Notes

1   Unfortunately, none of these locality studies was written up as a separate account from the national investigation.
2   The full list of wards and their z-scores is given in Appendix 4 to Townsend *et al.* (1987).
3   Under some circumstances, deprivation can comprise what Lockwood terms 'civic exclusion'. This occurs when social practices are aimed at excluding groups from the status of citizenship.
4   The causes of household poverty were seen to lie in low income, and Townsend supports, implicitly, the 'conventional' view of class and gender put forward by Goldthorpe (1983).
5   The survey was written up in Mack and Lansley (1985) and revised in the second edition (1993). See the comments on the first phase of the study in Townsend's review (1985).
6   Mack and Lansley also tested a number of new items in 1990, and

found that insurance, fresh fruit, adequate decoration, and savings were recognised as necessities.

7 Mack and Lansley (1985: 96, Table 4.3) show that 'choice' was responsible for the lack of perceived necessities in the most prosperous households.

8 A washing machine was lacking in 'only' 31 per cent of households lacking seven or more necessities, whereas a regular meat or fish meal was lacking in 88 per cent of cases. See Mack and Lansley (1985: 135).

9 Further evidence on income and property distribution can be found in Diamond Commission (1975).

10 The range of 8 per cent to 12 per cent is given because of variations in ways of estimating the value of pensions.

11 A slightly different situation arises with respect to the value of housing. An invididual could, in principle, sell his or her house and purchase a smaller one or enter into a rental agreement. For this reason, ownership of a house does represent a convertible asset, the value of the asset being greatest for those whose houses are valued above the average for the population.

12 The value of housing is included in this calculation.

13 In the following discussion I have slightly simplified Harbury and Hitchens's sample dates by referring to '1925' instead of '1924–6' and to '1957' instead of '1956–7'.

14 Harbury and Hitchens point out that the trend towards smaller family size would produce a countervailing trend.

15 The Wills family wealth tree is contained in an appendix to Harbury and Hitchens (1979).

16 The researchers did try to estimate the values of these hidden assets whenever possible, generally when it was known that a wealth holder had recently sold or altered them. Full details on the methods and procedures employed are contained in Beresford (1990: 13–15).

17 It is worth noting that the study makes different assumptions about family shareholdings from those that would be made in a study of business control. The Leverhulme charitable trust, for example, is not – quite rightly – regarded as constituting a part of the wealth of the Leverhulme family. It is, though, an important element in the control of the Unilever company, in which the Lever family plays a continuing part.

18 A final qualification to make about the *Sunday Times* data is that the study does not consistently use 'individuals' or 'families' as its unit of analysis. The investigation switches from one to another without any discussion of the consequences for the analysis.

19 The significance of these sectors in an earlier period is discussed in Marriott and Jones (1967).

20 The 'generations' referred to are the generations of wealth. The families themselves, of course, go back much further. As I shall note below, however, it is difficult to be precise about the historical point at which a family becomes wealthy.

21 The fate of the Maxwell fortune after Maxwell's death is still being decided by the courts at the time of writing.

22 The argument has been debated in America between Drucker (1976) and Rifkin and Barber (1978). For Britain see Minns (1980, 1982).

CHAPTER 5

Poverty and wealth:
a comparative view

The central concern of this book has been with the distribution of poverty and wealth in Britain. I have tried to show, using contemporary studies, that Britain is – and has for a long time been – a highly unequal society. Yet it is difficult to know whether the British pattern of inequality is truly high by international standards. I have shown that the extent of inequality in Britain has, in fact, altered significantly over time, but I have not shown whether these fluctuations have occurred around a level of inequality that is high or low when viewed comparatively. The purpose of this chapter is to provide a broad sketch of the comparative context within which poverty and wealth in Britain must be considered. These kinds of explorations serve an important descriptive purpose, but they are also essential when the question of explanation is considered. The pattern of poverty and wealth that can be found in Britain today can be explained only if its similarities to and differences from those of other countries are known.

The problems of measurement that arise when poverty and wealth are studied on a comparative basis are, of course, far greater than those that are involved in a single-nation study. Where official statistics are employed, for example, researchers must take account of the highly varied definitions and practices that are used by the governments and agencies that collect and collate the statistics. These variations are rooted in national differences in social and economic policies and in varying historical experiences, and it is unlikely that any degree of uniformity will be found in official conceptions of poverty and wealth. Any valid measure of poverty must be defined in relation to the prevailing social standards that constitute a society's conception of citizenship. Such standards will obviously vary from one society to another.[1] A purely statistical focus on inequality, on the other hand, would fare much better, as the position of, say, the top or bottom 10 per cent of the population can be compared with some certainty across a range of countries.

Despite these limitations, it is possible to construct the broad outlines of a comparative framework for Britain and similar modern industrial societies. These societies, for all their variations, form a comparable group for study, while comparisons with non-industrial societies are hardly meaningful. A study of income in 125 countries in the late 1970s found that per capita income in the industrialised societies varied between $5 and $40 per day. In 38 non-industrial countries, on the other hand, per capita income fell below $1 per day, and countries such as India, Bangladesh, Ethiopia, Nepal, Burma and Vietnam had income levels that put them at or below starvation levels (World Bank 1980). In this chapter, then, I concentrate on the broadly uniform industrial societies. In the following section I will sketch such an outline, and in later sections I will try to pursue some of the features of this comparative framework in greater detail. I will, in particular, look at the contrasting patterns of poverty and wealth that can be found in the United States and in Russia.

A cross-national sketch

Looking first at comparative levels of inequality, Tables 5.1 and 5.2 show that, in 1970, the top 10 per cent of the population in Britain received 24.2 per cent of income before tax and 23.5 per cent of income after tax. These data, drawn from a multi-nation study, are in line with those given for Britain in the previous chapter. They also bring out the fact that the taxation system had little effect on the relative positions of the top and bottom sections of the population. Most striking, however, is that Britain appears to have been the most egalitarian of all the major European Community countries, so far as the wealthiest groups are concerned. In every other country listed both the before-tax and the after-tax incomes of the top 10 per cent were more unequally distributed than was the case in Britain.[2] France and

Table 5.1 Income before tax in Europe, 1970

| | % of income received by: | |
	Top 10%	Bottom 20%
United Kingdom	24.2	5.6
Denmark	26.0	4.0
Italy	28.8	4.5
Netherlands	30.5	4.3
France	31.0	4.3
Germany	31.1	5.9
Belgium	32.6	5.7

Source: Lawson and George (1980: 236–7, Table 8.3)

Table 5.2 *Income after tax in Europe, 1970*

	% of income received by:	
	Top 10%	Bottom 20%
United Kingdom	23.5	6.5
Belgium	28.6	6.6
Germany	30.3	6.5
France	30.4	4.3
Italy	30.9	5.1

Source: Lawson and George (1980: 236–7, Table 8.3)

Germany showed significantly higher levels of after-tax income concentration, and – despite the redistributive effects of taxation – Belgium remained a far less egalitarian society than Britain.

The picture is rather more complex for those at the bottom of the income hierarchy, though one uniformity comes out very strongly. Those countries in which the top 10 per cent of the population held a high proportion of income were also the countries in which the bottom 20 per cent of the population held a relatively high proportion of total income. In these countries 'top' and 'bottom' were advantaged relative to those in the 'middle'. In Belgium and Germany, for example, the relative advantages that were enjoyed by the top 10 per cent had not been gained exclusively at the expense of the bottom 20 per cent. In Britain and France, however, there was a very different situation. In Britain, the top 10 per cent held a relatively low proportion of national income because the pre-tax and post-tax incomes of those in the bottom 20 per cent of the population had, to a limited extent, been protected. While the share of the bottom 20 per cent was a mere quarter of their 'fair' share, they were, nevertheless, doing relatively well by international standards. In France, on the other hand, the top 10 per cent had gained their advantages at the expense of the bottom 20 per cent. The lower-income groups in France were – in relative terms – among the most disadvantaged in the European Community. The French taxation system had little influence on this pattern of disadvantage. A similar situation held in Italy, where the share in total income that was held by the top 10 per cent of households in total income had remained constant at around 30 per cent over the whole of the post-war period. Similarly, the share of the bottom 30 per cent had remained constant at between 10 per cent and 11 per cent (Moss and Rogers 1980: 168). Those with low incomes in Italy have been concentrated in the agricultural sector, which accounts for about one in six of the labour force.

Table 5.3 uses information that was calculated on a slightly different basis and for a different selection of countries for various

Table 5.3 *Income distribution before tax, 1970–77*

	% of income received by:	
	Top 20%	Bottom 20%
Australia	38.9	6.3
United Kingdom	39.4	5.7
Eire	44.5	4.1
Japan	46.2	3.8
USA	46.4	3.8
France	47.0	4.3

Note: Data relate to various dates between 1970 and 1977, but Australian data relate to 1966–7; these data were originally compiled by the Royal Commission of the Distribution of Income and Wealth.

Source: Atkinson (1975: 26, Table 2.4)

years during the 1970s. The United States and Japan appear to have had similar patterns of income inequality to those that were to be found in France, and all three countries showed a much greater degree of concentration than could be found in either Britain or Australia. Atkinson has suggested that inequality in Britain and the United States had, in fact, been at a similar level through most of the 1950s but that they had subsequently shown a divergence of patterns. The share of the top 20 per cent of the population in the United States declined slightly between 1947 and 1957, but thereafter it crept up again until, in 1977, it was at the same level as it had been in 1947 (Atkinson 1975). In Britain, on the other hand, there had been a sustained long-term fall in the concentration of income. This is apparent also in the fact that the bottom 20 per cent of income recipients were, in relative terms, worse off in the United States than they were in Britain.

The earliest studies of the very wealthy in the United States date from the 1880s, though these were of variable quality. Only in the 1930s, following the introduction of federal income and property taxes some twenty years earlier, were more reliable studies undertaken. Lundberg's (1937) investigation of the 'super rich' of the 1930s suggested that there were 11,800 millionaires in America in 1936. This estimate was comparable with the numbers that had existed up to the end of the First World War, but was much lower than the number of millionaires that had been produced during the boom conditions that preceded the great crash of 1929 (see also Sorokin 1925). Lundberg's millionaires included members of such families as the Vanderbilts, the Morgans, the Rockefellers, the du Ponts, and the Fords. Many of these families were multi-millionaires. Jaher's report has suggested that this figure increased only slowly until the beginning of the 1950s (1980: 196). The number of millionaires rose to over 40,000 in 1958 and over 180,000 in 1972. Much of the increase since 1950 was, of course, a consequence of inflation in the value of money: a million dollars in 1936 represented far more spending power than the same sum in 1972. To set against this effect, Jaher produced evidence to show that 3,413 people in 1969 had wealth of $10 million or more (1980: 221). The principal sources of this wealth were the financial and commercial undertakings of New York and the north-east, though a substantial number of millionaires came from the industries of Chicago, Cleveland, and Detroit (Mills 1956). The millionaires are a very small proportion of the population, but some evidence is available on the position of the wider group of the wealthy. The top 1 per cent of the American population held around one third of all property during the 1920s and 1930s, but their share fell to less than a quarter during the 1940s and 1950s. In 1972 their share stood at 20.7 per cent (Rubinstein 1986: 147).

Table 5.4 shows the absolute levels of per capita income for the United States and a number of East European countries for 1981. Average income in the United States was more than twice that in the former Soviet Union, though the differential would not, perhaps, have been so great if the comparison had been made between the United States and Russia. While Russia itself had a large and impoverished agricultural sector, it was an industrialised society. The wider Soviet Union combined industrial and relatively advanced areas such as Russia and the Ukraine with backward agrarian societies such as those of Central Asia. As a result, average income for the Soviet Union was somewhat lower than that for Russia alone. The importance of industry in generating relatively high levels of per capita income is apparent from the fact that East Germany, Czechoslovakia, and Hungary all had higher average income than the Soviet Union. Daily per capita income in the Soviet Union and other East European countries in the late 1970s ranged from $5 to $15, while that for

Table 5.4 GNP per capita, 1985

	Per capita GNP ($)
United States	12,661
German Democratic Republic	9,731
Czechoslovakia	8,958
Hungary	5,943
USSR	5,863
Poland	4,986

Source: Matthews (1986: 156, Table 7.1)

the non-Soviet industrial societies ranged up to $40 per day (World Bank 1980).

There has been a very limited amount of research into poverty in the United States. The official poverty line that has been employed in American studies was devised for the Social Security Administration in 1963 by the United States Bureau of the Census. The Bureau aimed to establish a subsistence measure of the kind that had been used by Rowntree and, to this end, its staff calculated the cost of meeting the assumed needs of families of various sizes. While the costs have subsequently been updated to take account of rising prices, the underlying estimates of 'needs' have not been reconsidered and they remain as they were in the early 1960s. Earlier estimates, using a more loosely formulated measure, had found that the proportion living in poverty had fallen from 48 per cent in 1935 to 33 per cent in 1940, 27 per cent in 1950, and 21 per cent in 1960 (George and Howard 1991: 62; see also Harrington 1962). Use of the newly established official measure in 1965 suggested a level of just over 17 per cent.

The amount of poverty in the United States continued to fall during the following decade and it stabilised at a level of between 11 per cent and 12 per cent for most of the 1970s. In 1979, however, the level began to rise again, though it fell back to its 1980 level in 1988 (see Table 5.5). In broad terms, then, the American poverty level of 1988 was approximately the same as it had been in 1968 (Wilson 1987: 171–2; George and Howard 1991: 65). Further light is thrown on this by considering the level at which the official line had been set. The official poverty line in the United States for a family of four was set at $3,000 in 1965, and by 1988 it had reached $12,092, though a survey undertaken in the same year discovered that majority opinion held that $15,017 was a more realistic figure. Popular judgements thus pointed to a poverty line that was almost 25 per cent higher than the official poverty line. While the official line defined 32 million people as poor in 1988, the popularly estimated line recognised 45 million poor (Wilson 1991: 3).

Studies undertaken since the 1930s have consistently shown that poverty in America has been concentrated among rural and urban African Americans, and the black ghetto has been widely identified as the principal locale of urban poverty. Throughout the 1970s and 1980s approximately two thirds of poor families

Table 5.5 **Poverty in the USA, 1965–88**

	1965	1970	1975	1980	1985	1988
% of poverty	17.3	12.6	12.3	13.0	14.0	13.1

Source: George and Howard (1991: 65, Table 3.1)

were white and one third was black: an African American family had a three times greater chance of experiencing poverty than did a white family (George and Howard 1991: 72). Defining a ghetto as a neighbourhood where the rate of poverty is greater than 40 per cent, Wilson (1991) has shown that the number of people living in ghettos – principally in New York and Chicago – had reached 2.4 million by 1980. Two thirds of these poor people were African Americans, and a further quarter was Hispanic. The ghettos – areas of extreme poverty – housed 21 per cent of poor black families and 16 per cent of poor Hispanic families (see also Wacquant and Wilson 1989).

The pattern of international variation is also clear from a recent study that has used the European Poverty Line (EPL) to explore the actual levels of poverty in a number of European countries. According to the EPL – it will be recalled – a household can be said to live in poverty if its income is 50 per cent or more below the national average income. On this EPL measure, the Benelux countries and Germany appeared as the countries with the lowest levels of poverty in Europe (see Table 5.6). Across Europe as a whole, 13.9 per cent of households lived in poverty in 1985; but in Germany and the Benelux countries less than 10 per cent of the population were living in poverty. The highest levels of poverty – over 20 per cent of the population in each case – were to be found in Portugal, Greece, Ireland, and Spain, the countries with the lowest per capita gross domestic product. Britain and Denmark fell in the middle of the range, either side of the European average, with France having an above average level of poverty and Italy having slightly below the average for Europe as a whole. In most of the countries of Europe the period from the mid–1970s to the mid-1980s saw only minor fluctuations in the level of poverty, but Ireland, Portugal, and Britain showed large increases in poverty over the period. The greatest increase in the whole of Europe was that experienced in Britain.

A study of poverty that was undertaken for the European Community in 1987 had as its focus so-called new poverty, a rather confused and simplistic attempt by the EC commissioners to describe recent trends in economic development. The ranks of the poor today include not only the old and the low paid but also the long-term unemployed, who are dependent on social assistance, single-parent households, and the homeless. In his summary of this research Room has pointed to the inadequacy of this concept, but he recognised the powerful evidence that the economic trends of the 1980s had produced a substantial increase in the numbers that were living in poverty (1990: 54–6). As significant as this growth in poverty is the evidence of the changing composition of the poor: fewer of the poor are now elderly, while many more are unemployed. This shift neatly reverses that which Rowntree and Lavers (1951) had identified as having occurred between

1936 and 1951. I showed in Chapter 3 that Rowntree believed that economic affluence and full employment had removed most of the labour market causes of poverty and had left the residual – but very serious – problem of the poverty of the old and the sick. Townsend's early studies had suggested that this conclusion was over-optimistic, and worsening economic conditions led to the operations of the labour market, once again, becoming an important factor in the generation of poverty. Room's analysis demonstrates that this was a Europe-wide phenomenon, resulting from a general deterioration in economic conditions during the 1980s:

The high rate of unemployment during the 1980s, together with associated changes in the labour market, has had a number of major effects on the extent and distribution of poverty in the countries of the European Community. There is, first, clear evidence of significant gaps and limitations in income support and social protection for the unemployed. In addition, however, recent years have also revealed growing disparities of income and welfare between those confined to insecure and low-paid jobs and those who are fortunate enough to remain in relatively stable and secure occupations.

(1990: 70)

Those who have suffered particularly badly across Europe have been ethnic minorities, women, and young people (Room 1990: 78–82). Direct labour market discrimination and more indirect exclusionary practices have meant that resident and migrant workers from ethnic minorities have been particularly likely to experience unemployment. In the Netherlands, for example, foreign workers – especially Turks and Moroccans – had a higher unemployment rate and lower chances of re-entry to the labour market. Similarly, the occupational segregation of women and their concentration in insecure, low-paid, and part-time employment have meant that they are far more prone to unemployment than are male workers. This 'feminisation of poverty' is especially important when there is an increase in the number of female-headed single-parent families (Room 1990: 96). Youth unemployment and delayed entry to the labour market have combined with the failures of training schemes in many countries and have produced large numbers of welfare-dependent young people who have never experienced employment and so have had no chance of building up an entitlement to proper unemployment benefit.

On a broader comparative basis, a study of data for 1979 showed that the level of poverty in the United States, as measured on the EPL, was about twice the level found in Britain in that year. While 9 per cent of the British population lived in poverty, 17 per cent of the American population did so – about the same level as in France. Canada, also, showed a relatively high level of poverty at 12 per cent, about twice the German level (Smeeding *et al.* 1990, cited in Oppenheim 1990: 122).

*Table 5.6 **Poverty in the European Community, 1985***

	% of households below EPL
Portugal	28.0
Greece	24.0
Eire	22.0
Spain	20.0
France	17.5
Denmark	14.7
United Kingdom	12.0
Italy	11.7
Federal Republic of Germany	8.5
Luxembourg	7.9
Netherlands	7.4
Belgium	7.2

Source: Oppenheim (1990: 121, Table 26)

The income inequality and poverty level that are found in a country are, of course, influenced by its aggregate national income. A country with a high national income is better able to pursue a policy commitment to greater equality than is a country with a lower national income. The European countries with high and growing gross domestic product for most of the post-war period included Germany, France, and the Benelux countries. The lower-income countries were those that had large agricultural sectors – such as Spain, Portugal, Ireland, and Greece. While Britain has a relatively high gross domestic product, its growth rate has been extremely low and it falls into an intermediate position between these extremes. These variations in productivity and growth rates are the constraints within which any political strategy must operate. Observed patterns of inequality, wealth, and poverty are the outcome of the complex interplay of economic, political, and cultural forces.

In France, for instance, there has been a high degree of social inequality and a high level of poverty by international standards. This is reflected in public perceptions of class division and widespread feelings of social injustice. Despite this, there has been little academic discussion of poverty and wealth and, as a result, there has been no agreed official definition or measure of poverty. The evidence that is available, however, suggests that poverty is concentrated among the elderly and the disabled, and among low-paid workers in agriculture, domestic and catering services, and the textiles industries (Sinfield 1980). A particularly large section within the poor has been the immigrant and foreign workers from North Africa, Spain, and Portugal whose employment opportunities have been limited to precisely these low paid industrial sectors. France's large agricultural sector – where much farm work is technically and economically backward – has created a massive pool of rural poverty. Poverty in France has been geographically concentrated in such rural areas as Corsica, Brittany, and the Midi, while wealth has been overwhelmingly concentrated in Paris and a few other urban areas (Daumard 1980: 101). French social structure, then, combines an advanced industrial economy with a backward agrarian sector, and this has served to differentiate its pattern of poverty and inequality from that found in industrial Germany or in agrarian Spain.

The economic prosperity of West Germany was a consequence of post-war growth following its industrial reconstruction, but this pattern of growth and prosperity has been put under strain following its reunification with the East. The long-term implications of political reunification for inequality and poverty are, as yet, uncertain, and it is not clear whether Germany can continue to combine a relatively high level of inequality with the moderate levels of poverty that have been apparent throughout the post-war period (Lawson 1980). The 'economic miracle' of the post-war years permitted a general rise in incomes and living standards and resulted in a stretching of the upper bands of the economic hierarchy without any significant increase in the amount of poverty. While the percentage of total income that is held by the wealthy is comparable with that found in France, these high incomes have been facilitated by a depressing of the middle range of incomes rather than by any specific pressure on the lowest incomes. Germany has been a high-wage and low-unemployment economy throughout the post-war period, and this has allowed the state to channel welfare benefits into pension provision rather than see it being eaten up by unemployment benefit or income support. As a result, the level of poverty is somewhat lower than that which has been found in Britain. Despite this impressive record, Germany is far from having the lowest levels of poverty in Europe. Lawson (1980) has pointed out that much poverty can be found among the massive number of migrant workers – the *Gastarbeiter* – that have bolstered German economic growth. The number of foreign workers in the German labour force increased continually throughout the post-war period, reaching a high point of around 10 per cent of the labour force (Castles and Kosack 1973). Restricted to short-term, insecure, and low-paid work, they have borne the brunt of poverty in Germany.

A study using a slightly modified version of the EPL measure of poverty has thrown an interesting light on the distribution of poverty across Europe as a whole. If average household income is calculated for the European Community as a whole, the numbers in poverty can be defined as the number of households whose income is 50 per cent or more below this Community standard.

Table 5.7   Poverty in the European Community: Community basis, 1985

	% of Europe's poor in each country
Spain	26
Italy	16
Portugal	16
France	12
United Kingdom	11
Greece	10
Eire	3
Germany	3
Netherlands	2
Denmark	1
Belgium	1
Total	101

Note: Figures add up to 101 because of rounding

Source: Oppenheim (1990: 121, Table 26)

This measure allows an investigation of the national distribution of the poor in Europe (see Table 5.7).

A quarter of all the poor families in Europe, on the basis of this revised EPL measure, were to be found in Spain, and over a half were in Spain, Portugal, and Greece combined. By contrast, Germany, the Benelux countries, and Denmark together accounted for just 7 per cent of Europe's poor families. This brings out very clearly the association between poverty and backward agriculture – responsible also for the fact that over a quarter of Europe's poor were to be found in France and Italy. The more advanced agriculture of Denmark and Ireland did not result in comparable levels of poverty.[3] While a positive correlation between poverty and backward agriculture and the negative correlation between poverty and industrialism can be discerned in the table, neither correlation is clear-cut. Britain, for example, combines a relatively modern agriculture with a predominantly industrial economy, yet it houses 11 per cent of Europe's poor.

It is extremely difficult to find the kind of longitudinal data that would be necessary to put these cross-sectional comparisons into context. Britain is unique in having the well-established research tradition on poverty and wealth that I have drawn upon in the preceding chapters. Some idea of broad trends can, however, be gleaned from Wedgwood's (1929) study of income and property distribution, which used a range of official sources for a number of countries.

Table 5.8 **Property distribution before the First World War**

	England	*Prussia*	*France*	*Australia*
	% of property held by top percentiles of population			
Top 0.1%	34	25	26	16
Top 1.0%	68	50	57	39
Top 5.0%	87	75	75	65
Top 10.0%	91	84	83	79

Note: Actual dates for data are England 1911–13, Prussia 1908, France 1909–13, Australia 1914–15

Source: Wedgwood (1929: 121)

Table 5.8 shows Wedgwood's findings on property holding for England, Prussia (a former Germany state), France, and Australia in the period before the First World War. It can be seen that England had a much higher level of concentration in property ownership than Prussia and France, and it was considerably more concentrated than in Australia. Whereas the top 0.1 per cent of the English population held over one third of all property, the same proportion held less than a half of this amount in Australia. In all countries except Australia the top 1 per cent of the population held over a half of all property, and in England they held over two thirds. The relatively greater equality that was found in Australia was also apparent in the distribution of income. Table 5.9 shows a striking similarity between Australia and the United States in terms of income distribution, reflecting their common global standing as 'new' and expanding societies at that time. By contrast, pre-war Prussia showed a higher degree of

Table 5. 9 **International income distribution, 1910–1920**

	England	*Prussia*	*USA*	*Australia*
	% of income received (before tax)			
Top 0.1%	10	8	6	6
Top 1.0%	29	18	14	14
Top 5.0%	43	31	26	26
Top 10.0%	52	40	34	33
Top 20.0%	–	52	47	45

Note: Actual dates for data are Britain 1910, Prussia 1913, USA 1918, and Australia 1920

Source: Wedgwood (1929: 121)

concentration at each level of the hierarchy and England showed an extremely high degree of concentration. These data suggest a three-fold classification of the societies that were studied by Wedgwood. First, England stood alone as an old, closed society with an extremely high level of inequality. Second, Prussia and France were old societies with relatively high levels of inequality. Third, the United States and Australia were new, 'open' societies with moderate levels of inequality. Wedgwood's own discussion of these patterns identified the longevity of inheritance as an important factor. The United States and Australia, he argued, had shorter histories as national economies and national states and so there was less chance that stable patterns of inheritance would have been established.

		Degree of poverty		
		Low	Medium	High
	High	Germany Belgium Netherlands	France USA	Spain Portugal Greece
Degree of inequality	Medium		Italy	Eire
	Low	Australia	Britain Denmark	Russia

Figure 5.1　A typology of societies

I have tried in Figure 5.1 to summarise some of the broad comparative conclusions about poverty and wealth. Contemporary patterns of inequality and poverty in modern societies have each been classified into three categories, according to whether they can be regarded as 'high', 'medium', or 'low' by comparative standards. The most polarised social structures are to be found where a high level of inequality is combined with a high level of poverty. In such societies – for example, in Spain, Portugal, and Greece – a large and archaic agricultural sector and low gross domestic product have created fertile conditions for the emergence of great disparities in economic resources whereby a large section of the population is excluded from the enjoyment of those things that are taken for granted by the majority. Societies such as Australia, on the other hand, have prosperous, modern agricultural sectors and growing economies, conditions that are favourable to a low level of inequality and the inclusion of the great majority of the population above the widely shared minimum standard of living. Britain and Denmark, which for a long time shared a similar 'social democratic' outlook on welfare, have combined relatively low levels of inequality with moderate levels of poverty. While levels of poverty are comparable with those in both France and the United States, these societies have shown a high degree of inequality and, therefore, the existence of larger numbers of wealthy individuals and families. This is true also of Germany, Belgium, and the Netherlands, but these societies are more inclusive in terms of their standards of living and they show rather less poverty. The pattern of Russia is particularly interesting. The agricultural and industrial backwardness of the country has produced massive disparities in income, but official practices have suppressed the overall level of incomes and so have prevented the development of the kind of inequality that is found in the United States.

The discussion so far has concentrated on the statistical features of poverty and wealth, but it is important to try to say something about the social composition of the poor and the rich and about their economic foundation. The wealthy owe their position to the structure of property and the uses to which it is put, and so their nature varies with the system of capital mobilisation that is found in a society. A number of systems of capital mobilisation can be identified in the modern world, the most important of which for my purposes are the 'Anglo-American', the 'Latin', the 'German', and the 'Japanese'.[4]

The 'Anglo-American' economies of Britain, the United States, Australia, and Canada share a common cultural heritage and have common patterns of legal and business organisation. In all of these societies the growth of joint stock companies as the characteristic form of large-scale business enterprise has involved a gradual transfer of the bulk of company shares from propertied families to financial institutions, such as insurance companies, pensions funds, and banks. Instead of holding controlling blocks of shares in particular companies – the characteristic pattern for entrepreneurial capital – the property of increasing numbers of business families in the Anglo-American economies has taken the form of diversified portfolios of financial assets. The system of 'institutional' capital is the means through which these assets are managed and it creates the incomes from which the privileged families benefit as property holders and as top employees.

In the 'Latin' economies such as France and Belgium no system of institutional capital mobilisation has developed. Instead, large scale business undertakings have come under the control of investment holding companies in which families often retain substantial controlling stakes. Such a system creates opportunities for the accumulation of large fortunes, but these fortunes are less secure for the families than is the case in the Anglo-American economies. The 'German' system of capital mobilisation is centred on the investment power of the big banks, which bolster family wealth and ensure that the major property owning families have benefited disproportionately from the bank-led growth in the economy. Finally, in the 'Japanese' system a depersonalised system of 'corporate capital' and an extremely low level of family share ownership has created relatively fewer opportunities for the making of large business fortunes. This suggests an ideal typical pattern in which the greatest concentration of economic resources would be found in Germany and France and the lowest concentration in Japan, with the Anglo-American economies falling into an intermediate range.

The position of the poor in a society is determined by the structure of the labour market. The balance of unskilled to skilled work, of casual and temporary work to permanent and full-time work, and the differentiation of the labour market into 'advanced' and 'backward' sectors are all factors that affect the relative power of the different groups of workers in the labour market. In countries such as Germany and Japan, where there is a great emphasis on training and a consequent high level of skill in the labour force, the impetus to poverty is weaker than in countries such as Britain and France, with their lower level of skills and more 'backward' regions and sectors. In periods of high economic growth such labour market differentials may be masked by a general improvement in living standards, but when an economy falters or stagnates they generate an increase in the numbers living in poverty.

The nature of poverty and wealth in a society can be seen as the outcome of these two sets of mechanisms – the structure of capital mobilisation and the structure of the labour market – but not of these alone. Political mechanisms of redistribution that shape the final outcome may operate alongside these 'economic' mechanisms. Tendencies towards the production of poverty and wealth that are generated by the operations of the capital and labour markets can, for example, be offset by political strategies of equality and redistribution on the part of the state agencies. The most important of the factors involved in the shaping of these political strategies are the conceptions of citizenship that prevail in a society, and it is to these that I turn in the following chapter.

Poverty and wealth in Russia

I have looked so far at the patterns of inequality that can be found in the main capitalist societies of the modern world. Russia and the other countries of the former Soviet Union and Soviet bloc now form part of that system, but their patterns of inequality continue to be shaped by their non-capitalist past. It will, therefore, be instructive to look at the case of Russia in some detail in order to compare capitalist and non-capitalist systems of inequality and to assess the patterns of poverty and wealth that are emerging in the new, post-communist Russia. As I will show, the inequalities that have emerged in contemporary Russia are not a new phenomenon, but date back to the earliest days of the Revolution.

Inequality in Russia has been shaped by its revolutionary break with its capitalist past in 1917 and the subsequent progress of the policies introduced by the makers of that revolution. The ostensible aim of the Bolsheviks, the leading force in the revolutionary take-over of the Russian Empire, was the establishment of a communist society in which there would be equality, freedom, and co-operation. The revolutionary government abolished private property, which Marx had seen as the basis of class divisions, and so sought to eliminate inheritance and wealth accumulation. A policy of equalisation in incomes, it was felt, would supplement this and establish the basis for social harmony. A necessary precondition for communism, however, was a substantial increase in the level of industrial development of the country, as its industry was, in 1917, incapable of sustaining an advanced egalitarian society.

Lenin's immediate aim after the Revolution of 1917 was to reverse the economic collapse that had taken place during the wartime years and to develop the industrial base. Before the First World War Russia had had a per capita gross national product of around a quarter of the British level and one fifth of the American level. This low level of income reflected the low level of economic development that it had attained. Russia was, at that time, a rather backward agrarian society with only limited pockets of industrial development. Inflation and famine had worsened this underlying situation, and Lenin sought to remedy the state of affairs by creating incentives for the technical specialists who, he believed, could be induced to put their skills to work to improve economic conditions and to help to build a communist society.

This policy of establishing economic incentives involved an abandonment of Lenin's intention to promote equality through maximum wage legislation, and it was recognised that it involved the re-establishment of 'bourgeois' patterns of motivation. Nevertheless, Lenin's policy was reinforced in the New Economic Policy of 1921, which encouraged both economic differentials and private enterprise. The private enterprise of the kulaks – the more productive and prosperous, market-oriented peasants – was given greater encouragement as a way of improving the food supply to the cities, and economic differentials were extended in favour of such groups as the political and military workers and the intelligentsia. At the same time a number of economic concerns were given autonomy in the allocation of wages to the various categories of worker that they employed. Through these and similar means, managers, engineers, party officials, military officers, doctors, lawyers, and writers were all accorded high incomes, bonuses, and special benefits. Alongside these privileged groups there arose many dealers and 'entrepreneurs' who were able to take advantage of the system and could build up substantial private business undertakings.

By the middle of the 1920s, then, Lenin the communist had established the basis of a highly differentiated pattern of inequality in which market incentives and private enterprise played a major part. With Stalin's rise to power from 1928, after Lenin's death, some elements of this system began to be reversed. Private enterprises in agriculture and trade were attacked through a forcible collectivisation of agriculture and the suppression of private commerce. The inequalities and differentials that had been established in industry, on the other hand, were allowed to expand, and the administrative and technical workers, party officials, military personnel, and intelligentsia all continued to improve their standing relative to the mass of industrial workers and peasants. The topmost levels of these groups – already highly privileged under Lenin – became more entrenched and distinct from the bulk of the population. The most significant change that Stalin made to the structure of inequality and economic differentials was to impose a cloak of secrecy around it: some of the central elements of Bolshevik policy may have been abandoned in order to secure rapid industrial development, but it was important that the industrial and agrarian masses on whom the system depended did not know this. The policy of rapid industrialisation that Stalin had initiated had, in fact, resulted in a doubling of the size of the industrial workforce and a tripling of the white-collar workforce. Many in the 'new' working class were living in conditions of extreme poverty by any standard.

Following the death of Stalin and the accession of Khrushchev there was some attempt to narrow the range of economic differentials that had been established. Minimum wage legislation was introduced in 1956, and there was the beginning of an endeavour to document the true extent of poverty. Khrushchev's efforts to remove the rigidities of the Stalinist system were, however, blocked by the vested interests of the powerful and the privileged. The policy was relatively easy for them to undermine, as the people whose job it was to implement government policy were, in fact, the beneficiaries of the very system that the policy was trying to reform. As a result, Khrushchev's period in office saw little change in the overall pattern of income differentials; the privileges of the inner group, tied to the centralised economy, persisted.

Social research that was carried out under Khrushchev's 1959–65 'Seven Year Plan' helped to establish an official 'minimum family budget', set at 205.6 roubles per month for a family of four. This official minimum can be compared with an average income of R175.7 for a family with two earners. The conclusion drawn by Matthews (1986: 19–21) was that about one third of urban manual workers in the Soviet Union were living below the officially recognised poverty line, and he claims that the proportion was higher among the lower levels of the white-collar workforce and among the peasantry.

The Brezhnev period saw a reaffirmation of differentials and privileges in official policy. Indeed, privileged groups once more began to improve their position as the structure of inequality began to ossify into a system of entrenched privileges. At the same time the amount of poverty increased. An updating of the minimum family budget for 1977 gave a figure of R266.4 per month for a family of four (R66.6 per capita), and also allowed for the inclusion of a larger range of 'necessities', such as better food and clothing, and an allowance for holidays. By this time average income for a two-income family had risen above the official poverty line, but many people still lived in poverty. Between 12 and 15 per cent of Moscow residents lived below the poverty line. In relatively prosperous Estonia 18 per cent were living in poverty, while 35 per cent of families in rural Novosibirsk were poor (Matthews 1986: 24).[5] Matthews concluded his review with the claim that about two fifths of the total population of the Soviet Union were living in poverty according to officially recognised standards.

Susceptibility to poverty in the Brezhnev period was particularly marked among pensioners and the disabled on the one hand and the low paid on the other (Matthews 1986: ch. 2). Pensioners numbered 33 million in 1980, and the level of the pension entitlement began at half the wage when in employment.[6] The official minimum level of pension provision was set at R45 per month, and the maximum was set at R120. These levels could be reduced, however, if a person had spent less than twenty-five years in qualifying employment. As inflation eroded the real value of pensions, retirement from a low-paid job was especially likely to cause distress. In many occupations pay was not sufficient to support a family unless both partners were in employment. The escape from poverty involved the combination of two low wages to form a single living income. The lowest-paid occupations were to be found among state and collective farm workers, among those employed in light industry, food processing, and service work, and in some areas of office and professional work – clerks, typists, cashiers, and teachers were all among the lowest paid in the population. Where employment in such jobs was the sole source of income for a family, poverty was the result. Thus, poverty was especially marked among single-parent households, which numbered 7.9 million in 1979. Even casual earnings in the 'black economy', where such opportunities were available, could not securely raise a family above the poverty line.

McAuley (1993) has shown the growth of poverty during the Gorbachev period. In 1988 40 million people – 14 per cent of the population – were living below the official poverty line and at least the same number could be said to be 'on the margins' of poverty. More than half of the people living in poverty had incomes that were less than three quarters of the official minimum. Inflation increased substantially and many basic food items disappeared from the shops. The introduction of markets in place of central planning exacerbated these problems and created further economic dislocation and an increase in unemployment. Family size was also a contributory factor in the generation of poverty. Even where there were two earners in a family, an increase in family size above three could undermine the family budget. One effect of this was to produce high levels of poverty in those Muslim areas – such as Tadzhikistan, Turkmenistan, Uzbekistan, and Azerbaidzhan – where families of six or more were especially common. Indeed, the regional concentration of poverty was especially marked in the Soviet Union. More than a half of the population lived in Russia, yet Russia had only one third of the country's poor. The Central Asian republics, on the other hand, included 17 per cent of the population but almost two fifths of the poor.

At the other end of the scale of inequality, an important study by Matthews (1978) has documented the extent of wealth and privilege in the Brezhnev period of the old Soviet Union. Matthews's argument is that the directive élite that had been solidified in the Soviet Union was at the core of a highly privileged group. While the extent of inequality and the kinds of advantages that they enjoyed were limited in western terms, they nevertheless enjoyed an exclusive lifestyle from which the mass of ordinary citizens was excluded. The existence of the privileged group and the qualitative break in the social hierarchy that set them apart from the rest of the population were a direct consequence of state policy, but they were also a matter of official secrecy and were not acknowledged in public statements. For this reason, of course, it was even more difficult to demarcate the boundaries of wealth in the Soviet Union than it was in Britain.

Paradoxically, however, the very existence of official secrecy provided an indicator of privilege. As government policy established strict censorship over the discussion of high incomes, it was possible to take the income level that was identified in the system of censorship as marking the level at which wealth began. The highest figures mentioned in official studies in the early 1970s were R400 per month above the legal minimum income. Thus Matthews held that it was possible to regard this as the lower limit for identifying the wealthy. Minimum wages at this time stood at between R60 and R70, and so Matthews takes R450 per month as an approximate cut-off point for wealth. This compares with an average wage of R130 per month (1978: 22).

The occupations with incomes above this wealth line of R450 were party secretaries, top industrial managers, academic administrators, top trades union officials, judges, and top military officers (Matthews 1978: 23–7). In these occupations incomes began at around the 'official' threshold and ranged up to R900 per month. On top of these basic salaries people earned 'extras' that could bring the income of a marshal of the Red Army, for example, up to R2,000. Academicians, officials in the Writers' Union, and others with access to foreign earnings could receive up to R1,000. The official exchange rate in the early 1970s would equate a monthly income of R450 into an equivalent British salary of £2,500 per year – about the salary level of a well-paid university professor at that time. A monthly income of R2,000 would equate to a British equivalent of £11,000 per year.

It was the party, industry, military, and intellectual hierarchies that were the sources of high incomes, though only those at the tops of the hierarchies secured incomes above R450. Matthews has estimated that this privileged group numbered about 227,000, about 0.2 per cent of the labour force. Of these people, more than three quarters were party or state officials or held top posts in the police or the military. The privileged group was thus closely linked with the *nomenklatura* system, under which top posts were filled through party nomination. The wealthy, Matthews argued, were 'virtually state registered' (1978: 33; see also Voslensky 1980).

The advantages gained by people in these occupations went beyond direct income. Indeed, basic occupational income was merely one of a range of sources available to them. The intelligentsia had access to foreign earnings from books and other writings published abroad, and many received payments in 'certificate roubles' that could be used as hard currency in special shops. Sinecures, consultancies, and second posts could also boost basic incomes: a seat in a Supreme Soviet, say, could pay up to R100 per month, while holding the rank of Academician could give anything between R350 and R500 per month. Bonus payments were widespread, with many officials being paid the so-called thirteenth month, and these bonuses were supplemented by payments in kind and subsidised goods in the form of the 'Kremlin ration'. This would typically involve the right of access to official suppliers that were inaccessible to the mass of the population and whose prices were low or nominal. Western goods and other goods in short supply could all be obtained through these outlets. Subsidised private dining-rooms and buffets, often with take-home or delivery services, were also available to the privileged. An especially important subsidy was high-quality housing at low rents and with subsidised services, to which could often be added chauffeured vehicles, private cars, and access to petrol. Private health care was organised through the Fourth Directorate of the Ministry of Health, entrance to selective schools that were feeders to the universities was generally available, and subsidised holidays and foreign travel were possible. In all these ways, then, the extent of the privileges that were enjoyed by top earners in the Soviet Union was greater than the sizes of their incomes alone would suggest. A typical family living above the wealth threshold in the Soviet Union had a monthly income of between R88 and R1,200 in money and other benefits – about five to eight times the size of the average wage.

The collapse of the Soviet Union and the fall of Gorbachev have strengthened the deep-lying sources of inequality in Russia. The *nomenklatura* have sought, and found, alternative ways of securing their privileges, and those who obtained advantages for themselves by operating in the margins of the old system have acquired new sources of legitimate wealth. Former party officials and black marketeers alike have become 'entrepreneurs' and traders, with ever greater opportunities to enhance their wealth: in early 1991 a group of such entrepreneurs set up the Moscow 'millionaires' club'. The *nomenklatura* began to enter business in the late 1980s, under official sponsorship, taking on commercial and trading responsibilities in the various regions of the Union. With the disappearance of the party and Komsomol organisational structures, they have simply continued their commercial activities, which have acquired increased importance with the collapse of the old system of central allocation. State property has been handed over to, or usurped by, these businesses, and they have benefited from the privatisation programme (see Burawoy and Krotov 1992). Black marketeers and dealers in the shadow economy prospered under Brezhnev, taking advantage of legal loopholes and 'surplus' resources. While their activities were illegal, and many were imprisoned, they played an important economic role and have flourished since the collapse of the old system and the legalisation of their activities.

A survey of opinions among Russian millionaires in 1991 (Kryshtanovskaya 1993) found that they had wildly inaccurate views about the extent of inequality in Russian society. They believed that the typical income for an ordinary citizen was R6,800 per month, whereas official data showed that average income was less than 5 per cent of this figure. Their estimate of the poverty line – actually set at R450 per month – was also inaccurate, the common view setting it at 1.5 times the average wage. These millionaires can be expected to have a more accurate impression of the wealth line, which they estimated to lie at R30,000 per month: only those above this line were felt to be 'rich'.

Table 5.10 tries to put the findings on wealth in the Soviet Union into context. Matthews (1978) claimed that the wealthy in the Soviet Union amounted to 0.2 per cent of the labour force, and Table 5.10 presents data for the equivalent group in the United States. The lowest after-tax annual income for an American in this category in 1970 was $64,000, but incomes ranged to well above $1.25 million. While such comparisons must be made with

Table 5.10 *Incomes of the top 0.2% of the population in the USA, 1970*

No. of persons	Average annual income after tax ($)
639	1,228,000
1,738	372,000
12,757	164,800
62,233	83,000
92,633	64,000

Source: Matthews (1978: 180)

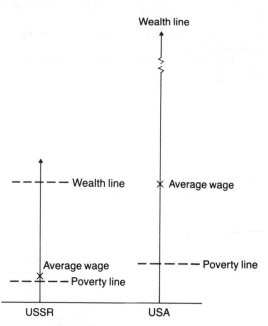

Figure 5.2 **The USA and the USSR compared**

care, Figure 5.2 tries to depict the implications of these differences between the two societies. In the Soviet Union the official poverty line was set at 0.95 of the average wage, while the 'official' wealth line began at around five times the average wage. The level at which wealth began in the Soviet Union, however, was close to the average wage in the United States, where immensely high incomes began at around twelve times the average wage. The official American poverty line, set at 0.33 of the average wage, was significantly higher, in absolute terms, than the Soviet average wage. The Soviet Union, then, was characterised by a much more compressed range of incomes than was the United States, and the top of this range was low by American standards. Nothing could more strikingly characterise the relativity of poverty and wealth: those who were regarded as the elite of wealth and privilege in the Soviet Union had a standard of living that was, in real terms, little better than that of the average American citizen.

Notes

1 A recent useful discussion of these problems can be found in Atkinson (1990). For international reviews of poverty see George and Lawson (1980) and R. Walker *et al.* (1984).
2 After-tax figures for Denmark and the Netherlands were not available.
3 These figures are, of course, also affected by the population size of the various countries.
4 This discussion draws on Scott (1985: ch. 5; 1991b; 1992a).
5 The Novosibirsk data are for 1975.
6 Retirement age was sixty for men and fifty-five for women.

CHAPTER 6

Citizenship and resources

I have used the concept of citizenship to organise the material that I have presented in this book. In Chapter 1 I examined the link between citizenship and the relative definition of poverty, and in Chapter 3 I showed the differing social policies that have been informed by liberal and by social democratic citizenship. In this chapter I return to address these questions more directly and to examine some recent developments in the sphere of citizenship.

Views of citizenship

Theoretical concepts are frequently appropriated from everyday life before being given their specialised and technical meanings. The sociological concept of citizenship – a second-order construct – relates closely to the first-order constructs that, in various societies, have been described by the terms 'citizen' or *'citoyen'*, but it cannot be simply equated with any one of these first-order constructs. The concept may, equally, be used to understand social conditions in some societies that recognise no such legal status.

The construction of a sociological concept of citizenship, therefore, must work at one remove from specific legal and constitutional terminology. In France, for example, all full members of the society have, since the Revolution, been described as *citoyens*, and most societies with revolutionary or republican traditions have followed a similar practice. In Britain, on the other hand, full members have been legally defined only as 'subjects' of the Crown. Not until recently has British law become seriously concerned with the legal status of a 'British citizen', and then only in connection with the questions of migration and nationality.

The legal terminology and constitutional arrangements for defining what sociologists call 'citizenship' vary considerably from one society to another, and the sociological concept itself is not concerned with the purely legal aspects of status. Citizenship is not simply an official category. An especially important connection between the official, legal rights of citizenship and the standards, powers, and obligations that are held in public opinion is provided by the electoral mechanism. A government whose policy runs too far away from widely held views is less likely to be re-elected, and so the electoral mechanism sets limits to the variation between official and unofficial views. Unless a government can suppress the electoral mechanism itself, these limits will be an important constraint on official policy. Citizenship, then, comprises a whole complex of institutions, practices, and conventions that may become embodied, in often contradictory ways, in the cultural and subcultural perspectives of a society, and which will inform its political and ideological struggles.

A first priority must be to distinguish the sociological concept of citizenship from the specific legal and political definitions of citizenship that have been espoused by constitution builders and political theorists. An important feature in T.H. Marshall's account of citizenship was that he contrasted 'full membership' of society with all other forms of membership. Citizenship describes the institutionalised conception of what it is to have 'full membership' in the public world of society. It thus refers to the norms and practices that define who possesses the rights – and the corresponding obligations – that permit full participation in public life. While all societies have some conception of 'membership', and of its various levels and types, only those that have a differentiated public sphere will have a conception of citizenship.

In classical Greece citizens were distinguished from 'slaves' and other lesser members of the society, only the citizens having rights of participation in the public life of the *polis*. In medieval Europe, on the other hand, no real public sphere existed, and the various members of society were simply subordinate 'subjects' of a ruler: they had no public status independent of their personal subordination to the monarch. Only in the cities of medieval Europe did there exist a public, 'bourgeois' sphere of life in which an idea of citizenship could develop (Turner 1990: 203). Modern societies exhibit, as one of their central characteristics, a structural differentiation of a public sphere, and this has permitted the development of the status of citizen.[1]

The connection of citizenship with the public sphere is reflected in its connection with the ideas and assumptions that classical political theorists described as liberty, equality, and fraternity (see King and Waldron 1988: 425–7). These ideas were seen as applying only among the citizens of a state and not among non-citizens or between its citizens and non-citizens. Liberty can be said to exist when all citizens are capable of autonomous action, of action that is unconstrained by coercion or by ignorance. Equality has not normally been seen as a condition of absolute homogeneity but as a condition in which the degree of inequality among citizens is limited so as to ensure that their liberty – their power and autonomy – is not compromised. Liberty and equality, then, are complementary ideas. Fraternity exists when citizens have achieved a degree of solidarity or community among themselves. When there is a sense of community and belonging, citizens can work together to pursue their common interests.

These abstract philosophical ideas have shaped modern debates about citizenship. As I argued in Chapter 3, the interplay of elitist and universalist views has resulted in the emergence of liberal, social democratic, and radical conceptions of citizenship in the modern world. These three conceptions are ideal types through which it is possible to understand the complexities and contradictions within the ideological formations of contemporary culture.

Michael Mann (1987) has highlighted some of the peculiarities of the British pattern of citizenship. The British monarchy of the eighteenth century took a constitutional form, rather than the absolutist form that was found through most of continental Europe.[2] In the constitutional regime a firm framework of civil rights was established and the members of the propertied classes all had full political rights. The development of liberalism, during the nineteenth century, allowed the expansion and strengthening of these civil and political aspects of citizenship and laid the basis for a subsequent institutionalisation of the social component of citizenship. In Germany, on the other hand, absolutism laid the foundation for more authoritarian structures of citizenship of the kind that also evolved in Japan and in pre-revolutionary Russia. In these countries there was a strong development of civil rights combined with very limited political rights and minimal social rights. Japan still shows this restricted pattern of citizenship, while Germany – following the suppression of civil rights under the Nazi regime – has evolved a system of social rights that is built on a combination of liberal and social democratic principles. These variations are seen by Mann as the outcome of the balance of class forces in a society and, in particular, of the power of organised labour to demand the establishment of social rights. In the United States, for example, the development of a strong labour movement was precluded by the early extension of the civil and political rights of a constitutional regime to all white members of the society. As a result, only a minimal structure of social rights developed in the American system of liberal citizenship, and African Americans for long remained outside the framework of civil and political rights.

The liberal conception of citizenship links the rights and duties of citizens to action within private, market relations. This idea has a long history in liberal thought, where the emphasis was originally placed on the property market (Macpherson 1962). The citizen was, in this view, the property owner. This emphasis set limits to the ways in which liberal citizenship rights could be universalised, and the property basis of rights was gradually enlarged into a work-related basis. From this point of view it is the worker, not merely the property holder, who has a legitimate claim to the status of citizen. It is this form of liberal citizenship that has been expressed in the 'New Right' thought that influenced the Reagan and Thatcher governments of the 1980s (Mead 1986). According to this position, the private contract of employment is made the basis of the public status of citizenship. The citizen is a worker. The rights of citizenship are grounded in the obligation to work, and are sanctioned through such means as 'workfare' or through restricting welfare benefits to those in low-paid jobs or on training schemes. Through such mechanisms, it is held, the 'dependency' status of those who receive benefit is avoided. Such a view tends to be highly gendered in its implications. Given the different patterns of labour market participation that characterise women and men, a strict liberal model would, for example, encourage married women to return to the labour market as a condition for receiving adequate welfare benefits.

Wilson has used survey data to document the continuing impact of liberal ideas in public opinion. He has shown the 'individualistic' views of poverty that have prevailed in both Britain and the United States, and it is clear that such attitudes underemphasise the social rights of citizenship (Wilson 1983: 13). Surveys undertaken in America during the 1970s found that between 89 and 93 per cent of respondents were in favour of seeing work obligations as the basis of welfare provision. These attitudes, argued Wilson, hardened during the 1980s. Nevertheless, sharp differences existed between Britain and the United States. A cross-national study in 1985 found that 43 per cent of the American population agreed that the government had a responsibility to provide a decent standard of living for old people, the corresponding figure in Britain was 79 per cent. Similarly, only 17 per cent and 16 per cent respectively of Americans saw a role for the government in maintaining high standards for the unemployed and in reducing income inequalities. In Britain three times as many people held these views (Taylor-Gooby 1989: 41).

Further aspects of the liberal concept of citizen include the linking of citizenship rights to taxation and to 'responsible' action. Citizens, it is held, should all contribute to social expenditure through public taxation: there should be no representation without taxation. Universal income tax, therefore, is seen as the primary fiscal basis of liberal citizenship. Income tax, of course, is generally limited to income from work and from property, and some New Right liberals have seen this as being too restrictive. If taxation is to be a universal obligation for all citizens, then all incomes – including welfare benefits – must be taxed. On the same principle, the use of other forms of taxation that apply to all adults (such as a universal poll tax) would be encouraged. It is important to be clear about the purpose of such taxation in the liberal view, as it is not viewed as a way of funding welfare schemes or other forms of public provision. Taxation is seen by liberals as a means through which citizens can exercise control over public authorities. The political imagery is that of the citizen as a paying customer.

Responsible civic action on the part of the liberal citizen involves charitable giving and voluntary service. This is considered as a more responsible act of citizenship than the reliance on impersonal taxation to provide benefits for others, and it is reinforced by the assumption that the responsible citizen will secure his or her own welfare through private insurance contracts. Thus state provision is to be held at a minimum level, with welfare coming from private charity and from personal insurance schemes. Liberal citizenship, therefore, implies an essentially privatised welfare system.

The social democratic idea of citizenship has sometimes been described as the 'social liberal' or 'social market' idea, and it is described by Roche (1992: ch. 1) as the 'dominant paradigm' of modern citizenship. It is that which was developed by Marshall himself, and it needs little more elaboration here. Like the liberal, the social democrat sees welfare provision as an insurance-based system, but holds that this insurance must operate through compulsory government schemes rather than simply through private provision. The social democratic view supplements private insurance and private charity with social insurance and universal benefits. Benefits are seen as rights that are earned through compulsory contributions to a public insurance scheme and supplemented by a progressive tax system (Hannah 1986). This view also accepts the liberal emphasis on work obligations, but it complements this emphasis with a public commitment to the maintenance of full employment. If all citizens have an obligation to work, then the state must have a corresponding obligation to ensure the conditions under which that obligation can be fulfilled. Social democrats, then, accept the need for economic intervention and fiscal management of a 'Keynesian' type.

The radical concept of citizenship makes the universalisation of citizenship rights its starting point. Welfare benefits must be accorded to all, regardless of any 'contributions' that they may or may not have made through the fiscal system. Radicals therefore advocate the right of all adult permanent residents to enjoy the full rights of the citizen.[3] For this reason, they stress the need to build the social, economic, and cultural conditions under which all can achieve equal participation in society. The radical concept also places particular stress on the plurality of ways in which people can participate as citizens. While liberal and social democratic conceptions also recognise that there can be a number of equivalent forms of citizen participation, they tend to assume a degree of cultural homogeneity. The radical concept enthusiastically embraces the diversity of life styles and identities that characterise citizens.

Marshall concentrated his account on the development of the social democratic form of citizenship, which he saw as having been partially institutionalised in the welfare system of post-war

Britain. But this welfare system also embodied many of the assumptions and practices of the more restricted 'liberal' concept of citizenship in which more limited rights of social participation were recognised. Post-war Britain was by no means unique in this combination of contradictory assumptions. Contradiction is, perhaps, the rule rather than the exception. There will always be alternative and competing views of citizenship within any one society, there will be changing conceptions of citizenship over time, and there will be differences in the form of citizenship between nations.

Citizenship, privilege, and deprivation

Ideas of citizenship have influenced systems of welfare provision, in part because they imply particular views of 'poverty' and 'deprivation'. I have shown in Chapter 1 that Townsend has been the most forcible advocate for a view of poverty as 'relative deprivation'. To be deprived is to be denied the opportunities to enjoy the standard of living that is customary in one's society. The poor are those who are deprived of the resources that would allow them to participate to the full as a citizen of their society. I have also suggested that wealth must be seen in relative terms and that this is associated with a condition of 'privilege'. It is through the concept of citizenship that it is possible to understand the relationship between privilege and deprivation.

The words 'privilege' and 'deprivation' have, in fact, a common origin in the Latin word 'privatus', which is also the origin of the modern word 'private'.[4] According to the *Oxford English Dictionary*, the noun 'private' means withdrawn from public life, kept or closed from the public, or belonging to a particular individual. Its related verbal meanings are to keep something secluded or closed off from the public world, or to dispossess someone from something. It is in this last sense that 'to private' someone is equivalent to 'depriving' them. To deprive means to divest, debar, or dispossess, and it involves an act of exclusion from that which is public. Deprivation is the social condition that results from being deprived.

Deprivation has always involved the idea of a negative sense of loss: the person who is deprived is unable to enjoy those things that are available to other members of the public. In this sense, therefore, the etymology of the word 'deprivation' underlines my argument that deprivation must be defined in terms of exclusion from the publicly recognised lifestyle and living conditions of the citizen. This is also apparent in the fact that the words 'public' and 'citizen' themselves have a very closely associated history.

If it is possible for people to be deprived – to be excluded from public life – it is also possible for people to be privileged in relation to that same public world. To be privileged originally meant that a person was advantaged or benefited from a special ordinance referring to them as a particular individual. By extension, a privilege came to mean any special advantage or benefit or a special right or immunity that was attached to a status. A privilege is thus a 'private' benefit that is unavailable to the public. To be privileged is to enjoy such private benefits.

Deprivation implies a *loss* of public participation, as a result of the exclusionary actions of others. Privilege implies a *gain* over the participation available to the public and it results from the ability to exclude others from the enjoyment of this benefit. The deprived are excluded from public life; the privileged are able to exclude the public from their special advantages. These two social conditions involve an institutionalised 'closure' of powers and opportunities at each end of the hierarchy of inequality. Deprivation involves an exclusion from the full rights of citizenship and, most particularly, from its 'social' component. Privilege involves the gaining of *de facto* (and sometimes *de jure*) civil, political, and social advantages that allow the development of a distinct and superior lifestyle.

The socially acceptable lifestyles of citizens are defined most clearly by a social minimum, the basic standard of living that all should be able to enjoy. Superior lifestyles above the 'normal' range are also recognised – and criticised – in public opinion, but the dividing line, for much of the present century, has been drawn less sharply than the poverty line. This reflects, in part, a growing homogenisation of citizen lifestyles, somewhat inadequately depicted in the ideas of 'mass society' and 'mass culture'. Despite this homogenisation, considerable variation in lifestyles persists, and the difficulty in drawing a sharp line to indicate where privilege begins is due to this continuing heterogeneity of citizen lifestyles. Despite the greater ease with which 'deprivation' can be identified, however, it is important to recognise that deprivation and privilege are interdependent. Deprivation and privilege, then, are complementary processes and conditions, and each can be understood only in relation to the establishment of the public status of the citizen. Marshall has, implicitly, raised some of the implications of this argument for those societies in which the social democratic concept of citizenship is institutionalised in a system of welfare. He saw the public status of citizen – as defined in the social democratic view of citizenship – as confronting the class inequalities of capitalism. The unfettered operation of a capitalist economy, he argued, constantly threatens to generate levels of inequality that make it impossible for some members of the society to participate fully in its public life. They are excluded by the way in which the economy operates, and their exclusion results in their deprivation. It is in this sense that Marshall argued that citizenship and the capitalist class system were at war.

This insight is undoubtedly correct. Indeed, it underlines the recognition that if a capitalist economy generates deprivation it must also generate privilege. Those who are privileged – the wealthy – are those whose location in the economic system means that the resources available to them are such that they are able to establish 'private' lifestyles and modes of consumption from which others are excluded. The level of their resources is such that they have access to a level of living that is inaccessible to others. Deprivation and privilege do not simply define the 'bottom' and the 'top' of a statistical distribution. They are polarised social conditions that are generated by the confrontation between the public sphere of citizenship and the operations of the economy. They are complementary modes of exclusion from the public life of the citizen.

If privilege is to be studied objectively, it is necessary to measure it in an analogous way to deprivation. Privilege arises at a particular point in the distribution of resources, which can be termed the 'wealth line'. It may be hypothesised that the wealth line marks a point in the distribution of resources at which the possibility of enjoying special benefits and advantages of a private sort escalates disproportionately to any increase in resources. The wealth line, like the poverty line, is a threshold point at which exclusionary mechanisms come into operation.

Figures 6.1 and 6.2 summarise the expected relationship between the wealth line and the poverty line under conditions of social democratic citizenship. These figures represent two different views of what is actually a three dimensional structure. The three dimensions are defined by (1) the total level of resources, (2) the total level of participation in social life, and (3) the level of participation in public life.[5] Figure 6.1 shows the relationship between dimension 1 and dimension 2, while Figure 6.2 shows the relationship between dimension 1 and dimension 3.

These figures should be regarded as illustrative rather than definitive. In particular, the fact that 'participation' is charted as a continuous variable should not be taken as suggesting that it is exclusively a quantitative matter. While it is true to say that the deprived are *less* able to participate in society than are full citizens, it is also the case that the nature of their participation is qualitatively *different*. In the same way, the range of normal citizen participation is shown as varying from lower to higher standards of living, but there are many qualitatively distinct lifestyles at each level in this range.

The figures attempt to show that the privileged have a total level of participation in social life, to the extent that this is quantitatively measurable, that is greater than that of other

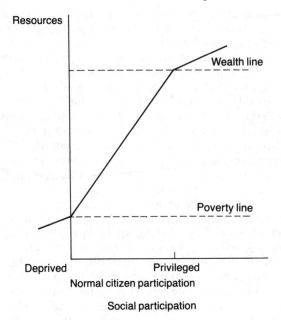

Figure 6.1 Resources and social participation

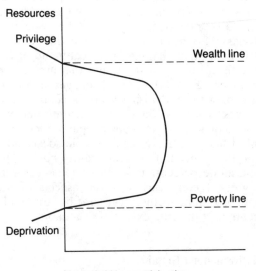

Figure 6.2 Resources and public participation

citizens and that this participation increases with resources (see Figure 6.1). At the same time their public participation as citizens may decrease: while the very wealthy – the privileged – are, in general, able to participate in society to a greater extent than other citizens, the nature of their participation is qualitatively distinct. The withdrawal of the privileged into an insulated and exclusive 'private' world, indicated by the turn of the curve at the upper level in Figure 6.2, leads them to have less participation in the public world than do other citizens. The majority of the population are neither privileged nor deprived – they participate fully, though in varying ways and at varying levels, in the lifestyle of the citizen. It is certain sections of the working class that become deprived, and it is certain sections of the middle class that are able to join the capitalist class in the realm of privilege.[6]

Runciman's work (1966) showed the way in which judgements of the relative standing of different groups in a society depend upon the accuracy of the knowledge that the various groups possess about other groups and the overall structure of inequality. This suggests some important aspects of the processes through which wealth and privilege come to be recognised. Gallie's summary of cross-national opinion surveys carried out in the 1970s has highlighted some important aspects of this. He has shown, for example, that workers in Britain have tended to define the privileged or wealthy group at the top of the economic hierarchy in very narrow terms, as compared with workers in France. Their immediate bosses and those who headed the large enterprises for which they worked were not seen as being especially 'privileged'. Instead, the top section of society was seen as a small 'aristocracy' or 'upper class'. It can be suggested that this reflects the lower degree of visibility that characterises wealth and privilege. While people may regard many of the things that are enjoyed by their employers as being 'luxuries' or advantages, most are likely to be unaware of who in British society is actually able to enjoy such privileges. There is, then, an inaccurate perception of the structure of inequality, which leads people to identify advantaged groups only where there are highly visible social indicators such as titles and the ownership of great country houses. Just as there may be inaccurate perceptions of the extent of poverty, despite a high degree of consensus over the aspects of lifestyle that constitute deprivation, so there can also be, for similar reasons, a misperception of the true extent of wealth.

Citizenship in modern Britain

The language of citizenship provides a framework of legitimation, a vocabulary of motive that draws on prevailing cultural ideas and provides the discursive conditions for discussions of social policy. The extent to which restrictions of class, gender, and ethnicity are challenged will depend on the nature and relative strengths of the various conceptions of citizenship that co-exist in a society. Similarly, forms of citizenship and attitudes towards them will vary from one society to another and from one period to another. In a society such as the United States, where a more purely liberal form of citizenship has been established, less deprivation and less privilege may be recognised than in a society where the social democratic concept has been institutionalised. In post-war Britain liberal and social democratic conceptions have co-existed in an uneasy combination, leading to research debates in which citizenship has become a highly contested concept. Much important work by British researchers, for example, has criticised welfare arrangements for their failure to fully match social democratic ideals.

Townsend's work combined two standards for the recognition of deprivation. On the one hand was Marshall's social democratic view, as reflected in the principal welfare institutions and in the widespread social recognition of a basic standard of living below which most people in modern Britain did not feel it acceptable to live. On the other hand was a radical concept of citizenship that assessed the extent of the discrepancy between actual and potential lifestyles. Townsend estimated the standard of living that would be available to all members of the society if its resources were to be distributed in an egalitarian way, and he then estimated the extent to which people were denied these opportunities by the actual structure of the distribution of resources. Much of Townsend's work has been directed towards showing that, in the British welfare state in the second half of the twentieth century, the number of people that were living in poverty was far greater than would be acceptable to social democratic opinion and that this number could be significantly reduced if resources were differently distributed.

A similar strategy has been used by Rentoul (1987), who adapts Townsend's radical view of poverty in order to estimate the level of wealth in Britain. He holds that the cut-off threshold for identifying the rich can be defined by the amount of money that is needed in order to eliminate poverty. His first step is to calculate the amount of money that would need to be redistributed to the deprived in order to eliminate their poverty. The second step is to estimate the point in the distribution of resources above which this amount of money could be made available through the imposition of taxes and a maximum income policy. Taking Mack and Lansley's (1985) study as his baseline, but updating it to 1986, he calculated that 10 million people were living in poverty and that £12,000 million a year would be required to remove their deprivation. In order to raise such a sum, he suggests, an income ceiling would have to be set at £22,000. This income might consist of £16,400 in salary, together with interest on personal assets of £110,000 (Rentoul 1987: 99). Interestingly, this figure corresponds closely to public perceptions of wealth. A study carried out in 1986 found that a majority of the population believed that a person with an annual income in excess of £20,000 and assets greater than £100,000 would be 'rich' (Schifferes 1986: iii). This level, then, can be suggested as a wealth line for 1986, and on this basis Rentoul identified 800,000 adults – 2 per cent of the adult population – as living a privileged existence above the wealth line.

Research into popular and official views of poverty also discloses the existence of competing conceptions of citizenship. Official calculations of the level of poverty, for example, vary not only with structural changes in the pattern of resource distribution, but also according to whether a liberal or social democratic criterion is used for the assessment of deprivation. For much of the post-war period official policy has reflected an acceptance of certain key elements in the social democratic conception of citizenship, but liberal conceptions have become far more prominent since the 1970s.

The dominance of social democratic citizenship within the British welfare system was associated with American dominance of the world economic system in the post-war period. This established an economic framework that underpinned Britain's adoption of 'Keynesian' economic policies and 'Fordist' practices in industry.[7] The dominance of social democracy could not survive the break-down of that economic pattern, which came under increasing strain during the 1960s and 1970s. Rights in health, welfare, and education were all eroded during the 1970s and 1980s through a comprehensive move away from universalism and towards greater 'selectivity' as successive governments attempted to consolidate state provision around more restricted liberal principles of welfare. A decade of 'Thatcherism' and the entry into the political arena of a generation of 'citizens' who were born when the decay of the post-war settlement was well under way raise the possibility that socially recognised standards of living may have altered in line with this restructuring of official citizenship rights (Goldthorpe 1984a; Sinfield 1986).

Within the strengthening liberal view of citizenship, individual effort and achievement have received much greater emphasis, and perceptions of the legitimacy of social inequalities have altered. As a result, the association between resources and participation that is shown in Figures 6.1 and 6.2 may also have begun to change. Resources remain unequally distributed – indeed, I have produced much evidence that they have become more unequally distributed as the commitment to equality has diminished – but a lack of resources is now less likely to be seen as an illegitimate departure from the lifestyle of a citizen. What was formerly regarded as the deprivation of a necessity may come to be seen, perhaps, as an incentive to greater effort. Popular and official perceptions of 'need' and 'necessity' may alter in such a way that fewer people are regarded as being 'deprived' of these necessities. In such circumstances, majority opinion might come to regard a low level of living as the acceptable ground floor of the house of citizenship.

To the extent that people come to believe that their society is open to ability and effort and that there are no socially generated obstacles to individual achievement – whatever the evidence to the contrary – a lack of resources and participation may come to be regarded as a necessary sanction on individual behaviour. The 'second class citizenship' of those who are dependent on dwindling state benefits may be seen in a positive light as an encouragement to greater effort which, effectively, re-establishes the Poor Law principle of less eligibility.

It might be anticipated that the consolidation of a purely liberal form of citizenship would strengthen these attitudes and result in a much greater willingness to countenance extremes of income and wealth (Smith 1989: 69–70). Government ministers have, in fact, already begun to reject estimates of poverty that are based on the Supplementary Benefit criterion that has been accepted in official estimates of poverty for most of the post-war period. Official recognition of poverty after the Second World War had been based on the 'subsistence' measures made by Beveridge, using methods similar to those of Rowntree. This official measure was, in fact, also taken up by governments in Australia, Canada, and South Africa. Townsend, the leading critic of this viewpoint, has argued that, for all its limitations, the Beveridge subsistence standard 'gave coherence to social security and it gave historical legitimacy to the formulation of citizens' rights' (1989: 27; see also Townsend and Gordon 1989). The defence of the official minimum by its fiercest critic was motivated by the government's decision in 1985 to abandon the idea of a subsistence minimum. The official view was that the welfare system had raised living standards and so had successfully achieved its goal of eliminating the kind of poverty that existed in the 1930s. Some ministers mischievously asserted that a relative view of poverty involved the use of value judgements and so the concept of poverty could, in modern Britain, be given no objective meaning. For this reason, they held, it should play no part in the determination of levels of welfare provision. If neither an absolute nor a relative standard of poverty can be used, the very concept of poverty must be abandoned. It was no longer necessary to compile the statistical measures that had, hitherto, been produced. Entitlement to income support was left unanchored in any other conception of a social minimum. The entitlement to benefit was *sui generis*: the minimum level of living for a citizen is whatever the government of the day says it is.

Townsend has claimed that this is reflected in a recent change in the procedures used by government statisticians to measure poverty and low income. A new series of statistics was introduced in 1988, and these were interpreted as showing a rise in the real incomes of the poorest 10 per cent of the population. Apart from a number of technical problems with these figures, Townsend pointed out that they are no longer related to the level of social assistance and so no longer constitute even an approximation to a properly relative concept of poverty. Indeed, the Director of Statistics at the DHSS confirmed this in his reply to Townsend's comments, as he suggested that the measured increase in the number living in poverty as a result of an increase in benefit levels constituted merely a 'spurious' increase in poverty. The assumption that was being made was that poverty is a matter of absolute living standards and not of deprivation relative to an officially recognised basic standard.[8]

Similarly, socially recognised standards of 'advantage' and 'luxury' may alter, and what was formerly regarded as the privileged enjoyment of a luxury may come to be seen as the natural and legitimate reward for achievement. The notions of privilege that survived into the nineteenth century and the first half of the twentieth century drew on older notions of public 'responsibility': the 'élite' of citizens who were fortunate enough to enjoy privileges that were not available to other members of society felt some obligation to help those in poverty through charity and philanthropic action. This sense almost of *noblesse oblige* co-existed with a liberal emphasis on self-help and private provision, and the establishment of a degree of social democratic citizenship in the post-war period supplemented these views with more universal principles of state provision. Social democracy also fostered the idea of equality of opportunity and the related ideas of 'merit' and 'ability' as justifications for inequalities of social condition. From a social democratic point of view, those inequalities that were legitimised on the grounds of merit or ability were to be contained by a framework of real equality of opportunity and a limitation on the overall extent of permissible inequality.

But the language of merit and ability was a two-edged sword, as it created the seeds of a system in which privileges could be legitimised as the rewards of effort and ability. The 'traditional' notion of the obligations of the privileged, rooted in ideas of the 'subject' rather than the 'citizen', had decayed as a significant ingredient in social order (Goldthorpe 1978). And when the official commitment to equality of opportunity also declined and the acceptable floor and ceiling levels of inequality were altered, the way was open for the dominance of a rhetoric of judgement in which existing inequalities, however extensive, were, *ipso facto*, to be judged as legitimate.

Such tendencies have become more marked over the past

decade or so. Changing attitudes have been most apparent in official policies and practices, and the *Breadline Britain* restudy has produced some evidence that social democratic views will remain a strong element in public opinion. In the climate that has been created by the erosion of the welfare state and the establishment of an 'enterprise culture' the rich have become less defensive about their privileges and less likely to feel any obligations towards the poor. The Townsend survey of London (Townsend *et al.* 1987) did produce some evidence that the wealthiest members of British society were more willing to countenance a greater degree of inequality among citizens and were less likely to recognise the existence of poverty. There were signs that the more conventional attitudes of compassion and a willingness to help the deprived were changing. These attitudes have been supplemented by a strengthening of fatalistic views. Fatalistic attitudes have become more widespread and deep-rooted, though they have always existed in a contradictory combination with more compassionate and critical views.

Fatalism creates the feeling that there is nothing that can be done about such poverty as exists. Poverty is seen as a result of impersonal and anonymous forces, such as the climate and international economic processes, that are beyond human control. For this reason, it is felt, there is no point in individuals worrying about it or trying to influence social policies that are, in any case, unable to affect these powerful forces. No matter how much, or how little, compassion might be felt for the poor, fatalism leads people to believe that there is simply nothing that can be done, either by governments or by individuals. Individuals should simply get on with their own lives, doing the best that they can for themselves. There is a fatalism about wealth as well as poverty. Gallie's summary of evidence on working-class attitudes, for example, showed that British workers recognised the importance of inheritance in the production of large fortunes, but they did not draw the conclusion that these fortunes were undeserved or that they should – or could – be eliminated through government policy. Inequality and inheritance were seen as residual features that had survived from the past and would continue in the future. There was nothing much that could be done about them and so they were, like the weather, simply to be accepted (Gallie 1983; see also M. Mann 1970).

This fatalism is congruent with the strengthened liberal views of welfare, and it complements the growing emphasis on ability and effort, and justifies the denial of reformism and welfare policies. It legitimates the pursuit of personal privileges by denying that they have any implications for the level of deprivation in society. A retired oil company executive living on a pension of £23,000 (at 1986 values) and with £100,000 in investments and a £100,000 house showed clearly the influence of such an outlook. For this man, poverty was seen in terms of hunger and starvation. It was a problem of the past in Britain and of the present only in less developed countries: 'The Third World. I tend to measure things by this. There are very serious problems there.' He believed that there were few poor people in Britain today, but accepted that the gap between rich and poor was too wide. He was unwilling to support any of the redistributive policies that had been current in social policy for much of the post-war period. Higher taxation of the income and wealth of the rich was not seen as a solution, and nor was an increase in welfare benefits, though he did suggest that many of those who were living in poverty were simply not claiming the benefits to which they were entitled. His preferred policy solution was a general rise in living standards through economic growth.[9]

A corporate acquisitions executive in a large clearing bank, earning a basic salary of £45,000, was even less willing to see any room for compassion in matters of income and wealth distribution. He did not believe that the gap between the rich and the poor was too wide, and so he saw no need for special policies aimed at closing it. The number of people who were living in poverty was very small, and this residual problem could be resolved through economic growth. He held, however, that many of those who were apparently in poverty and claiming benefits were not really entitled to them, and he felt that further cuts could safely be made in National Health Service expenditure without increasing the level of poverty. Here was a man, in his early forties, who was adopting a particularly strong and strident justification for inequality. These same attitudes were held by the group finance director of a large catering and entertainment firm, earning £45,000 and with £27,000 in investments, who supported a subsistence definition of poverty and saw unemployment as its main cause.

It seems clear from the London survey that harsh market-based attitudes are becoming more prominent in public discourse and policy options. This is also apparent in some of the results from Pahl's (1989) research on young merchant bankers, which suggests that the language of ability and effort had become especially strongly rooted in the 'yuppies' who epitomised the new harsh attitudes on income and wealth distribution. These people earned between £25,000 and £40,000 in 1988, but, as none of them claimed to feel rich, they felt no guilt about the level of their earnings relative to those in the professions and the public services – they did not compare themselves with those who were in manual work or were out of employment altogether. They worked long hours and so felt that their incomes were appropriate rewards for their efforts.

It is possible to recognise here an implicit acceptance of a market-based, functionalist justification of inequality – the existing distribution of resources is seen as a reflection of the relative importance of different kinds of employment. Such a view looks on inequality as a necessary aspect of the competitive drive to achievement in a market economy, and it is for this reason that inequality is seen as being both inevitable and just. The outcome of the competitive struggle to rise up the economic hierarchy is a system of stratification that rewards those who most deserve to be rewarded. It is held, for example, that the talented who have worked hard and employed their talents in the service of those activities that are in greatest demand by their fellow citizens have every right to enjoy a higher income. The distinguishing element of the 'Thatcherite' variant of this functionalist view was the claim that greater inequality – indeed, *unrestrained* inequality – provided the best possible framework for motivating the wealth-creators in society. This view was centred on the vision that attainable great wealth, and its unashamed enjoyment, would spur on entrepreneurs to ever greater achievements.

Pahl suggested that this individualistic and achievement-centred language was adopted by wealthy young financiers in a somewhat unreflective way, as they had little time or inclination to pursue its full implications. In discussion with a professor of sociology they were prepared to recognise some of its limitations and to recognise the validity of alternative viewpoints, but such discussions were hardly relevant to their day-to-day preoccupations. In everyday life this way of thinking was accepted unquestioningly and fatalistically. It would seem that a new language of discourse about inequality – centred on merit, ability, effort, and achievement as measured in the market – was becoming more widely accepted, uncritically and unreflectively, among those who had just begun their careers in what Pahl calls the 'K culture', a culture within which people were appraised solely by the number of thousands of pounds that they earned and in which all values were translated into monetary terms.

Is there an 'underclass'?

Changing attitudes of the kind that I have described have involved the resurgence of an imagery that dates back to the nineteenth century. In this imagery there is an attempt to distinguish those whose poverty is caused by factors that are beyond their control and those whose poverty can be regarded as being their own fault. Thus, Victorian liberal opinion had characterised those at the bottom of the economic hierarchy as the 'undeserving poor', a label that served to blame the poor for their own deprivation. The undeserving poor were the 'dangerous class', the major threat to social order. In more recent years commentators have spoken of an 'underclass', involving much the same kind of social imagery (Westergaard 1992). The immediate origins of the idea of the underclass can be found in the discussion of the 'culture of poverty' and the associated idea of a 'cycle of deprivation'. For many opponents of universal welfare provision in the 1960s and 1970s, these terms were employed to characterise the position of the poor. It was held that the environmental and cultural conditions of social deprivation generated characteristic patterns of motivation and attitude that were inimical to the kinds of educational and economic success that would allow individuals to escape from their poverty. The conditions of deprivation were self-perpetuating. 'Undeserving poor', 'culture of poverty', and 'underclass', then, can be seen as alternative images for describing and legitimating the subordinate position of the poor. But it is important to try to assess whether there may not be more to these ideas. The concept of the underclass, for instance, emerged first in academic social investigations and it only subsequently became a tool of political discourse. While such concepts may be used by the powerful and the privileged to blame the victims of poverty for their own circumstances, they may also point to important structural characteristics of poverty and inequality.

The intellectual value of the concepts of culture of poverty and underclass can be assessed by tracing the development of these ideas in the United States, where there has been considerable controversy over their relevance for social analysis. The Community Action Programs of the American governments of the early 1960s gave political expression to these concepts, promoting a social policy that was aimed at altering the community structures and cultural outlook that were seen as being responsible for the vicious circle through which poverty was reproduced over the generations (Moynihan 1969; see the review of the debate in Valentine 1968).

The 'Great Society' policy and its associated poverty programmes were inspired by President Kennedy's recognition of what he described as 'poverty amid plenty', but Kennedy was merely voicing conclusions that had been reached in the writings of Galbraith and Harrington. Galbraith (1958) had discerned the co-existence of what he called 'private affluence' and 'public squalor', while Harrington (1962), in a more radical vein, claimed to have discovered a part of American society that was set apart from and invisible to the mainstream of American society. This 'other America' was the America principally of impoverished inner-city African Americans, and Harrington maintained that the total number of American people living in poverty at the beginning of the 1960s was 40 million – about one fifth of the population. Such claims shocked public opinion, as the belief was widespread that poverty had disappeared with the development of the 'affluent society' of the post-war period. While it was recognised that large cities such as Chicago and New York had long histories of poverty in their inner city districts and that this poverty had increased during the depression years of the 1930s, it was widely held that full employment and economic growth had removed the final vestiges of this social problem. But, as Harrington remarked, the invisible poor of the 1960s were those who were 'at the wrong place in the economy at the wrong moment in history' (1962: 8).

The recognition of poverty in the slum districts of Chicago dated from a number of influential studies that had appeared since 1890. Riss's *How the Other Half Lives* (1890) had achieved some public attention at the turn of the century – though not so much as Booth's contemporary study of London – as did Breckinridge's *The Tenements of Chicago* (1936) (see Wilson and Aporite 1987). Chicago figured in American public opinion in much the same way as did London in British public opinion, and the period between the turn of the century and 1936 saw the appearance of a number of influential studies of the city by members of its University Department of Sociology. The context for much of the work that was undertaken by members of the Chicago school of sociology was Park and Burgess's *The City* (1925) and Wirth's classic essay 'Urbanism as a way of life' (1938). Inspired by these theoretical ideas, members of the school explored the slum conditions of the black ghetto, the most important of these studies being *The Ghetto* (Wirth 1928), *The Gold Coast and the Slum* (Zorbaugh 1929), and *The Negro Family in Chicago* (Frazier 1932).

The work undertaken by Frazier (1932, 1936, 1957) on African American families in the 1930s was highly influential. He focused his attention on the question of black poverty, seeing this as rooted in long-term changes in the social position of African Americans. Frazier held that the authentic 'peasant' culture of post-slavery rural black society had fragmented as African Americans moved north and east to settle in the big industrial cities. In these cities an emerging black middle class was adopting the dominant, white culture, while the poorer African Americans inhabited a 'disorganised' community and were socialised into a 'deviant' subculture. Urban migration had resulted in family breakdown and personal demoralisation for the black lower class. In Frazier, then, poverty and culture were seen as integrally linked to one another. He initiated a tradition of thought in which, as summarised in Valentine's critical review, 'the principal causes of the plight of the poor are found in the internal deficiencies of their own way of life' (1968: 28). Here, in germinal form, is the thesis of the culture of poverty.

It was in the work of the social anthropologist Oscar Lewis in the 1960s that the idea of the culture of poverty received its classic expression (1959, 1961, 1966). Lewis's work emphasised that deprivation was associated with a particular cultural outlook that reinforced that deprivation. Investigating the lives of poor Mexicans and Puerto Ricans in America, Lewis argued that the culture of poverty insulated the poor from the wider national culture and created a high degree of alienation and apathy among them. The poor were 'disengaged' and they rejected dominant values. Their culture centred around uncontrolled violence and sexuality and was manifested in gang formation, criminality, illegitimacy, and family breakdown. This deviant subcultural pattern was passed on from generation to generation through socialisation within the family. Shortly after Lewis's analysis of Mexican and Puerto Rican Americans, Daniel Moynihan (1965) produced a report on inner-city poverty that, restating Frazier's arguments, suggested that a similar culture of poverty could be found among poor black families. Such concerns were highlighted when Gunnar Myrdal (1962) coined the term 'underclass' to describe those who had become economically marginalised by the growth of what he called 'post-industrialism'.

Moynihan's report, written for the American Department of Labor, was entitled *The Negro Family: The Case for National Action*, and in it he claimed that social research had demonstrated the exclusion of African Americans from full citizenship in American society. Moynihan sought to mobilise social scientists in the search for a strategy to reverse this exclusion. Lyndon Johnson, then the American president, was convinced of the case and he planned a major speech to launch a new campaign against black poverty. The speech – delivered in June 1965 – was drafted by Moynihan and had been approved in advance by Martin Luther King and other civil rights leaders. The central tenet of the report and of the presidential speech was that black poverty could not be resolved through the general 'war on poverty' that had been launched by Kennedy. The poverty experienced by African American families was of a particular and deep-rooted kind that required special action.

In the wake of Johnson's speech, however, many activists in the civil rights movement along with many academic social scientists began to voice serious criticisms of Moynihan's argument. The principal point of contention was that Moynihan had highlighted 'the Negro family' as the main problem. This implied that the causes of black poverty were to be found in the structure of the disorganised family life of African Americans.

What, then, did Moynihan actually argue? Moynihan was concerned with what he saw as the deterioration of the fabric of black urban society in America. As a result of a historical accumulation of disadvantage and prejudice, of discrimination and social exclusion, 'the Negro community is . . . dividing between a stable middle-class group that is steadily growing stronger and more successful, and an increasingly disorganised and disadvantaged lower-class group' (Moynihan 1965: 5–6). But the emergence of a black middle class was not a sign that African Americans had achieved acceptance and full citizenship. On the contrary, Moynihan argued that the polarisation of African American society had proceeded hand in hand with a progressive deterioration in the very fabric of the lower-class black community. The inner-city black ghetto had become the focus of intensive and chronic deprivation. A symptom of this deprivation, and a contributory factor in its perpetuation, was the breakdown of the black lower-class family.

Moynihan highlighted four central processes in the deterioration of the African American family: a growth in marital breakdown, a rise in illegitimacy rates, the virtual disappearance of the male head of the household, and an increase in welfare dependency. He first showed that, by 1960, almost a quarter of African American marriages were likely to end in divorce or separation. At the same time there had been an increase in the illegitimacy rate among African Americans, the rate of increase being much higher than that for the general population. Between 1940 and 1963 the rate of illegitimacy in the African American community rose from 16.8 to 23.6 per cent. Divorce, separation, and illegitimacy meant that an ever larger proportion of black families were headed by women as 'single parents'. By 1963 this figure had reached almost 25 per cent, only a minority of black children reaching the age of eighteen in a two-parent household. Finally, this growing trend of family breakdown had led to rising levels of welfare dependency. At the time of Moynihan's investigation 14 per cent of black children were receiving Aid for Dependent Children (AFDC) social assistance, and a majority of black children received social assistance at some stage in their lives.

The roots of this 'deterioration' in African American family life, argued Moynihan, were to be found in the urbanisation that took place in a context that was shaped by the historical experience of slavery. Urbanisation produced inner-city slum conditions, and African Americans were disproportionately likely to be sucked into these slums. Drawing on the work of Frazier (1936), Moynihan saw this as the prime cause of family disorganisation:

In every index of family pathology – divorce, separation, and desertion, female family head, children in broken homes, and illegitimacy – the contrast between the urban and the rural environment for Negro families is unmistakable.

(1965: 19)

As a result, 'the Negro community has been forced into a matriarchal structure which . . . is . . . out of line with the rest of the American society' (Moynihan 1965: 29). Mainstream American society presumed male dominance and male leadership in both public and private affairs, and the African American community was disadvantaged by its cultural emphasis on matriarchy. Its members tended to find themselves unable 'to establish themselves as stable, effective units' (Moynihan 1965: 29) and so were unable to conform to the dominant social standards. They were, in this sense, denied the opportunities that were central to the status of citizenship. Even the black middle class was unable to escape from all of these disadvantages. Because of the segregation in housing that existed between black and white families, the African American middle classes lived in or near the inner-city slums and so were 'constantly exposed to the pathology of the disturbed group and constantly in danger of being drawn into it' (Moynihan 1965: 29–30).

The matriarchal structure of the African American community resulted in a poor record of educational attainment for black males, and Moynihan argued that this was responsible for characteristic patterns of disadvantage in the labour market. Young African American men grew up with little knowledge of their fathers or of their patterns and traditions of work – they had no male role models and so were not properly socialised for entry to the world of work. The result of this was a high level of alienation from the mainstream of American society. They withdrew even from those few channels of opportunity that were open to them and became involved in welfare dependency and drug use. Moynihan concluded that

Three centuries of injustice have brought about deep-seated structural distortions in the life of the Negro American. At this point, the present tangle of pathology is capable of perpetuating itself without assistance from the white world. The cycle can be broken only if these distortions are set right.

(1965: 47)

Moynihan's language and analysis are reminiscent of Victorian writings about the poor, though Moynihan regarded himself as a 'liberal' in the sphere of public policy.[10] He held that the problems of the black poor could be rectified only through a strategic policy formulated by the central government. The solution was for the national government to aim its social policy at the problem of the black family structure: African American families needed to be given the opportunity to live according to the dominant American pattern:

The policy of the United States is to bring the Negro American to full and equal sharing in the responsibilities and rewards of citizenship. To this end, the programs of the Federal government bearing on this objective shall be designed to have the effect, directly or indirectly, of enhancing the stability and resources of the Negro American family.

(1965: 48)

Moynihan's solution appears rather limited in relation to the 'problems' that he identified. While many of his remarks about African Americans and about the role of women might be regarded as rather patronising, he did document a very real process of economic exclusion and social disadvantage. But a solution that addresses itself to the features of family organisation rather than to aspects of the economic organisation of the society must be seen as, at best, a partial solution. This was, perhaps, why Moynihan's report and the presidential statement that followed it aroused such a political storm.

An important factor triggering this storm was a spate of 'race' riots in the late summer of 1965. The supposed 'disorganisation' of the urban lower-class African American family was seen by Moynihan as being most marked in the Harlem district of New York (Glazer and Moynihan 1963). In areas such as Harlem, he held, growing levels of unemployment and low pay had created the material circumstances that were responsible for social disorganisation. But the riots that proved fateful for the Moynihan report occurred on the other side of the continent, in the Watts district of Los Angeles. The eruption of street violence during an August weekend led many mass media commentators to turn to the Moynihan report for an explanation: they informed the public that the violence was a direct consequence of the disorganised state of the African American family and community.

This public use – and misuse – of the report proved fateful for subsequent research on poverty. The report was seen as stressing the causative role of African American family structure rather than the influence of the employment, housing, and deprivation with which that family structure was associated. Moynihan was widely seen as having blamed the African Americans themselves for their poverty. It must be said, however, that this misrepresentation was not completely without foundation, as Moynihan had concentrated on the symptoms rather than causes of poverty. Leaders of the black civil rights movement were perhaps justified in criticising Moynihan for having deflected public attention away from the need for structural change. It was clear, furthermore, that poverty was not exclusively a problem for America's ethnic minorities. Harrington had shown very clearly that the 'other America' included whites in the poor rural districts of the Appalachians and southern states and in the industrial towns of the north east as well as the African American and Hispanic families of the inner-city slums.

The acrimonious controversy that surrounded the Moynihan report led many radical writers to eschew the idea of an underclass of deprived and alienated African American families (see Rainwater and Yancey 1967; Moynihan 1969). Indeed, the fear that this idea would reinforce and encourage racism led to a virtual abandonment of research into inner-city ghetto conditions. The language of the underclass and the culture of poverty became the preserve of the New Right.

In Britain, also, the idea of the culture of poverty became increasingly associated with Conservative and New Right writings. The idea had been promoted by Sir Keith Joseph when he was secretary of state for social services during the early 1970s. At his instigation a programme of research into 'transmitted deprivation' was set up to investigate the so-called cycle of deprivation as it operated in Britain. Joseph's argument was that poverty persisted, despite economic improvement, because of deep-lying factors within the structure of the family itself: 'People who were themselves deprived in one or more ways in childhood become in turn the parents of another generation of deprived children' (Joseph 1972, quoted in Rutter and Madge 1976). The family was at the core of the vicious circle that reproduced poverty. Poverty would not, therefore, be eliminated through income redistribution or through higher welfare payments. What was required was a change in the attitudes and values of poor families.

A review of evidence on the cycle of disadvantage in Britain started out from a recognition that there was inter-generational continuity of economic position: those born poor were likely to grow up to have children who would live in poverty; and those who were born wealthy were likely to have children who were destined for wealth (Rutter and Madge 1976). The crucial question, of course, was whether this continuity could be explained as the outcome of a cyclical cultural process rooted in the attitudes and motivation of individuals. Rutter and Madge, the authors of the review, held that the culture of poverty idea, whatever its relevance to the United States might be, had no application to the situation of the poor in Britain (1976: 30). Inter-generational continuities occurred in Britain with respect to education, occupation, criminality, health, and economic circumstances, but this was by no means inevitable and deterministic. Significant numbers of individuals 'escaped' the cycle; and large numbers of newcomers became deprived as first-generation 'entrants'. Rutter and Madge concluded that 'familial cycles are a most important element in the perpetuation of disadvantage, but they account for only a part of the overall picture' (1976: 304).

Joseph's views, unsubstantiated by the research that he promoted, gave life to Conservative use of the ideas of the culture of poverty and the underclass. As Conservative writers became increasingly drawn to the idea of the underclass, so radicals abandoned it as irretrievably value-laden. Conservative commentators rejected structural explanations of inner city poverty of the kind that had been proposed by researchers such as Gans, who had explained inner city poverty in terms of the limited economic opportunities that were available to poor families. Instead, they emphasised the role of cultural factors, and the cultural values of the underclass were seen as being responsible for its members' continuing deprivation. These values, they held, were in conflict with the work ethic, and they were passed on from generation to generation, through socialisation and internalisation. The result was the creation of a 'culture of poverty' which reinforced long-term poverty and welfare dependence.

This led to very specific views about social policy. The American commentator Charles Murray (1984, 1990), for example, claimed that reformist social policies were a major contributory factor in the perpetuation of poverty. Welfare benefits were frequently *too high* and encouraged people to prefer welfare to work. The unemployment benefit that could be received by a single, unmarried mother in Britain, Murray claimed, was so high that many unmarried women were able to have a baby without worrying about the consequences (1990: 29). Such benefits could be significantly reduced, so inducing these women to remain in work or to marry.

For Murray, the concept of the underclass refers not to the fact of poverty or to its extent, but to a particular *type* of poverty. Whereas the majority of the poor 'simply lived with low incomes' or were 'doing their best under difficult circumstances' (1990: 1, 2), the underclass comprised what British writers of the nineteenth century had described as the undeserving or disreputable poor. In language reminiscent of Booth, Murray describes the members of the underclass as being those whose poverty is associated with particular deviant patterns of behaviour: they had dirty and unkempt houses, they were unable to hold a job, they were characterised by drunkenness and criminality, and so on (1990: 1). They were the ne'er-do-wells, who contaminated all those with whom they came into contact.

Murray identified three main indicators of underclass membership. The first of these was that underclass members 'drop out' from the labour force: 'large numbers of young, healthy, low-income males choose not to take jobs' (1990:17). The consequence of this was the disappearance of the work ethic and a consequent decline into barbarism. These young males do not work and do not marry:

Men who do not support families find other ways to prove that they are men, which tend to take various destructive forms. . . . Young men are essentially barbarians for whom marriage . . . is an indispensable civilising force.

(1990: 23)

The second indicator was a high rate of illegitimacy, which Murray regarded as symptomatic of deviant attitudes towards family and parenthood. Illegitimacy rates, he claimed, were rising and were concentrated among the unskilled and the unemployed. The result is communities without families and children without fathers. The withdrawal of young men from the workforce, then, was reinforced by a general lack of discipline and by the absence of appropriate male 'role models' who would demonstrate the work ethic and the morality of responsible parenthood. The third indicator of underclass membership was violent crime:

'the habitual criminal is the classic member of the underclass' (1990: 13). The disorganised 'community' generates a criminal subculture.

Wilson's influential study of inner-city poverty (1987) has sought to rescue the concept of the underclass from its usage by the New Right and to use it, instead, in the radical way that Myrdal had originally intended. He shows, like Moynihan, that the problem of urban poverty in the United States is essentially a *racial* problem that is rooted in the specific historical processes through which the ghettos had been produced and transformed.

African Americans in Harlem and other ghettos in the 1930s suffered deprivation, but they were characterised by 'social organisation' and not disorganisation. They had 'a sense of community, positive neighbourhood identification, explicit norms and sanctions against aberrant behaviour' (Wilson 1987: 3). Such communities were characterised by 'a vertical integration of different segments of the urban black population' (Wilson 1987: 7). Middle-class, working-class, and lower-class African Americans were all found in the same community and used the same facilities. There was a diversity of economic circumstances that was overlaid by a common experience of ghetto life. Black doctors tended black patients, for example, and black children were taught by black teachers. The presence of middle-class and working-class African Americans 'provided stability to inner-city neighbourhoods and reinforced and perpetuated mainstream patterns of norms and behaviour' (Wilson 1987: 7).[11]

By the 1960s this had changed. Wilson claims that

Poverty in the United States has become more urban, more concentrated, and more firmly implanted in large metropolises, particularly in the older industrial cities with immense and highly segregated black and Hispanic residents.

(1991)

There was considerable social dislocation and social disorganisation in the inner cities by the 1960s. The black middle class and black working class had moved out of the ghettos to the suburbs, and the ghettos were now occupied exclusively by the most deprived African Americans. As economic conditions for inner-city residents worsened during the 1970s and 1980s, these people were left in a state of 'disorganisation' by the absence of other classes. A continuing presence of the middle and working classes would have created a 'social buffer' against the worst of the effects of the economic dislocations of the 1970s and 1980s. Wilson holds that

even if the truly disadvantaged segments of an inner-city area experience a significant increase in long-term spells of joblessness, the basic institutions in that area (churches, schools, stores, recreational facilities, etc.) would remain viable if much of the base of their support comes from the more economically stable and secure families. Moreover, the very presence of these families during such periods provides mainstream role models that help keep alive the perception that education is meaningful, that steady employment is a viable alternative to welfare, and that family stability is the norm, not the exception.

(1987: 56)

Instead, large American cities produced the same kind of slum conditions that had characterised London and other large British cities in the nineteenth century. Inner-city districts were occupied by an underclass of low-income families and individuals who were living in truly deprived circumstances and whose behaviour contrasted sharply with the behaviour of the general population.

Wilson holds that the term 'underclass', which had been appropriated by Conservative writers, must be used to describe the inner-city deprivation of American cities today. The deprived inner-city African Americans are 'individuals who lack training and skills and either experience long-term unemployment or are not members of the labor force, individuals who are engaged in street crime and other forms of aberrant behaviour, and families that experience long-term spells of poverty and/or welfare dependency' (1987: 8).

Most inner-city families experience periods of long-term unemployment, and they lack the kinds of social networks and connections through which jobs might be obtained. They seldom interact with others who are in steady employment and so joblessness and welfare dependence become a way of life. Children see no point in acquiring work skills, and so they grow into adults who are unlikely to find opportunities for employment: 'A vicious cycle is perpetuated through the family, through the community, and through schools' (Wilson 1987: 57).

In short, the communities of the underclass are plagued by massive joblessness, flagrant and open lawlessness, and low-achieving schools, and therefore tend to be avoided by outsiders. Consequently, the residents of these areas, whether women and children of welfare families or aggressive street criminals, have become increasingly socially isolated from mainstream patterns of behaviour.

(Wilson 1987: 58)

Wilson concludes that the key idea is not that of the 'culture of poverty' but that of *social isolation*. The central issue is the nature of the contacts that exist between groups with different class and ethnic backgrounds. Culture is a response to structural constraints and opportunities: it is possible to change the culture of the underclass by altering its opportunities and constraints. A central feature of this structural change must be to reduce their social isolation from larger networks of social relations (1987: 137–8). Wilson's position is, then, less pessimistic – in some senses – than that of the culture of poverty writers. The cultural traits are not so deeply ingrained that we have virtually to write off the present generation and look to educational changes to shape future generations. It is possible to alter the economic constraints and opportunities, and people's cultural outlook will alter in response to this.

A number of social democratic and radical writers in Britain have, also, seen a sociological value in the concept of the underclass (Field 1989; Giddens 1973; Dahrendorf 1987; see also Runciman 1989; K. Mann 1992; Bagguley and Mann 1992). Field has accepted much of Murray's diagnosis, though he argues that the underclass does not have the racial characteristics that were found in the United States, and he rejects the 'culture of poverty' explanation. Such a view leads him to a structural conception of the underclass. Like Wilson and Myrdal before him, Field rejects the moralism of the New Right and looks to structural causes of the existence of an underclass.[12] The groups that make up the underclass in Britain, he claims, are very frail, elderly pensioners and single parents with no chance of escaping welfare dependence under the existing social assistance rules. The growth of poverty in single-parent, female-headed households, which is seen by Murray as an indicator of illegitimacy and deviant social values, has been seen by more radical writers as pointing to a fundamental 'feminisation' of poverty (Glendinning and Miller 1987).

In his most recent work, however, Wilson (1991) has begun to distance himself from the concept of the underclass, while maintaining his emphasis on social isolation. His reasons for this lie in criticisms made by writers such as Gans (1990), who argued that the term had become virtually synonymous with the phrase 'inner-city blacks' and that it functioned simply as a restatement of the nineteenth-century idea of the undeserving poor. Wilson has, therefore, begun to talk of the 'ghetto poor' rather than the underclass. This viewpoint accords with the conclusions of many British commentators. Alan Walker, for example, holds that the 1980s produced 'a severely deprived group' in Britain but that this cannot be described as an underclass (Walker 1990a; see also Walker 1990b; Walker and Walker 1987).[13] Walker argues that the problem of poverty worsened significantly during the 1980s and that there has been a growing polarisation of living standards between the poor and the rich:

At one extreme there is a severely deprived group whose behaviour is predictably influenced by their abject poverty but who still do not resemble an underclass in any sociological sense.

(1990b: 16)

They are not alienated from the rest of society and their position is not the outcome of the inter-generational transmission of pathological values. Those differences in lifestyle that separate them from the mainstream of society are a manifestation of the poverty that deprives them of choice. At the other extreme are the wealthy, living an exclusive and distinct lifestyle that is a true result of choice.

I have tried to show that deprivation and privilege can be understood as polarised departures from the normal range of lifestyles that are enjoyed by the citizens of a society. These two social conditions, then, are not to be understood as being simply the 'bottom' and the 'top' sections of a statistically defined hierarchy. They are distinct conditions and social statuses defined, in many situations, by 'catastrophic' boundaries in the distribution of resources. These boundaries are to be seen as the consequence of processes of exclusion. The deprived are excluded from public life, while the privileged are able to exclude the mass of the public from the enjoyment of their special advantages. Yet it would be a mistake to see these status divisions and differences in standard of living and lifestyle as corresponding in any simple way to class divisions. If it is incorrect to describe the deprived as an 'underclass', it is equally misguided to identify it with a 'working class'. Similarly, the privileged – sometimes semi-seriously misdescribed as an 'overclass' – should not be equated with an upper or capitalist class.

A modern capitalist society generates complex patterns of class division, which can be understood, at its simplest, as involving a division into a capitalist class, a service class, and a working class.[14] The capitalist class is structured by the system of capital mobilisation that exists in a society (Scott 1991a), while the working class is structured by the nature of its labour market. The service class owes its position in the structure of economic power to the intersection of both of these systems of class structuring, and this has led some to describe them as occupying a 'contradictory class location' (Wright 1978; on the service class more generally see Goldthorpe 1982).

The operations of the labour market and the system of capital mobilisation, under the prevailing conditions of state intervention and redistribution that follow from the society's pattern of citizenship, produce a distribution of resources that can be described in statistical terms (see Figure 6.3). The distribution may, for example, follow the pattern of the 'normal distribution', or it may be more or less skewed towards one 'tail' or the other. Variations in the shape of the distribution over time and from one society to another have constituted a principal focus for the majority of studies of inequality that have been undertaken. The statistical categories that are identified in the distribution of resources must not, however, be confused with social classes and their underlying class locations or with the polarised conditions of privilege and deprivation.

Privilege and deprivation are most likely to be identified as sharply bounded and polarised conditions when there are sharp

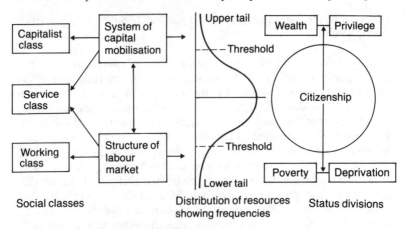

Social classes   Distribution of resources   Status divisions
                        showing frequencies

*Figure 6.3 **Poverty, wealth and the class structure***

thresholds in the distribution of resources that define the wealth line and the poverty line as points of catastrophic escalation. In some circumstances, the capitalist class may comprise all of those whose resources place them above the wealth line, and in these circumstances there will be a direct correspondence between that class and the category of the privileged. But such circumstances are unusual. While the advantages of the wealthy are dependent on the resources that are generated in the system of capital mobilisation, these advantages can rarely be monopolised by the capitalist class alone. More typically, the privileged in a society will comprise its capitalist class together with some of those at the upper levels of the service class.

In a similar way, the resources of many of those within the working class are sufficient to allow them to live the life of an ordinary citizen, and so the 'lower tail' of the distribution of resources will normally include only a part of the working class. As I have shown in my review of the American debate on the so-called 'underclass', the deprived in a society are likely to include disproportionate numbers of those who are excluded from full citizenship rights on such grounds as 'race' and ethnicity.

Questions of class analysis, then, are highly germane to the questions of poverty and wealth, but these are to be seen as social statuses that arise from the ways in which the status of citizen is institutionalised in a society and enters into complex interrelations with its class system.

Notes

1   The general concepts of status and status divisions are usefully reviewed in Turner (1988), which explores the 'politico-legal' and the cultural aspects of status.

2   See also Turner (1990). On the development of citizenship in European nation states and in Japan see Bendix (1964) and Heater (1990).

3   The emphasis on adults is qualified by a recognition of the rights of children. Equally, the radical view tends to link with wider concerns over the (non-citizen) rights of animals and of responsibility to the natural environment. The radical view is influential in the 'New Times' debate, and is outlined in Hall and Held (1989). See also Lister (1990).

4   It is surprising that this striking fact has gone unremarked by researchers in the past, as it offers important clues to the analysis of privilege. I owe the recognition to Williams (1976; 203–4).

5   Any continuous scale will show three levels of social participation: deprived, normal, and privileged.

6   It is important to note that those who are privileged are not simply to be equated with the capitalist or upper class. This class is discussed more fully in Scott (1991a, 1982). See also the discussion of 'civic gain' in Lockwood (1986).

7   This argument draws on the varying arguments of Gamble (1988) and Hall and Jacques (1983). See also Jordan (1987).

8   These arguments were made in an exchange of letters in the *Guardian* on 30 May, 16 and 30 June, and 14 July 1988.

9   This and the following paragraph draw on unpublished data from the Townsend *et al.* study (1987). I am grateful to Peter Townsend for allowing me access to this material.

10 In American usage, 'liberal' denotes social democratic or radical views.

11 Wilson's study, of Chicago, is referring to the kinds of ideas set out in Suttles (1968).

12 Murray's comment on Field's contribution to Murray (1990) points out that Field defines the underclass by its *condition* and not by its *behaviour* or cultural attributes.

13 See on this debate Lister (1990) and Golding (1986).

14 It hardly needs to be said that this is too simple to serve as an adequate description of the class structure of any modern society. My purpose is to try to make the general links between class location and status divisions as clear as possible.

BIBLIOGRAPHY

Abel-Smith, B. and Townsend, P. (1965) 'The Poor and the Poorest', *Occasional Papers on Social Administration*, 17, London: Bell.

Abercrombie, N., Hills, S. and Turner, B. (1980) *The Dominant Ideology Thesis*, London: George Allen and Unwin.

Abercrombie, N., Hills, S. and Turner, B. (1983) *Sovereign Individuals of Capitalism*, London: George Allen and Unwin.

Abercrombie, N., Hills, S. and Turner, B. (1990) *Dominant Ideologies*, London: Unwin Hyman.

Atkinson, A. B. (1969) *Poverty in Britain and the Reform of Social Security*, Cambridge University Press.

Atkinson, A. B. (1972) *Unequal Shares*, Harmondsworth: Allen Lane, (revised edition, Penguin, 1973).

Atkinson, A. B. (1973 ed.), *Wealth, Income and Inequality*, Harmondsworth: Penguin.

Atkinson, A. B. (1975) *The Economics of Inequality*, Oxford: Clarendon Press, (2nd edition 1983).

Atkinson, A. B. (1990) 'Comparing Poverty Rates Internationally', *Welfare State Programme Discussion Paper*, WSP/53, London School of Economics.

Bagguley, P. and Mann, K. (1992) 'Idle Thieving Bastards: Scholarly Representations of the Underclass', *Work, Employment and Society*, 6.

Bateman, J. (1876) *The Great Landowners of Great Britain and Ireland*, Fourth Edition 1883, Leicester University Press, 1971.

Bean, P. and Whynes, D. eds (1986) *Barbara Wootton: Social Science and Public Policy*, London: Tavistock.

Bendix, R. (1964) *Nation Building and Citizenship*, New York: John Wiley.

Beresford, P. ed. (1990) *The Sunday Times Book of the Rich*, London: Weidenfeld and Nicolson.

Beveridge, W. (1942) *Social Insurance and Allied Services*, CMD 6404, London: HMSO.

Booth, C. (1889) *A Descriptive Map of London Poverty*, London Topographical Society, 1984.

Booth, C. (1902–3) *Life and Labour of the People of London*, 17 vols, London: Macmillan.

Bowley, A. L. (1920) 'Changes in the Distribution of National Incomes, 1883–1913', in Bowley (1938) *Three studies on the National Income*, London: London School of Economics.

——and Burnett-Hurst, A. R.(1915) *Livelihood and Poverty*, London: G. Bell.

——and Hogg, M. (1925) *Has Poverty Diminished?*, London: P. S. King.

——and Stamp, J. C. (1924) 'The National Income', in Bowley (1938) *Three studies on the National Income*, London: London School of Economics.

Bradshaw, J. (1992) *Household Budgets and Living Standards*, Social Policy Research Findings, no. 31, Joseph Rowntree Foundation, York.

Breckinridge, S. (1936) *The Tenements of Chicago 1908–35*, University of Chicago Press.

Burawoy, M. and Krotov, P. (1992) 'The Soviet transition from socialism to capitalism', *American Sociological Review*, 57.

Carlyle, T. (1831) 'Characteristics', *Edinburgh Review*, 54, No. 108.

Castles, S. and Kosack, G. (1973) *Immigrant Workers and the Class Structure in Western Europe*, Oxford University Press.

Checkland, S. G. and Checkland, E. O. A. (eds), (1974) *The Poor Law Report of 1834*, Harmondsworth: Penguin.

Chiozza-Money, L. G. (1905) *Riches and Poverty*, London: Methuen.

Crompton, R. and Mann. (eds) (1986) *Gender and Stratification*, Cambridge: Polity Press.

Crosland, C. A. R. (1956) *The Future of Socialism*, London: Jonathan Cape.

Crowther, M. A. (1981) *The Workhouse System 1834–1929*, London: Batsford.

CSO (1990) *Households Below Average Income, 1981–1987*, London: HMSO.

D'Aeth, F. G. (1910) 'Present tendencies of class differentiation', *Sociological Review*, 3.

Dahrendorf, R. (1987) 'The erosion of citizenship', *New Statesman*, 12 June.

Daumard, A. (1980) 'Wealth and affluence in France since the beginning of the nineteenth century', in Rubinstein 1980.

Dean, M. (1991) *The Constitution of Poverty*, London: Routledge.

Desai, M. (1986) 'Drawing the line', in Golding 1986.

DHSS (1969) *The Right to Help*, Department of Health and Social Security, London: HMSO.

Diamond Commission (1975) *Royal Commission on the Distribution of Income and Wealth*, Reports nos 2 and 3, CMD 6172/6173, London: HMSO.

Digby, A. (1989) *British Welfare Policy*, London: Faber & Faber.

Disraeli, B. (1981) *Sibyl*, Oxford: Oxford University Press.

Drucker, P. (1976) *The Unseen Revolution: How Pension Fund Socialism Came to the United States*, New York: Harper and Row.

EC (1984) *Council Decisions on Specific Community Action to Combat Poverty*, Council of the European Community, Article 1.2, 85/8/EEC, Brussels.

Eden, F. (1797) *The State of the Poor*, 3 vols, London: J. Davis.

Elias, N. (1970) *What is Sociology?*, London: Hutchinson, 1978.

Engels, F. (1845) *The Condition of the Working Class in England*, London: Panther, 1969.

Field, F. (1989) *Losing Out*, Oxford: Basil Blackwell.

Fraser, D. (1973) *The Growth of the British Welfare State*, London: Macmillan.

Frayman, H. (1991) *Breadline Britain 1990s*, London: London Weekend Television.

Frazier, E. F. (1932) *The Negro Family in Chicago*, University of Chicago Press.
——(1936) *The Negro in the United States*, New York: Macmillan.
——(1957) *Black Bourgeoisie*, New York: Macmillan.
Galbraith, J. K. (1958) *The Affluent Society*, Harmondsworth: Penguin, 1962.
Gallie, D. (1983) *Social Inequality and Class Radicalism in France and Britain*, Cambridge University Press.
Gamble, A. (1988) *The Free Economy and the Strong State*, London: Macmillan.
Gans, H. J. (1990) 'Deconstructing the underclass', *Journal of the American Planning Association*, 56.
George, V. and Howard, I. (1991) *Poverty Amidst Affluence*, Cheltenham: Edward Elgar.
George, V. and Lawson, R. (1980) *Poverty and Inequality in Common Market Countries*, London: Routledge & Kegan Paul.
Giddens, A. (1973) *The Class Structure of the Advanced Societies*, London: Hutchinson.
——(1981) 'Class division, class conflict and citizenship rights', in Giddens 1982.
——(1982) *Profiles and Critiques in Sociology*, London: Macmillan.
——and Mackenzie, G. (eds) (1982) *Social Class and the Division of Labour*, Cambridge University Press.
Giesen, B. and Haferkamp, H. (eds) (1987) *Soziologie der sozialen Ungleichheit*, Opladen, Westdeutscher Verlag.
Glazer, N. and Moynihan, D. P. (1963) *Beyond the Melting Pot*, Cambridge: MIT Press and Harvard University Press.
Glendinning, C. and Miller, J. (eds) (1987) *Women and Poverty in Britain*, Hassocks: Wheatsheaf.
Goffman, E. (1961) *Asylums*, Harmondsworth: Penguin, 1968.
——(1963) *Stigma*, Harmondsworth: Penguin, 1968.
Golding, P. (ed.) (1986) *Excluding the Poor*, London: Child Poverty Action Group.
Goldthorpe, J. H. (1978) 'The current inflation: towards a sociological account', in Fittirsch and Goldthorpe (eds) 1978 *The Political Economy & Inflation*, Oxford: Martin Robertson.
——(1982) 'On the service class, its formation and future', in Giddens and Mackenzie 1982.
——(1983) 'Women and class analysis: in defence of the conventional view', *Sociology*, 17.
——(1984a) 'The end of convergence: corporatist and dualist tendencies in modern western societies', in Goldthorpe 1984b.
——(ed.) (1984b) *Order and Conflict in Contemporary Society*, Oxford: Clarendon Press.
Hall, S. and Held, D. (1989) 'Left and right', *Marxism Today*, June.
——and Jacques, M. (eds) (1983) *The Politics of Thatcherism*, London: Lawrence & Wishart.
Hannah, L. (1976) *The Rise of the Corporate Economy*, London: Methuen.
——(1986) *Inventing Retirement*, Cambridge University Press.
Harbury, C. and Hitchens, D. M. W. N. (1979) *Inheritance and Wealth Inequality in Britain*, London: George Allen & Unwin.

Harrington, M. (1962) *The Other America*, New York: Macmillan.

Heater, D. (1990) *Citizenship: The Civic Ideal in World History, Politics and Education*, Harlow: Longman.

Hollingshead, J. (1861) *Ragged London in 1861*, London: Dent, 1986.

Ignatieff, M. (1978) *A Just Measure of Pain*, New York: Pantheon.

Jaher, F. C. (1980) 'The gilded elite: American multimillionaires, 1865 to the present', in Rubinstein 1980.

Jordan, B. (1987) *The State*, Oxford: Basil Blackwell.

Jowell, R., Witherspoon, S. and Brook, L. (eds) (1989) *British Social Attitudes*, Aldershot: Gower.

Keating, P. (ed.) (1976) *Into Unknown England*, Glasgow: Fontana.

Kincaid, J. C. (1973) *Poverty and Equality in Britain*, Harmondsworth: Penguin.

King, D. S. and Waldron, J. (1988) 'Citizenship, social citizenship and the defence of welfare provision', *British Journal of Political Science*, 18.

Knightly, P. (1981) *The Vestiery Affair*, London: Macdonald.

Kryshtanovskaya, O. (1993) 'The emerging business elite', in Lane 1993.

Land, H. (1969) *Large Families in London*, London: Bell.

Lane, D. S. (ed.) (1993) *Russia in Flux*, Cheltenham: Edward Elgar.

Lawson, R. (1980) 'Poverty and inequality in West Germany', in George and Lawson 1980.

Lawson, R. and George, V. (1980) 'An assessment', in George and Lawson 1980.

Lewis, O. (1959) *Five Families*, New York: Basic Books.

———(1961) *The Children of Sanchez*, New York: Random House.

———(1966) *La Vida*, New York: Random House.

Lister, R. (1990) *The Exclusive Society*, London: Child Poverty Action Group.

Llewellyn Smith, H. (1932) *The New Survey of London Life and Labour, Survey of Social Conditions: The Eastern Area*, London: P. S. King.

———(1934) *The New Survey of London Life and Labour, Survey of Social Conditions: The Western Area*, London: P. S. King.

Lockwood, D. (1986) 'On the incongruity of power and status', in Strasser and Hodge 1986.

———(1987) 'Schichtung in der Staatsburgergesellschaft', in Giesen and Haferkamp 1987.

Lundberg, F. (1937) *America's Sixty Families*, New York: Vanguard Press.

McAuley, A. (1993) 'Poverty and underprivileged groups in the USSR', in Lane 1993.

Macpherson, C. B. (1962) *The Political Theory of Possessive Individualism*, Oxford University Press.

Mack, J. and Lansley, S. (1985) *Poor Britain*, 1st edn, London: George Allen & Unwin; 2nd edn, London: Routledge, 1993.

Mann, K. (1992) *The Making of an English Underclass*, Milton Keynes: Open University Press.

Mann, M. (1970) 'The social cohesion of liberal democracy', *American Sociological Review*, 35.

———(1986) 'A crisis in stratification theory', in Crompton and Mann 1986.

———(1987) 'Ruling class strategies and citizenship', in Mann 1988.

——(1988) *States, War and Capitalism*, Oxford: Basil Blackwell.
Marriott, O. and Jones, R. (1967) *The Property Boom*, London: Hamish Hamilton.
Marsden, D. (1969) *Mothers Alone*, London: Allen Lane.
Marshall, D. (1965) *The English Poor in the Eighteenth Century*, London: Routledge & Kegan Paul.
Marshall, T. H. (1949) 'Citizenship and social class', in Marshall 1963.
——(1963) *Sociology at the Crossroads*, London: Heinemann.
——(1965) *Social Policy*, London: Hutchinson.
Marx, K. (1864) *Capital*, vol. 3, Moscow: Progress Publishers, 1972.
Mass Observation (1943) *The Pub and the People*, London: Century Hutchinson, 1987.
Matthews, M. (1978) *Privilege in the Soviet Union*, London: Allen and Unwin.
——(1986) *Poverty in the Soviet Union*, Cambridge: Cambridge University Press.
Mayhew, H. (1861) *London Labour and the London Poor*, London: Frank Cass, 1967.
Mead, L. (1986) *Beyond Entitlement*, New York: Free Press.
Mills, C. W. (1956) *The Power Elite*, New York: Oxford University Press.
Minns, R. (1980) *Pensions Funds and British Capitalism*, London: Heinemann.
——(1982) *Take Over the City*, London: Pluto Press.
Morrison, A. (1896) *A Child of the Jago*, London: Penguin, 1946.
Moss, D. and Rogers, E. (1980) 'Poverty and inequality in Italy', in George and Lawson 1980.
Moynihan, D. P. (1965) *The Negro Family*, Washington DC: Office of Policy, Planning and Research, US Department of Labor. Reprinted in Rainwater and Yancey 1967.
——(1969) *Maximum Feasible Misunderstanding*, New York: Free Press.
Murray, C. (1984) *Losing Ground*, New York: Basic Books.
——(1990) *The Emerging British Underclass*, London: Institute of Economic Affairs.
Myrdal, G. (1962) *Challenge to Affluence*, London: Victor Gollancz.
Novak, T. (1988) *Poverty and the State*, Milton Keynes: Open University Press.
Oppenheim, C. (1990) *Poverty: The Facts*, London: Child Poverty Action Group.
Pahl, R. E. (1989) 'St Matthews and the golden handcuffs', Unpublished paper, Darwin College, University of Kent.
Park, R. and Burgess, E. W. (1925) *The City*, University of Chicago Press, 1967.
Pember Reeves, M. (1913) *Round About a Pound a Week*, London: Virago.
Perkin, H. (1969) *The Origins of English Society*, London: Routledge & Kegan Paul.
Rainwater, L. and Yancey, W. L. (eds) (1967) *The Moynihan Report and the Politics of Controversy*, Cambridge: MIT Press.
Rentoul, J. (1987) *The Rich Get Richer*, London: Unwin Hyman.

Reports from Commissioners (1834) *Poor Laws*, Session 4 February to 15 August 1834, vol. 27. Reprinted in Checkland and Checkland 1974.

Return (1874a) *Return of Owners of Land, 1872–3*, England and Wales, Parliamentary Papers, 72, pts I and II.

——(1874b) *Return of Owners of Land*, Scotland, Parliamentary Papers, 72, pt III.

——(1876) *Return of Owners of Land*, Ireland, Parliamentary Papers, 80.

Rifkin, J. and Barber, R. (1978) *The North Will Rise Again*, Boston: Beacon Press.

Riss, J. (1890) *How the Other Half Lives*, New York: Scribner.

Roche, M. (1992) *Rethinking Citizenship*, Cambridge: Polity Press.

Room, G. (ed.) (1990) *'New Poverty' in the European Community*, London: Macmillan.

Rose, M. (1971) *The English Poor Law, 1745–1834*, London: Macmillan.

Rowntree, B. S. (1901) *Poverty: A Study of Town Life*, London: Macmillan.

——(1937) *The Human Needs of Labour*, London: Longmans Green.

——(1941) *Poverty and Progress*, London: Longmans Green.

——and Lavers, G. R. (1951) *Poverty and the Welfare State*, London: Longmans Green.

Rubinstein, W. D. (ed.) (1980) *Wealth and the Wealthy in the Modern World*, London: Croom Helm.

——(1981) *Men of Property*, London: Croom Helm.

——(1986) *Wealth and Inequality in Britain*, London: Faber & Faber.

Runciman, W. G. (1966) *Relative Deprivation and Social Justice*, London: Routledge & Kegan Paul.

——(1989) 'How many classes?', *Sociology*, 23.

Rutter, M. and Madge, N. (1976) *Cycles of Disadvantage*, London: Heinemann.

Scase, R. and Goffee, R. (1982) *The Entrepreneurial Middle Class*, London: Croom Helm.

Schifferes, S. (1986) 'The rich in Britain', *New Society*, 22 August.

Scott, J. P. (1982) *The Upper Classes*, London: Macmillan.

——(1985) *Corporations, Classes and Capitalism*, 2nd edn, London: Hutchinson.

——(1986) *Capitalist Property and Financial Power*, Hassocks: Wheatsheaf.

——(1990a) 'Poverty and comfort: the Booth studies of London life', *Family Tree Magazine*.

——(1990b) 'Occupation and industry: the Booth studies of London life', *Family Tree Magazine*.

——(1991a) *Who Rules Britain?*, Cambridge: Polity Press.

——(1991b) 'Networks of corporate power', *Annual Review of Sociology*, 17.

——(1992a) 'In search of wealth and power', Discussion Papers in Sociology, S92/3, Department of Sociology, University of Leicester.

——(1992b) 'Citizenship and privilege', Discussion Paper, Department of Sociology, University of Leicester.

Sen, A. K. (1982) *Poverty and Famine*, Oxford University Press.

Sinfield, A. (1980) 'Poverty and Inequality in France', in George and Lawson 1980.

———(1986) 'Poverty, privilege and welfare', in Bean and Whynes 1986.

Smeeding, T. H., O'Higgins, M. and Rainwater, L. L. (1990) *Poverty Inequality and Income Distribution in Comparative Perspective*, Hassocks: Wheatsheaf.

Smith, T. W. (1989) 'Inequalities in welfare', in Jowell *et al.* 1989.

Social Trends, (1992), 22, London: HMSO.

Soltow, L. (1968) 'Long run changes in British income inequality', *Economic History Review*, 2nd series, 21.

Sorokin, P. (1925) 'American millionaires and multi-millionaires', *Journal of Social Forces*, 3.

Spicker, P. (1990) 'Charles Booth: the examination of poverty', *Social Policy and Administration*, 24.

Stamp, J. C. (1922) *British Incomes and Property*, London: P. S. King.

Stedman Jones, G. (1971) *Outcast London*, Oxford University Press.

Strasser, H. and Hodge, R. W. (eds) (1986) *Status Inconsistency in Modern Societies*, Duisburg: SOCOOP.

Suttles, G. (1968) *The Social Order of the Slum*, University of Chicago Press.

Taylor-Gooby, P. (1989) 'The role of the state', in Jowell *et al.* 1989.

Titmuss, R. (1962) *Income Distribution and Social Change*, London: George Allen & Unwin.

Townsend, P. (1952) 'Poverty: ten years after Beveridge', *Planning*, 344.

———(1974) 'The concept of poverty', in Wedderburn 1974.

———(1979) *Poverty in the United Kingdom*, Harmondsworth: Penguin.

———(1985) Review of Mack and Lansley 1985, in *Poverty: Journal of the Child Poverty Group,* 61.

———(1987) 'Deprivation', *Journal of Social Policy*, 16.

———with Corrigan, P. and Kowarzik, U. (1987) *Poverty and Labour in London*, London: Low Pay Unit.

———(1989) 'Slipping through the net', *Guardian*, 29 November.

———and Gordon, D. (1989) 'What is enough? New evidence on poverty allowing the definition of a minimum benefit', in *Minimum Income*, House of Commons Social Services Committee, 1988–89, 579, London: HMSO.

Turner, B. (1986a) *Citizenship and Capitalism: The Debate Over Reformism*, London: George Allen & Unwin.

———(1986b) *Equality*, London: Tavistock.

———(1988) *Status*, Milton Keynes: Open University Press.

———(1990) 'Outline of a theory of citizenship', *Sociology*, 24.

———(1991) 'Prolegomena to a general theory of social order', in *Citizenship, Civil Society and Social Cohesion*, Swindon: ESRC, 1992.

Valentine, C. A. (1968) *Culture and Poverty*, University of Chicago Press.

Veit-Wilson, J. (1986) 'Paradigms of poverty: rehabilitation of B. S. Rowntree', *Journal of Social Policy*, 15, 1.

Voslensky, M. (1980) *Nomenklatura*, London: Bodley Head, 1984.

Waites, B. (1987) *A Class Society at War*, London: Berg.

Walker, A. (1990a) 'Blaming the victims', in Murray 1990.

——(1990b) 'A poor idea of poverty', *Times Higher Education Supplement*, 17 August.

——and Walker, C. (1987) *The Growing Divide*, London: Child Poverty Action Group.

Walker, R., Lawson, R. and Townsend, P. (eds) (1984) *Responses to Poverty: Lessons from Europe*, London: Heinemann Educational Books.

Waters, M. (1989) 'Patriarchy and viriarchy: an explanation and reconstruction of concepts of masculine domination', *Sociology*, 23.

Wedderburn, D. (ed.) (1974) *Poverty, Inequality and Class Structure*, Cambridge University Press.

Wedgwood, J. (1929) *The Economics of Inheritance*, Harmondsworth: Penguin, 1938.

Westergaard, J. H. (1992) 'About and beyond the underclass: some notes on influences of social climate in British sociology', *Sociology*, 26

Williams, R. (1976) *Keywords*, London: Fontana.

Wilson, W. J. (1983) 'The American underclass: inner city ghettoes and the norms of citizenship', The Goodkin Lecture, Harvard University.

——(1987) *The Truly Disadvantaged*, University of Chicago Press.

——(1991) 'Studying inner city social dislocations: the challenge of public agenda research', *American Sociological Review*, 56.

——and Aporite, R. (1987) Appendix, in Wilson 1987.

Wirth, L. (1928) *The Ghetto*, University of Chicago Press.

——(1938) 'Urbanism as a way of life', *American Journal of Sociology*, 44.

World Bank (1980) *Poverty and Human Development*, Oxford University Press.

Wright, E. O. (1978) *Class, Crisis and the State*, London: New Left Books.

Zorbaugh, H. W. (1929) *The Gold Coast and the Slum*, University of Chicago Press.

INDEX